Adult Education

Adult Education

H.D. Kamat

A. David

CRESCENT
PUBLISHING CORPORATION

[The responsibility for the facts stated, conclusions reached and plagiarism, if any, in this book is entirely that of the Author. And the Publisher bears no responsibility for them, whatsoever.]

Adult Education

First Published : **2014**

ISBN 81-8342-042-7

Published by :

CRESCENT PUBLISHING CORPORATION
4831/24, Prahlad Street,
Ansari Road, Darya Ganj,
New Delhi - 110002
Ph. : 23272541, 23257835
Fax : 91- 011- 23257835
e-mail : campusbooks@hotmail.com

Typesetting by :

Arjun Computers
Delhi - 110051

Printed at :
Roshan Offset Printers
Delhi

PREFACE

Adult education, offers of educational opportunities to those adults who have never been to school or were not able to complete their basic education due to certain reasons. In many countries, during last few decades governments have established departments of non-formal education as part of their education ministries and have given them responsibility for all adults and out of school education along with the responsibility of co-ordinating with adult education carried out by other ministries such as agriculture, health, rural development. Non-formal education occupies middle space between traditional school system and formal learning practices. Since a lot of changes have taken place in the national scenario of adult education, it is really essential to deal the subject extensively to give a comprehensive review and growth of adult education in India including the latest trends and issues. Literacy, critical factor for the knowledge are discussed along with emerging need, importance and challenges of the information/knowledge revolution in our country.

The book emphasizes on adult education as an important strategy for initiating a social change for good. Main objects of adult education can said to be : (1) Remedial : To elimate illiteracy by teaching adults or in other words to bring the entire normal population upto the level of secondary school; (2) Vocational : To provide them means and skill by which an adult can improve himself in way they earn a living and teach women how to perform their roles better as housewives and mothers; (3) Cultural : To give adults some understanding of natural world their cultural heritage, society in which they live. These purposes of adult education may seem to be too exiomatic to be worth telling.

It is hoped that this book will provide archivists, librarians and information specialists, as well as all those responsible for their theoretical and practical training, with new ideas for use in their teaching and in their professional activities and help in the task of learning how to write objectives, with due regard for the process of formulating them in precise terms, and that it will encourage those concerned to make proper use of them as a tool.

H.D. Kamat
A. David

Contents

1

The Significance of Adult Education Today

Adult Americans have lived, though few of them realize it, through a period of change momentous enough to be termed—adopting what has become a cliché—a social revolution. Many in this country, however, still lack the training necessary either for living the full life that our economic abundance makes possible, or for performing in sufficient number some of the most essential tasks in a complex industrial society. If the world were moving at a slower rate, we might be tempted to write off the under-educated portion of the adult population and wait until the longer schooling now being received by the country's youth significantly increases the average learning. But the United States cannot postpone a generation or two facing up to the tasks—technical and economic, cultural and political—that urgently demand more skills. We must try to develop the human resources available in that portion of the adult population capable of contributing more fully to their own welfare and that of their society. And in particular we must try to realize more of the potential at the level of university training.

The Twentieth-Century Revolution

Over the past fifty years the population of the United States has doubled. Average expectation of life at birth increased from about fifty years in 1900 to about seventy years in 1950.

In 1900, though industrialization was well under way, 38 per cent of the gainful workers were still occupied in agriculture; fifty years later this figure was only 12.5 per cent and continuing to decline. At the turn of the century, six Americans out of ten lived in rural areas; in 1950, 64 per cent lived in towns and almost 60 per cent in the country's 168 metropolitan areas. This shift is no longer a simple country-to-town movement; the differences between "urban" and "rural" are diminishing. The intermediate suburbs are growing much faster than either city centers or small towns and villages, and what were once urban amenities are becoming available to a larger and larger proportion of the remaining rural population.

Mechanical and electrical energy has been substituted for human. The production of electric energy increased over the half century from 6 billion to 389 billion kilowatt hours, while the average workweek of production workers in manufacturing fell from 51 hours (in 1909) to 40.5. The decline over the whole past century is even more spectacular: the average workweek in all occupations fell from seven 10-hour days in 1850 to five 8-hour days in 1950.

In spite of the rapidly growing population and the steady reduction of the average workweek, productivity increased fast enough to provide a steady, substantial rise in living standards. The average annual gross national product, expressed in billions of 1929 dollars, rose from 29.4 in 1891–1900 to 149.3 in 1941–1950. The tremendously increased national income, moreover, came to be distributed more equitably among the whole population.

Rapid as the change was between 1900 and 1950, in most respects it has accelerated since mid-century. During 1959 *Fortune* published a series of articles projecting to 1970 the progress to date in technology, production and living standards. The prognoses are extravagant, but to be at all realistic they must be. During the 1950's, some $60 billion was spent on scientific research and development; the sum for the following decade will be twice that, and we can expect a corresponding increase in both basic discoveries and practical applications. Productivity per man-hour, which increased by 1 per cent per year between 1850 and 1889, by 2 per cent between 1889 and 1919, by 2.5 per cent between the wars, and by about 3 per cent since 1945, will continue to increase at least this last rate during the 1960's. With a rapid increase in the labour force and a no more than moderate decrease in the workweek, the gross national product may well shoot up to a fantastic $750 billion by 1970.

According to *Fortune's* estimate, by 1970 some 25 million families, or nearly two-fifths of the total, will have an annual income after taxes of more than $7,500. About half of this will be spent on necessities like food, clothing and shelter; the other half will be discretionary, available for a widely increased range of consumers goods, personal investment, cultural activities. Certainly there will be more of everything; whether also more and better is a question, already much debated, that will depend on whether taste improves as rapidly as purchasing power rises.

Even today, before these projected developments, man's basic needs are better satisfied in the United States than at any time in all history. Social problems are now often the effects of the country's economic and cultural abundance, paradoxical as this still sounds. Overrating is a far greater threat to health than malnutrition. Infant mortality has all but disappeared, but the number of aged grows steadily. The new mass audience sometimes threatens to engulf high culture in *Kitsch.* With the rapid population growth, some of what economists term "free goods" have become, or are likely to become, commodities: water in the semi-arid West, air in smog-ridden Los Angeles, space in any city to park a car.

Apart from such anomalies, *the* problem of economic theory—how to allocate scarce goods among alternative uses—seems to be in the process of becoming obsolete. With productivity as efficient as it has become, it is often not necessary to choose one or the other commodity, but rather possible to have both. For instance, the classic example of the economic problem, the distribution of productive factors between military and civilian needs, had a brand new solution in the United States during World War II—guns *and* butter. To some degree, this unique affluence is disguised by a reversal in the traditional relation between supply and demand. In any nonindustrial society, demand comes first—the need for food, clothing, housing, or something almost as fundamental; and production tends to rise in an effort to meet this demand. In the United States today, on the contrary, supply often comes first, and the demand for the goods produced is then stimulated by advertising and other, more subtle means of exciting social emulation. Galbraith terms this relation the Dependence Effect: "The production of goods creates the wants that the goods are presumed to satisfy". So long as this kind of squirrel cage remains in operation, the economic system can never achieve psychological satiation in consumers goods, for with greater and greater production more and more economic "wants"—in this new sense—remain unsatisfied.

The Dependence Effect operates, however, only with respect to commodities sold on the market, not with respect to social services. It is now far less important to increase industrial production than to find means of redressing the balance between opulence in consumers goods and public poverty. Any American city shows a marked contrast between rising retail sales and, on the other hand, crowded schools, understaffed police forces, dirty street, and overworked transportation systems. Any discussion of education and particularly of adult education, must take cognizance of this contrast. In the wealthiest country in history, even so obvious a demand on the public purse as schooling is not adequately satisfied.

The Educational System: Achievements and Lacks

The economic and social metamorphosis of American society was accompanied, both as cause and as effect, by a no less complete change in its educational system. In the nineteenth century, the main problem was getting free public education established, especially at the primary level. A hundred years ago, less than half of those aged five to nineteen years attended school; and almost a tenth of the native-born white, plus virtually all of the slave population and a considerable portion of the foreign-born, were totally illiterate. The full establishment of a free universal school system during the second half of the nineteenth century made possible, among other things, the assimilation of millions of immigrants and their children into a unified culture.

At the end of the century, however, education beyond grammar school was still limited to a very small minority. Of those aged fourteen through seventeen years, the proportion enrolled in high school has increased from 7 per cent in 1890 to

88 per cent in 1959. Thus, in sixty years, the American high school has changed from a preparatory school for a small elite to an institution almost as universally accessible as elementary school; and this trend is continuing. Over the same period, college enrolment has grown even faster; only about 4 per cent of persons of college age entered college in 1900, and about 30 per cent in 1959. In absolute terms, college enrolment increased by more than ten times, or from about 237,000 in 1900 to about 2.7 million in 1955.

While the United States can be justly proud of this expansion in educational opportunities, its very rapidity left a gap among the substantial number of adults who had lacked these advantages. When today's very old people were children, about a quarter of the population were given no more than four years of schooling, an amount now considered so inadequate that it is used to define the upper limit of the "functionally illiterate". In 1950, the proportion functionally illiterate among whites ranged from 18 per cent of those aged sixty-five through sixty-nine down to only 3 per cent of those aged twenty-five through twenty-nine. Put another way, the median number of school years completed in 1950, 9.3 for the total adult population, ranged from 8.2 for those sixty-five and over up to 12.1 for the twenty-five to twenty-nine age group. The gradual improvement in the country's educational system during the past generation or too was not, of course, at an equal rate among all social classes, and differences persist by region, urban-rural residence, and race, as well as by age. Thus, rural Negroes in the South, by reason of all three of these characteristics, have both the least schooling and the poorest present educational facilities.

In short, millions of adult Americans have less education than would be most beneficial both to themselves and to their society. In 1950, three-tenths of the adult population had not graduated from grammar school, two-thirds had not graduated from high school, 94 per cent had not graduated from college. A portion, but only a portion, of these deficiencies was based on innate limitations, but accidents of birth played a greater role.

The rapid expansion of America's school system has not been without travail. As even the most casual reader of newspapers knows, the whole educational system has been undergoing a thorough, and often a hostile, review. Three topics in this important debate are worth summarizing here—the finances of education, the effect of the rapid population increase and the question of standards.

1. "Education costs money. Though expense does not guarantee success, more and better education always costs more". Obvious as this truism may appear to be, the question of how to pay for public education is a complex one. The increase in expenditures per pupil in elementary and secondary schools was spectacular—from $20 in 1900 (or $62 in 1949-1950 dollars) to $259 in 1950. But the rise in costs was even faster. Today the United States spends less proportionately on its public schools than it did in the depth of the interwar depression.

Public schools are locally financed, and their funds thus derive principally from the relatively inflexible general property tax. New sources of tax income are hard for local governments to find: personal and corporate income is already taxed by the federal government and many of the states. Municipalities have tried to keep up with their growing financial responsibilities by levying sales taxes or by broadening the property tax base; but these can be nothing more than stopgap measures. The solution for public education, in the opinion of some, is federal financing; but this attacks, or seems to attack, local control of the schools—one of the most reversed of America's large herd of sacred cows. Thus, the many bills introduced in Congress to establish federal aid to public education have all, for one reason or another, failed to pass. Only about 4 per cent of the cost of public education is now paid by the national government, which collects three out of every four tax dollars.

American higher education also rests on an inadequate and *ad hoc* financial base. College revenue is derived from student fees, which have risen alarmingly during the past decade; from municipal and state legislatures, which are under constant pressure of allocate monies elsewhere; from alumni and other donors, who are sometimes more interested in football than in education; from personal and foundation endowments, always inadequate in amount and sometimes arbitrarily restricted to certain uses; and from greatly underpaid faculties. This haphazard patchwork is not a satisfactory way of financing so important an institution as the country's higher education.

2. The difficulties in financing schools and colleges, moreover, have been considerably aggravated by the baby boom. During the first postwar decade, more than 36 million infants were born to American parents, and as these children move up into adult life, they are disrupting one institution after another built to accommodate more modest numbers. Greatly swollen student bodies have burst the grammar schools, and the flood is just beginning to engulf the high schools. Administrators of universities are well aware that their turn is coming. In their case, a double increase must be anticipated, one in the number of persons of college age and another in the proportion of this age group that attends college.

Today we have 3 million students in colleges and universities. By 1975 the college population will be at least 7.5 and perhaps as many as 12 million—a little less than 50 per cent of the eligible age groups...Today the total annual expenditure of higher education, including capital investment, is probably around $5 billion. Twenty years hence it may exceed $25 billion.

The rapid increase in the school population has effected an unprecedented strain on educational facilities and personnel. The so-called "normal capacity" of elementary and secondary schools is presently exceeded by some 2.3 million pupils, and their enrolment will increase by another 30 per cent over the next decade. Even if every person who gets a Ph.D. were to become a college teacher, the shortage in faculties would grow. "Unless the supply of competent college teachers is increased, the next 20 years may do damage to higher education in the United States which the following 100 years will find it impossible to repair".

3. Partly as a consequence of the shortage of funds and the overabundance of pupil, but partly also for other reasons, the quality of American education has suffered. There has been, depending on which books in this heated dispute one reads, either a shocking deterioration in educational standards or—at best, by the most optimistic appraisal—a failure to improve quality nearly fast enough to satisfy the educational prerequisites of an industrial democratic society. Differences are sharp

over where to put the blame—whether at the door of teachers colleges, or in the lap of a public unwilling to pay for a good educational system, or wherever. That the products of the American public schools are less knowledgeable and competent than they ought to be, however, hardly anyone would deny. Under the stresses outlined in the previous paragraphs, moreover, it will be particularly difficult for elementary and high schools to improve, or even to maintain, the quality of their instruction over the next decade or so. And if colleges will not be able to take it for granted, as seems reasonable enough in the abstract, that applicants for admission will be well prepared in basic subjects, then their talk of raising standards may well also remain—talk.

This short and incomplete review of the economics of American education has perhaps been sufficient to indicate how complex the question is. Automatically, on principal, all Americans are "for" more and better schools; *whether* there should be good educational facilities is never a political issue, with candidates and parties aligned for and against. Nevertheless, the proportion of the national income allotted to education is grossly inadequate. The subsistence financing of the schools is the product in large part of a rather inflexible institutional structure. A fundamental reform in the manner by which school revenue is allocated is called for, but this will not be accepted overnight. In the interim, some of the educational gaps that the school system leaves can be repaired by devoting more attention to the education of adults.

The Functions of Adults Education

Education as a lifelong process, at least for a portion of the population, is an ideal as old as Western civilization. For the Greek citizen, the medieval scholar, the Renaissance man, learning was an attribute of life, continuing until death. The central purpose of American adult education today is to preserve this ideal in the more formal structure of an organized programme, and to apply it to as large a portion of the total population as is capable, by both innate intelligence and interest, of continuing to learn. This purpose is sought at all levels, from remedying the lack of primary skills to keeping persons with graduate degrees up to date in their profession:

1. In 1950, there were nearly 10 million adults who were functionally illiterate, that is, who had had four years or less of schooling. While many of these, both Negro and white, were reared in the rural South, there are illiterates in virtually every state of the union. Many of those who can read and write, moreover, were never taught much more. One out of four of the healthy young men drafted into the Army are unable to learn any task more complicated than digging ditches or washing pots and pans; and while some of these soldiers are undoubtedly of low native intelligence, the staggering size of the inept proportion suggests that the principal cause of their deficiency is inadequate schooling.

2. Even the simplest function of an educational system, vocational training, is relatively complex in an economy changing as fast as ours. Among manual jobs, those that require no skill are becoming proportionately fewer; and in the labour force as a whole, the percentage of white-collar and professional positions is increasing even faster. The significance of these trends to each individual American is obvious: they mean that the traditional opportunity to raise himself up the social ladder still exists to a marked degree. The main prerequisite to a significant rise, however, has become the formal education appropriate to the position he is seeking. A degree pays for itself many times over: a four-year college education that costs a total of about $9,000 (including the amount that could be earned by a teenager at relatively unskilled work) increases one's lifetime income by about $100,000.

That the efforts of an individual to get ahead are commendable in terms of American values need hardly be said, and it is also a commonplace that the society as a whole is in great need of more highly educated specialists. The number of persons engaged in professions associated with industrialization has grown tremendously—from 30,000 engineers in 1890 to more than 530,000 in 1950, for example, and by similar ratios among chemists, physicists, biologists, accountants and, most recently, administrators. Even this growth has not been fast enough, however, and there are serious and in some cases increasing shortages in several essential professions. Which these are depends to some degree, of course, on one's definition both of "essential" and of "shortages".

The most obvious, though not necessarily the best, criterion of a shortage of professional personnel is a large number of unfilled openings and a consequent disproportionate rise in salaries or earnings. But this definition, in spite of the fact that it has the sanction of economic theory, applies only to professionals subject to market conditions, such as engineers working for corporations or physicians in private practice. Persons who work for a government and are thus paid out of a tax fund often have lower salaries even if their services are more important to society. The shortages of physicians in salaried positions in health departments, for example, or of nurses in hospitals, or of teachers, must be defined by comparing the number and quality of the supply with some standard of what the society needs. Sometimes such a need—for example, for a greater number of highly qualified theoretical physicists—can be appreciated only by one himself trained in the profession.

The principal reason for such shortages is that, in spite of the rapid expansion of America's educational system, too few young people are learning nearly as much as they can absorb. Furthermore:

Today, less than half of those capable of acquiring a college degree enter college. About two-fifths of those who start college—many with superior ability—do not graduate. For every high school graduate who eventually earns a doctoral degree, there are twenty-five others who have the intellectual ability to achieve that degree but do not.

A long term policy demands that greater incentives be devised to keep some of these "underdeveloped human resources" in school for a longer period. For the immediate future, the only remedy is more and better adult education.

3. The differentiation between vocational skills and general cultural knowledge that we have made is to some degree artificial. Indeed, it may be potentially dangerous.

Vocational education conceived as job-training represents the greatest threat to democratic education in our time. It is a threat to democracy because it tends to make the job-trained individual conscious only of his technological responsibilities, but not of his social and moral responsibilities. He becomes a specialist in "means" but indifferent to "ends" which are considered the province of another specialist.

In any case, if even a liberal arts degree generally results in a higher salary, and if a larger income is valued in part for the greater access to culture it makes possible, then economic roles are not really as rigidly separated from the rest of life as in the usual analysis. The function of a liberal education is to prepare a student both to earn his own living and to live fully with what he earns.

Perhaps the greatest boon that their technology has brought Americans, at least potentially, is more free time. Leisure has been increased in three ways: people generally work less hard and thus have reserves of energy at the end of the working day; as has been noted, over the past century the average workweek has been cut from 70 to 40 hours, and is still going down; and during the last fifty years the average life has been extended by twenty years, and is still going up. However, this free time is often less a boon than a burden, particularly for the aged.

So long as work was the main waking activity of the vast majority of the population, "leisure" was regarded simply as respite from work. This merely negative view of free time has been maintained in our value system after its relevance disappeared. Americans are a hard-working people. Veblen to the contrary notwithstanding, the United States has never had a leisure class. The so-called "ridle rich" have seldom been idle, for no matter how great their wealth they have been typically as much imbued as the rest of the population with the stem Protestant ethic epitomized in Benjamin Franklin's maxims. This moral imperative to work made possible the overnight conversion of a wilderness into a great civilization, and it still continues to be a conspicuous element of the American national character.

> In twentieth-century America, leisure is misconceived as idleness, vacationing (which involves "vacancy"), play, recreation, relaxation, diversion, amusement and so on... Leisure, properly conceived,....consists in activities which are neither toil nor play, but are rather the expressions of moral and intellectual virtue—the things a good man does because they are intrinsically good for him and for his society.

In theory, the whole rich storehouse of Western culture is now available for all to draw from, but many have not learned how to open the door.

By far the favourite reading matter of the wartime Army, that cross-section of young America, was comic books. Half of the students in a major state university do not know who Karl Marx is. A much larger proportion do not recognize the Bill of Rights of the United States Constitution when they see it. The failure of the educational system to teach students the elements of their own culture is greater even than the failure to provide the American economy with a sufficient number of trained persons.

4. "Popular government without popular education", in the words of James Madison, "is a prologue to a farce or a tragedy".

It is a truism that democracy requires a higher general level of education, and a much higher level of political understanding and experience, than other forms of government; yet it is difficult to be convinced that it is a truism which we have taken very seriously, and equally difficult to see how we can claim to be taking it seriously without a considerable development of adult education and of university participation in it.

In the American democracy the level of ignorance of the populace is an important determinant not only of public policy but, with the growing power of the United States, of world affairs as well. Over the past half century the relation between the United States and the rest of the world has changed at least as dramatically as its domestic social economy. In 1900, this country was still in many respects a cultural appendage of Europe, having just made in the Spanish-American War its first, brash entry on the world scene. Today the United States is the core of Western democracy. The rest of the nontotalitarian world looks to it, not always hopefully, for both material aid and political guidance. In a fundamental sense, this leadership is legitimate: the many demands of the peoples of the world can be summed up in two—political and social democracy, and mass-produced consumers goods—and these are significant features of American society today. In political terms, however, world leadership was thrust on the United States before the necessary experience and tradition had fully developed. America's national interest must be more effectively defined in the nation's schools and—again, to make up for past and present deficiencies—in adult-education programmes.

If, as we have tried to show, the many important changes that have taken place in American society over the past fifty years necessitate special educational facilities to help adults adapt to them, this does not mean that the role of adult education is only adaptive. Education, including adult education, ought to help people adjust to changing conditions—but also to see that they do not adjust too far. The *main* function of education is to furnish cultural continuity from one generation to the next, and the more rapid the change in society, the more essential it is to stress the enduring varieties response to what in articles on education is invariably termed our "dynamic" world is not simply flexibility, but flexibility combined with fundamental stability. "The greatest task of adult education and the greatest obligation laid upon state universities in this disordered present is to restate the cultural and political ideals of America".

To what degree are the tasks of adult education fulfilled? That it has failed to realize the potential that exists among the large number of possible participants, that it has not made good the gaps between existent and needed knowledge, even its own practitioners would hardly deny. The reasons for this partial failure are many and complex. One of the most important, according to the thesis of this book, is that, in spite of the vast literature on the subject, few people in adult education know precisely either what they are trying to do what means are appropriate.

If adult education is important, as we have tried to demonstrate in this chapter, a guide to policy concerning it is necessary; and in the following chapters we attempt to furnish this with respect to the university's role.

Summary

Over the past fifty years, the economy, social structure and educational system of the United States have all undergone a fundamental transformation. For many Americans, this rapid change has made possible a richer life, achieved by the vocational training and cultural orientation their education give them. For many other, however, the potential has not been realized; and both they as individuals and society as a whole suffer as a consequence. The under-educated sector of our population can be brought up to part only by offering it the opportunity to learn more. Of the many conclusions that might be drawn from this review of the past half century, thus, we wish to suggest only one—significant adult education may well be as worthy an object of public support as the primary school itself.

In general terms, the functions of adult education can be defined as follows:

1. *Remedial:* To elimate illiteracy, teach adult immigrants English, and in other respects bring the entire normal population up to the level of grammar school graduates.
2. *Vocational:* To provide the means by which adults can improve themselves in the way they earn a living, either within their vocation or by changing to another one; to alleviate specific shortages of professional personnel by teaching suitable adults; and to teach women how to perform better their roles as housewives and mothers.
3. *Cultural* : To give adults some understanding of the natural world, their cultural heritage, the society in which they live, and themselves, so that they can live more fully and make richer use of the increasing years of leisure available to them.
4. *Political* : To train adults as citizens and give them a better basis for taking sides on public issues; particularly, to correct the very serious deficiency in Americans' understanding of foreign affairs.

Stated baldly, these purposes of adult education may seem to be too axiomatic to be worth writing down. But neither these ends nor especially the means by whcih they might be achieved are agreed on among adult educators. On the contrary, whether we speak of aims, or content, or method, or whatever, there is hardly a thesis in adult education without its counter thesis. In Chapter 2, we will examine the most important of these disputes and attempt to resolve them.

2

Adult Education : Principles and Problems

American education is in a turmoil. Vigorous disputes over the philosophy of education, curricula, teaching methods, standards, the training of teachers, and so on and on, have engaged the attention of the entire teaching profession and a sizable portion of the general public. In some respects, the controversy in adult education is parallel to the more familiar one between progressive and traditionalist educators, between those who "teach children" and those who "teach subject matter". There are, however, several important differences.

Standard education (that is, all but adult education) has established a number of relatively inviolable functions: pupils in primary grades are to learn the three R's; college teaching is governed by the several disciplines. The complaint is that Johnny cant's read, and the dispute is over the efficacy of various methods of teaching him. No one so much as raises the question whether he should learn to read at all. Similarly, the range of the divergence concerning higher education is generally not so great that the opponents get out of sight of each other. Advocates of polar positions—say, Sidney Hook at one extreme and Mortimer J. Adler at the other—agree that the college's function is to transmit a "liberal education". The differences are over how to define the key term and especially over how to attain this goal. When all more or less agree on ends and differ mainly over means, it may be possible to resolve the dispute. Whether knowledge of Latin improves the student's English, for instance, or whether learning algebra teaches him to reason better, can be tested. However difficult it may be to devise such tests, the point is that in standard education evaluation is generally possible to some degree, and advocates of various philosophies usually find it expedient to argue in terms of the educational effects of the curricula and methods they propose.

Adult education is a different world. It is, most practitioners agree, unorganized, confused, chaotic; and some of them believe that this is as it should be. One of the things about an adult-education conference that, amazingly, "most cheered" a visiting colleague from Canada was that "a certain amount of confusion, apparent contradictions and unresolved difficulties not only were present but were tolerated". We would agree that a democratic movement must have a place for differing positions, and that a dynamic movement is likely to reflect past rapid change in present variety, but what is the value to education of confusion, even "a certain amount"? And any movement, even the most democratic and the most dynamic, is meaningful only if there is a minimum core of invariable consensus. Whether this exists in adult education is a moot question.

A potpourri of heterogeneous organizations interested in "reaching" adults, each in its own fashion and for its own purposes, defines each in its own way the institution, its functions, the means of achieving the goals set. Among adult educators the very word *education,* for instance, is markedly imprecise: for some, it means the process by which new knowledge or attitudes or skills are transmitted, and for others that by which persons participate together in an activity and come to feel a sense of identification with a group. Distinctions between such opposed positions are not ordinarily sharply drawn. White adult educators feel, or course, that the orientation they prefer is the best, they almost always concede that every other "approach" also has its value. Tolerance of others' views, flexibility, exciting experimentation, imagination, and creativity —these are seen by most practitioners as prime virtues, overriding such mundane characteristics as consistency, practicality and logic.

In order to analyze the basic trends in adult education, where should one begin in this welter of contradictory, sometimes self-contradictory, tenets and practices, most of which are neither validated nor even capable of being evaluated? One frequent device is to take the extreme positions and compare them. According to Birnbaum, for example, the "two major schools of adult education today" are as follow:

1. The "traditionalist"—"those who see mental functions or cognition as the central phenomenon in learning, who stress content as against method, who see their task as the liberal education of the individual, who stress the development of a mature value system, and who would, moreover, make substantial use of the content of past civilizations".

2. The "psychological"—"those who stress the importance of the emotions in learning, who are impressed with the influence of the unconscious in human behaviour, the powerful educational value of group learning, the role of experience in learning, and the frequent conflict between values and attitudinal systems".

Such a dichotomy has the advantage of giving the analyst an axis around which to arrange his ideas, but also several disadvantages that outweigh this:

1. On several important issues, there are not two but three or four significantly different positions. Collapsing these into a dichotomy, like the right-left continuum in a political analysis, loses more in clarity than it gains in convenience.

2. Very often the distinctions on which the dichotomy is based are false. The experimentation that is usually insisted on in adult education, for example, need not be at the cost of traditional standards. Or: the dispute over methods need not be in terms of absolutes; "it would be as ridiculous to assume that no true learning transpires within the organized study group as it is to hold that no learning occurs outside of it".

3. Some of the issues are false in another sense: a key word is used in several meanings, as in the slogan, democracy in education. Some who advocate this mean that the teacher should try to imbue his subject matter with the values of democracy, others that the teacher should give up his professional authority to student rule. According to one leading figure of the Adult Education Association, for example, "the adult is the one who decides his education, not the educator or

the educational agency". Here is a point significant enough to form an appropriate opening theme in a discussion of the principles of adult education.

On "Democracy" in Adult Education

Perhaps the most perplexing question in adult education, as it is ordinarily administered, is how to decide what programmes should be offered. With no firm educational principles themselves on what content is appropriate, adult educators generally turn to prospective participants and ask them what they would like. How prevalent customer satisfaction is as a determinant of adult education is indicated by the most extensive survey to date of how programmes are established.

In 1951, Kempfer analyzed 530 adult-education programmes in public schools and community colleges. Arranged in order from most to least "successful" in terms of his criteria, the programmes had been established by the following methods:

1. We systematically cultivate a group of "coordinators" in industry, business, and other community organizations and agencies who watch for every opportunity for education to perform a service.
2. We receive requests from business, industrial, labour and community groups.
3. We study deficiencies of adults (*e.g.,* poor nutrition, low educational level, lack of civic participation, poor methods of child rearing).
4. We maintain an extensive personal acquaintance with a wide range of community leaders and groups.
5. We examine data from the census and similar sources.
6. We make systematic surveys of the industrial, business, civic and cultural life of the community.
7. We examine published surveys of other communities and similar literature.
8. We examine catalogues, schedules, publicity materials and programmes of comparable institutions.
9. Through "hunch".
10. We try to be sensitive to civic, personal and social problems of people—problems which can be alleviated by education.

11. We check with other known interests of people (*e.g.*, library reading interests, newspaper and magazine readership surveys).
12. We utilize check lists and other "interest finders".
13. We receive individual requests.

These thirteen methods of establishing the content of an educational programme can be grouped into four classes, as follows:

Surveys of various types, either those already in existence (5, 7, 11) or those made specially for this purpose (6,12). In spite of their limitations, such surveys are obviously one important source of relevant background information.

Requests from groups or individuals, either spontaneous (2,4, 13) or solicited (1,4). Again, no one would deny that such requests should be taken into consideration by the director, as well as being solicited by any convenient means. The issue is whether they are taken as absolutes, or fitted into a prior policy that the administrator has set.

Following practices that were successful elsewhere (8) or that the administrator thinks would be successful (9). It is noteworthy that, according to this tabulation, the professional judgment of administrators is restricted to following their colleagues' examples or their own 'hunches". Were their knowledge and imagination relatively unimportant in setting up a successful programme because of their lack of ability, or because of the criteria by which a programme was adjudged to be "successful"?

Remedial education (3,10), "a negative approach to programme planning", which, according to Kempfer, has "long handicapped the full development of adult education". This depreciation of remedial education, usual in writings by adult educators, possibly derives from a comparison with the lofty goals they ordinarily set themselves and the more dramatic that these presumably demand.

According to this study, then, adult-education programmes are established mainly by what the participants would like. Quite apart from the educational principles on which these procedures are based, it is worth pointing out that most surveys are not very reliable. Even the simplest kind involves all of the weaknesses of public-opinion research. "An extensive personal acquaintance" with leaders and groups, thus, will not be representative unless there is a special effort to make it so. Respondents may be uncertain of their interests and thus inclined to reply to a question concerning them in terms of a momentary whim. Such answers, moreover, will tend to be biased in one direction: when asked whether they are "interested" in fine arts, literature, music, better citizenship, few persons will say No. Replies may be conditioned more by conventional attitudes than by the personal interests of the respondents. According to what seems to be the only check ever made of such a survey (in Radburn, New Jersey, more than twenty years ago), stated intentions do not correspond with later actual behaviour:

After the programmes were inaugurated, it was discovered that only slightly more than one third of the persons who had indicated interest in a particular activity actually took part in it; whereas nearly two thirds of the total number of actual participants had not previously expressed interest in the activities...Actual participation turned out to be inversely related to stated preferences.

This experience suggests that, at best, surveys can be useful only if they are made in accordance with the best practices of public-opinion analysts—with a carefully selected sample, a professionally constructed questionnaire, well trained interviewers, and coding and analysis of the results by persons who recognize the limitations as well as the value of this type of research.

In any case, a community survey should be no more than one criterion out of several in establishing the curriculum of adult education. What "the people" want, even if it were possible to judge this exactly, ought not to be the main determinant, not to say almost the only one, of the content of adult education. According to those who believe differently, "democracy" apparently means that persons must give up their special skills in the economy: the educator must abdicate his professional function of establishing an adequate and balanced curriculum and become "merely a waiter behind a cafeteria line". In the opinion of Nolte, it would be as logical for a physician to demand that his patients themselves prescribe the appropriate medicine. Or, in Houle's words:

> Great courses of study are not enunciated by popular demand...Adults aware of their own need for knowledge and insight rarely can articulate exactly what it is they want to know. If they could do that, the libraries and the museums would already have helped them to know it.

Why do some educators refuse to accept their professional responsibility? The most obvious reason is the notion that this makes their task easier. "The use of the concept of 'needs' for goal defining purposes is...an attempt to ease the burden of decision on the educator", who then is "content just to go about sleuthing for 'needs' in the belief that these 'needs' when 'discovered' will relieve him of the leadership task". Moreover, "the altruism" displayed in serving community needs "fools everybody and disarms potential critics". Whether an educator can really make it easier for himself by avoiding his responsibility, however, is another question. "The director is likely to be deluged with requests for all kinds of courses... His life can be made miserable unless he has a definite set of policies to back him up in screening such requests."

There is a more compelling reason for the prevalence of this type of "democracy" in adult education—that administrators are confronted with the dilemma of running programmes that are both educational and money-making, and try to save face by labelling customer satisfaction the "democratic" control of educational policy. Virtually all adult-education programmes have to pay their own way to one degree or another. According to Cohen's survey of world-affairs organizations, which may be taken as an example of private adult-education agencies generally, "the need for... funds is felt to be so great that many of the existing resources are applied not to education but to the search for new resources." Public schools are generally reimbursed for their adult-education programmes on the basis of average daily attendance. Foundations that give support to adult education also, though less formally, tend to measure "success" first by the size of the enrolments and eventually by whether the programme becomes self-supporting. And general-extension divisions, unlike any other sector of the university, are usually required to get a large proportion of their income from fees.

If the adult educator is forced to regard his students as customers, he must define his programme as commodities. Like any other businessman, he tries both to adapt his product to public taste and, through advertising, to induce the public to accept it. The choice between educational offerings is put on the same level as the choice among several brands of breakfast food. A group of evening-college administrators discussed recently "ways in which courses might be attractively packaged and marketed". In a chapter of his text entitled "Identifying Educational Needs and Interests of Adults," Kempfer recommends the community survey as the equivalent in education to market research in business.

The notion that in adult education the patients cure themselves is not only professionally degrading but also hypocritical. No one really wants to write himself out of his profession, though he may try to give others that impression. According to Kempfer, for example, "the imposition of goals is authoritarian," but "if the formulation of objectives is left to individuals without control or agreement, on the principle of *laissez-faire,* anarchy is the ultimate result." Similarly, "in a democracy the participants are often the final judges of the worth of an adult-education programme," though "few programmes should ever be judged solely on consumer satisfaction." If in the opinion of an adult educator a programme (for example, on the principles of democratic theory or race relations) would do the community good, he would ordinarily attempt to set it up whether or not anyone had expressed a desire for it.

Needs—Felt, Unfelt and Other

The conflict between the shibboleth that the content of every programme in adult education must be determined by the "felt needs" of the individual or the community, and the actual refusal of educators to abrogate their professional responsibility entirely, has resulted in a remarkable variation in the meaning of this phrase. In most contexts *need* is a good English word with a reasonably precise definition. In the field of adult education, however, the abuse inflicted on it has pommelled this term into a misshapen mess. In order to re-establish a modicum of communication, we shall here replace *need* by the half-dozen nonsynonymous words that it has ousted. Let us begin by breaking down "felt need" into its several component parts.

The first recognizable meaning of "need" is *interest,* which we define as a vague, low-level desire to be associated with an activity or subject either for its own sake or for the social contacts it affords:

> The teachers recognized that many students had interests other than information...best described as "social" or "recrea-tional". ...Concerning their own aims as teachers, all of them expressed a strong feeling in one way or another that they should try to meet the *needs* of their adult students.

One of the important criteria defining interest is its low level—needs "best described as 'social' or 'recreational.' A person who becomes involved in an adult-education programme out of loneliness or boredom may become "interested" in painting or ancient history or child psychology and enroll in any one of these courses, but in an educational context it is useful to distinguish the student who does not choose his programme merely out of indifference.

The second meaning of "need", then, is *concern,* which we define as a spontaneous, high-level, noninstrumental desire to be associated with an activity or subject for its own sake. A person "concerned" with painting, that is to say, would take the initiative in enrolling in a course in painting, but not in just any subject:

> The people themselves know their *needs.* A careful block-by-block survey of adult education needs in Denver disclosed what 63 per cent found most lacking—an understanding of what is going on in a world at war.

Some "felt needs" are instrumental; that is, the knowledge or activity is desired not for its own sake, as an end, but as a means toward achieving another goal. A women with her first baby may take a course in child psychology even though she finds the subject boring, or her husband may try to improve his vocational skill. Let us define "needs" in this sense as *wants:*

> Sometimes an adult finds that he has prepared himself for a field in which later he discovers himself unhappy or ill-adapted, and so feels the *need* to prepare for an entirely new field.

In seeking to satisfy his "wants," a person retains the possibility of choice but some vocational "needs" are essentially coercive: a man has been told by his employer that he will be fired unless he improves his level of skill; a public school teacher cannot get an increase in salary unless she accumulates "alertness credits." A vocational "needs" with a significant degree of coercion by the employer (or other persons or circumstances) we define as a *requirement.*

There are not only "felt needs" but also, at least by implication, "unfelt needs," that is, "needs" of which the individual is not aware. (It is almost too bad that a Freudian has not wanmdered into this field, so that the "felt needs" would be interpreted as mere symbols of the individual's unfelt—in the sense of unsconscious—"needs." The already unique confusion would then achieve perfection.) But what does this implied distinction between "felt" and "unflet" needs mean, if not that though adults may know what they want, they are not able to define a sound educational programme? However, it is unfashionable, not to say authoritarian, to put this so bluntly; and adult educators ordinarily prefer to say that "the director must understand not only the needs felt by adults but those which they may not recognize" and must be "led to recognize." In other words, adult students must merely be given the impression that they have made a choice on their own.

The first type of communal "need", which may be "felt" or "unfelt" by the individual, comes close to the literal meaning of the word—a functional prerequisite to societal survival or health (or, at the lowest level of intensity, improvement). "Needs" for such institutions or facilities as new school buildings, more industry or retail trade in the community, sanitary programmes, various kinds of educational or cultural activities, and the like, we define as *necessities:*

> Another approach to the problem of more adequately meeting adult *needs* is illustrated by ... a community-action checksheet... as the basis upon which a programme of action can be recommended.

A second type of communal "need" relates to the purposes of social life. Necessities have been defined as the means by which democracy, a high standard of living, and other social ends can be achieved. "Needs" in the sense of such ultimate goals we define as *moral imperatives:*

> The common man...*needs* to understand this life in all its local and remote relationships and he also needs to participate actively in creating conditions whereby democracy has some tangible meaning.

These six separate concepts—interest, concern, want, requirement, necessity and moral imperative—do not exhaust the range of meaning included in "need", but they are sufficient to demonstrate the utter ambiguity involved in the adult educator's use of the word. It is not merely that "need" can mean any one of several things, but that in many contexts it seems to mean several of them together:

> It is always a good idea to start with some planned procedures to determine *needs* and interests...We are all tempted to think in terms of what people ought to have rather than what they *want*... There are several ways of finding out what people need and want...

Or, as another example:

> The newer type of community or adult-education center programme...is more flexible and adaptable, covers a broader range of interests, and endeavours to take into account the recreational and cultural *needs* of adults as well as their vocational ones.

This confusion helps the educator in not taking a definite stand for or against anything. In particular, as we have noted, he can both propound the students' "right" to set their own education and also defend his professional prerogative to determine the best programme, without permitting this contradiction to appear above the surface. In part as a result, nothing is too frivolous, too far removed from education, to escape endorsement by some adult educator as a legitimate part even of a *university's* function:

> Courses in ice skating, square dancing, or totem pole carving would certainly be less academic in nature than investment analysis, agricultural, mathematics, or construction and maintenance of aircraft; but if the students believe they have some *need* for the training and skill they can secure by doing the work, only an extremely narrow concept of adult education would preclude the possibility of setting up such courses.

> Although many of the courses that adults require are not of an academic nature, every effort should be made to provide good training.

The educator's canon that he must "begin with people where they are" puts no limit on the legitimacy of the "felt needs" that determine the content of an educational programme. Yet obviously there is such a limit—whether legality, good taste, middle-class conventionality, or whatever.

You have an adult programme. It includes classes in bridge. And in how to cheat at bridge? Any in safe-cracking? Seduction? I suppose not; the question is, *why* not? Offered with discretion, they might be both popular and profitable...Your town has a high divorce rate. Should you offer classes in better ways to divorce?

Wherever the line is drawn, the fact that it is drawn is decisive. Since "the people" do not rule absolutely, the limit of their legitimate option might well be set by an *educational* criterion.

The fuzzy thinking typical in adult education touches bottom in the discussion of this crucial issue—to what extent should needs, however defined, determine programmes? "Nothing provides such a splendid cover for obscure educational thinking as the underbrush of platitudes that perpetually flourishes about the main moral issues of education". Consider the queer kind of democracy to which this illogical application of political principles to an inappropriate field has led adult educators. Democracy implies not merely the right to choose but the power to make a free choice, and "there can be no free choice unless alternatives are seen and their probable consequences explored. Not to reveal alternatives is to restrict choice". An adult educator who bases his programme mainly on surveys and similar indications of students' "needs" deprives them of the possibility of opting for something that, in their relative ignorance, they had never thought of.

Content

The supposed absolute rule of "felt needs" does not apply even in theory. If adult educators took seriously their maxim that "democracy" demands that they give "the people" what they want the way they want it, there would be no point in further cogitation on the matter. Yet there is a good deal of discussion of both the appropriate content of adult-education programmes and of the best methods of teaching them.

At the most abstract level, the question is whether adult education ought to benefit mainly the individual participating in it or society as a whole. The aim of adult education, we are told, "is to inspire grown-ups to be something more than they are now and to do their work better than they now do it," so that they will learn "some content material worth learning and understanding, something that will make their individual lives richer and more meaningful." Other educators insist, on the contrary, that "mere extension of personal knowledge on the part of individual adults does not constitute an adult education movement"; that "the major task of adult education is the reduction of alienation in our society"; that "one of the major areas of adult education is that of training people in the skills of productive group membership."

The difference does not reflect a real dilemma. To the question of whether adult education should benefit the individual or society, the only reasonable reply is: both. In a democracy there is no contradiction between individual improvement and a more viable community life. Where there are rigid class lines, a man can move up from his father's station only by disturbing what is felt to be the suitable relations between himself and his betters. But in the United States, both the democratic credo and in large part actual practice encourage each man to establish himself at the highest level his abilities permit. In a society governed by a totalitarian party, individuals who acquire some uncomfortable facts or, more important, learn to be critical of official dogmas, constitute a danger to state security. But in the United States, again, both theory and practice demand that citizens be taught how to think critically, how to judge political issues objectively; and this educational philosophy has been one basis of what is probably the most stable government in the world today.

The difference over whether it is the individual or society that is to be served by adult education is really one over content. Apart from the thesis that the content ought to follow "felt needs," three major positions are discernible:

1. The content of adult education ought to be whatever is necessary to bring about social reform—to solve "family problems, deliquency, labour difficulties and national and international problems," or, in a word, to "help save the world within the next few years." Or, as stated in the guiding principles of the Adult Education Association: "*Social action on behalf of reasoned social change is the functional raison d'etre of a modern adult education movement.*"

There is a basic confusion apparent here. Social reform, in the sense of the establishment and extension of a democratic society, rests in part on popular education. This observation is so obvious at the level of primary schooling that it is generally agreed (though, as has been noted, sometimes with little grace) that one legitimate function of adult education is to remove fundamental educational deficiencies like illiteracy. But those who believe in liberal education maintain that at any level it gives support to democratic society. If a person learns to appreciate a Bach cantata, or to read Catullus in the original Latin, or to use a microscope, his richer inner life will help make him a better member of society. "Should a group of adults appear, asking for a course in astronomy, for example, not because they hope to rearrange the stars and improve the universe, but solely because they are filled with wonder, and would like to know more about the heavens, this is warrant enough." in the last decades of the nineteenth century, when the courts decided in favour of tax support to high schools teaching foreign languages, algebra and geometry, and other "useless frills" previously reserved for the children of the rich, the creed of liberal education became American law.

If in this general sense *all* of education is relevant to the establishment of the good society, in a more specific instrumental sense, very little of it is. There is no evidence, for instance, that the innumerable "marriage and family" courses set up during the past decades have reduced the incidence of divorce; and if anything we know even less about how to use education to eliminate other "national and international problems." What education can do—and what adult education in particular ought to do—is to give people the basis for understanding, for example, the relation between the United States and the rest of the world. If American citizens acquire such an understanding, and if in part because of their more informed participation in public affairs the United States develops a better foreign policy, and if this policy is successful in maintaining world peace without loss of national honour—then we can say that education helped solve the social problem of war. In this circuitous route, however, many other factors would exert their influence; and educators would play a significant role only to the degree that they stuck to their last and concentrated on transmitting knowledge, ideas and values to those lacking them.

Education has a function in democratic society, an important but a limited one. This apparent truism is attacked both by educational utopians, who believe that society can be changed only by first changing its system of education, and by educational defeatists, who believe that education can play no significant role until a just society is first established. These extreme positions have common their extremism.

2.The second important doctrine with respect to the content of adult education is that this is relatively unimportant, or, in an absolutist version, that there should be no content. What matters is *that* a group interacts, not *what* it interacts about.

Democracy cannot be taught by precept, but can only be learned through experience. This means that in the operation of our adult education programmes people should always be gaining experience in the democratic process, this means that the way they learn is even more important than what they learn.

If content is unimportant, then it is not necessary to have a teacher.

The focus of adult education is the *local community*. Adult citizens meeting together in face-to-face groups for the purpose of exchanging knowledge and experience constitutes [sic] the sociological nexus of adult education.

In a sense this thesis is a special version of the notion that social reform is the function of adult education. *The* problem in modern society, it is maintained, is the alienation of the individual, and this can be solved only by incorporating him into group life. We comment on this thesis first by questioning its validity and secondly by denying its relevance, if it were true, to adult education.

Any viable society is based on an underlying consensus, and this has been challenged in Western society by the effects of the urbanization, industrialization, and secularization during the past several centuries. The countryman's organic identification with his village cannot be maintained in a mobile urban world; and an attempt to re-establish in the latter setting a feeling of belonging based on mere propinquity results only in a caricature of village life. Too often, in his effort to reduce his alienation from his fellow, modern man has become simply a joiner of groups, a Babbitt of the type that Sinclair Lewis parodied. This is the kind of "education" that the group dynamicists advocates: they seek to dispel one characteristic flaw of "mass society," the alienation of the individual, by fostering another, his other-directed conformity to the current style in faiths, patterns of behaviour, or whatever.

It is possible, however, to reduce alienation not by discarding one's principles but by associating with others whose principles one shares. Education in a complex urban society has as one of its important functions the establishment of a common understanding of jointly held basic values. A villager is at ease with his neighbours because he grew up with them and knows them as he knows his family; but a resident of New York or London can feel at home from his knowledge that the rest of his world shares his concept of what fundaments define a good society. To maintain this consensus does not call for crude indoctrination. It is a misunderstanding of democracy to hold that this political system has no place for individualists. It could be one of the proudest functions of adult education, on the contrary, to furnish to mavericks—the square pegs who could never fit into the round holes of the standard educational system—the opportunity to develop their potential later in life. Some of the most notable figures in Western society, men like Harry S. Truman or Henry Mencken, have been self-educated; and often their greatness was part of a cantankerous individuality, an inability to adjust to the group.

3. The content of adult education, like that of any other kind of education, ought to be the society's cultural heritage, transmitted for the sake of individual improvement. This third position, to which we adhere, needs little comment—except perhaps amazement that it has to be defended against

professional educators. In Powell's words:

> I am...astonished...that, in discussing a field called "education," it is necessary to argue in behalf of *knowledge*...Adult education, apart from formal courses, has sought to achieve its goals almost wholly through the elaboration of process rather than the enrichment of content...I am quite serious in saying that we are in some danger of leaving "curiosity" to be satisfied by gossip, "creativeness" by a do-it-yourself kit, and "comprehension" by the mere acquisition of tolerance for other people's views.

Method

As this quotation suggests, in adult education the relation between content and method has often been conceived of as an opposition, as content *versus* method. The notion that method is more important than content, to the degree that it derives from similar statements in the works of John Dewey and his followers is based on a lack of understanding. When a student of Dewey like Sidney Hook writes, "Far more important than knowledge is the method by which it is reached," he means by this that it matters less, for example, whether a student learns the specific facts of chemistry or of astronomy than that he learns in general terms what constitutes scientific evidence. "Educational institutions...must build up in students a critical sense of evidence, relevance and validity against which the multitudinous seas of propaganda will wash in vain." There is a contrast here not between learning and nonlearning, but between learning matters of first and second priority. When adult educators use the term "method," however, they generally mean "how we may guide the class without dominating it, keep the atmosphere informal without letting it become disorganized, help the student to feel himself a part of the group without feeling submerged in it,"etc. "Scientific method" in the context of adult education designates not a mode of thought and behaviour that is taught but an alternative to education in this sense:

> It is [the authors'] belief that an adult-education programme should be oriented to meet the felt needs of people and that these felt needs are not generally satisfied by methods designed to pass subject-matter information efficiently from authorities (the textbooks, the reading references, or the instructor) to the

student. Felt needs are more likely to be satisfied by methods which involve the use of scientific method—that is, the identification of the problem or the block to needs satisfaction, the gathering of data, the formulation of a hypothesis, and finally, the testing of this hypothesis through an action programme.

"Group discussion is the basic method of adult education." This aphorism, repeated so frequently by adult educators, can refer to either of two quite different contexts:

1. *Discussion as a pedagogic device.* Many studies have been made to test whether lectures or discussion (or, sometimes, a combination of the two) is the more effective means of transmitting knowledge and attitudes. A recent survey of this research by Dietrick includes a bibliography of 186 items. Many of these studies are not wholly comparable, however, since neither "discussion" nor "effective" is uniformly defined. When the amount of information acquired was taken as the criterion of efficacy, most of the studies showed no difference between the two methods; and "where significant differences have been found, they have generally...[indicated] the superiority of the lecture method." But adult educators (particularly those who pay lip service to scientific method) have tended to resist this conclusion. The fact that many of the studies were made with college students rather than adults is often used to dismiss the evidence. Let us grant that it is far from conclusive; and for the sake of the argument, let us yield to the bias in favour of discussion. In that case, we must be quite clear what has been accepted. If (a) there is an attempt to transmit a specific content and teach certain facts or attitudes or behaviour patterns, and if (b) an expert participates as such in the discussion, group discussion is a valid and often useful pedagogical method. No one would deny this, or even perhaps that discussion may be more important in adult than in standard education. More generally, the efficacy of a teaching method depends mainly on the educational end being sought.

An objective defines the possible processes of education which may be used for its accomplishment. If the presentation of an ordered body of principles is desired, it is necessary to use a lecture, a film, a book, or some other similar approach. If a skill is to be taught, demonstration and practice are required.

If a group wishes to examine its existing knowledge to crystallize a set of convictions or principles, it must ordinarily use discussion. To be sure, the objective does not finally determine the means; it merely limits the range of choice.

2. *Discussion as a means of strengthening group feeling.* For group dynamicists, the superiority of group discussion lies not in effectiveness as a pedagogic device, but in the simple fact that a number of individuals have coalesced into a group. Brought together into a "face-to-face situation," they benefit from the consequent reduction in alienation. Among this kind of advocates of the discussion method, "learning" is good but teaching must be avoided: "It seems to me that anything that can be *taught* to another is relatively inconsequential, and has little or no significant influence on behaviour." Subject-matter competence on the part of the discussion leader, if there is to be one, is thus positively forbidden (if such an authoritarian term may be used):

I have often, myself, argued that it is perilous for a man a lead groups in the field in which he *is* expert. As Robert Blakely puts it, "It is harder for a subject-matter expert to keep his special knowledge in check than it is for a layman to acquire the subject-matter orientation and discussion techniques to lead a group well."

And when a subject-matter expert is present, he need not—according to the proponents of this view—restrict himself to the area about which he knows something. For example, a man teaching public speaking to members of a trade union discovered that "the fellows who were taking the course were learning speaking so they could throw over the old union leadership." Having discovered their "felt needs," the teacher of public speaking, in Powell's opinion, "should have started a new course on union politics."

> Discussion among equally ignorant fellow learners, with no such dangerous expert present, "somehow... is more consistent with a democratic philosophy and more conducive to good mental health upon the part of both leader and learners."

The dispute in adult education about group discussion, thus, is not really one over method but rather, like that about whether the individual or society shall benefit from education, a disagreement on content. If content of one sort or another is to be taught, and learned, then no educator would even deny that discussion is one effective means of achieving this end. But to denote mere participation in a group for a therapeutic purpose as "education," and indeed as all of adult education, is "noxious foolishness."

Evaluation

The purpose of evaluation in adult education, it is generally agreed, is "continuous programme improvement." It is also an accepted maxim that knowledge of his own progress encourages the student to greater effort. Adult educators agree, finally, that programme evaluation, though of crucial importance, takes place far too infrequently. Beyond these generalizations, the usual confusion reigns.

What is it we want to evaluate? What is "good"? "Unless we know where we are going and what we are trying to accomplish, no design for measurement and evaluation of results can possibly be formulated." Nevertheless, most of the works on adult education that discuss the matter elaborate on *how* to measure educational programmes without considering precisely *what* they want to evaluate. This would be legitimate only if programmes were established with a clear notion of their specific purpose, but except in credit courses, where evaluation also is less of a problem, the contrary is the typical case. "To educate the community", for example, is much too general an objective for a library to be useful for purposes of measurement.

The questions that the various types of evaluation are designed to answer can be summarized into four basic queries:

A. Are the consumers satisfied—with the facilities, accessibility, administration, fees, quality of instruction, etc.?

B. Is the programme meeting the "needs" of the community?

C. Do the participants experience "growth"?

D. Have the participants acquired new knowledge or skills, or have their attitudes changed?

Each of these will be discussed in turn.

A. CONSUMER SATISFACTION

The usual type of programme evaluation is, quite simply, a counting of noses. Most directors of adult education maintain more less elaborate enrolment records, from which they can tell how many participants they have, how much continuity there is from one season to the next, which are the popular programmes, and so on. Additional information is often sought through questionnaires or interviews. At the Rochester Institute of Technology, for example, "it has been the practice...to find out what the 'customers' think, on the assumption that nothing is too good to be improved," and students' opinions are solicited on courses, teachers, staff, store, equipment, parking facilities the catalogue of courses, and registration procedures. Favourable replies to such questions, however, need indicate nothing about educational content. Students' satisfaction with courses may be based on such irrelevant matters as "prices" or the accessibility of the extension center. In general, according to Knowles, students range from "Pollyannas" to "chronic complainers" through a normal distribution curve, like the one that he designed to help directors evaluate this type of evaluation.

Kempfer's "composite superiority ratio," similarly, was based on: size of programme, number of population segments served, flexibility of schedule, number of approaches used, number of co-ordinative practices, number of cooperative practices. The "best" programmes, in other words, are those that enroll the highest proportion of the population, that meet at times and places convenient to participants, and that do not conflict with the schedules of other institutions. No reasonable person would challenge the theses that if a programme was adjudged "good" by educational standards, generally the more participants it had the "better" it would be, and that such an increase in participation could be furthered, for example, by careful scheduling. But such criteria, while relevant, ought to be subordinate to what Kempfer himself—in a different work—terms "the truest test of the merit of an adult-education programme," namely, "the results produced."

> Most "evaluation" rests on how many people will "buy" a new programme in a certain length of time; and on subjective reports from the participants. But what these "measure" no

one knows; *de gustibus non disputandum est;* and an education should have to meet profounder tests than will do for a toothpaste.

B. ARE COMMUNITY "NEEDS" MET?

Certainly the outstanding example of such an evaluation is the baltimore Cooperative Survey and Work-Study Conference (1947-1948). This was a joint enterprise of the Baltimore public schools, all other adult-education agencies in that city, and the relevant department of the National Education Association. Eighteen local committees, formed to survey as many areas of adult education, met regularly over a period of seven months and gathered data about local programmes and resources. A final committee on coordination and evaluation surveyed the city as a whole and acted as liaison among the other committees. Nineteen parallel committees were set up to survey the surrounding area. All this work culminated in a three-day conference called to discuss the committees' reports. For nearly two years thereafter, an enlarged committee on coordination and evaluation met monthly to plan for further activity and improvement.

It can be assumed that the information accumulated in the Baltimore survey was useful in establishing new courses and eliminating duplications, if only because it resulted in the organization of the Baltimore Association for Adult Education, which provides "some coordinating services for the various participating agencies". More citizens of Baltimore also may have become aware of the adult-education offerings available to them. One might imagine from the enthusiastic appraisal given them, for example bv Benne (who participated as a National Education Association expert), that the Baltimore survey and conference had also achieved their stated purpose. He described them as "the marriage of two promising democratic youngsters in the adult education field,... the *work-group conference movement* and the *cooperative action research movement,"* and thus as "an *historic event in the history of adult education."* We should not be misled by the turgid language into supposing that the survey accomplished what it had been set up to do, the "evaluation of adult education." It was appraised as excellent because of the impressive number of committees created, the many times all these persons met together—in short, because of the process rather than the results. Like the discussion method, the survey is seen less as an effective means toward a worthwhile end than as a good in itself.

C. DO PARTICIPANTS EXPERIENCE "GROWTH"?

According to group-actionists, only the participants themselves, as individuals or preferably as a group, can judge the value of what they are doing.

In every genuine adult education enterprise it happens that the individuals who participate tend to become a *true group.* The principal distinction to be made here, that is, between true groups and mechanical collectivities, pseudo-groups, is this: the former tend always in the direction of fellowship and friendship, whereas the latter tend always to create a semblance of unity through concealed coercions. ... Only participants will know how true groups come into existence and what dynamic principles they follow.

If "only participants will know," a skeptic might ask, how do they know? It is often admitted that "satisfactory measures of the growth of adult learners have not yet been developed." In general, however, adults' "real satisfaction and that of their teachers comes [sic] when they are aware that the unique personalities are finding ways to express themselves more completely." The path to this awareness is often paved with the most prosaic stones —evaluation questionnaires of various types.

While recognizing that the full evaluation of discussion lies beyond the process of discussion, it is important that a group recognize that they can find intermediate checks on the quality of their discussion by evaluation from time to time their own group process and the difficulties and problems which it presents. It is also true that the latter two objectives of discussion growth of members in insight and skill in managing group participation and the growth of the group as a group may also be well-served by a group's evaluation of its procedures.

One evaluation scale, as an example, ranges from "It was one of the most rewarding experiences I have ever had" to "It was a complete waste of time."

D. RESULTS

The discussion of how to evaluate programmes is, thus, largely a dispute over whether there should be any subject-matter content in adult education. If content is irrelevant, then the main question becomes whether the consumers are satisfied, or whether they are experiencing "growth" in a "true group." If, however, education is understood in the usual sense—the transmission of new facts, ideas and values to persons who lacked them—then evaluation also has a definite meaning. If the goal of a programme is to teach the participants conversational French, or to give them a better understanding of American foreign policy, or to change their attitudes toward Negroes, whether such a goal has been achieved can be gauged with reasonable accuracy.

Perhaps the main difficulty in measuring the objective results of adult education is that the authority of the evaluator is ambiguous. As we have remarked in several contexts, advocates of "democracy" in education cannot accept forthrightly the dominance of the teacher in any learning situation, and their ambivalence is particularly notable when they discuss evaluation. Thus, according to a committee of the Adult Education Association of which Kempfer was chairman:

> Difficulties often arise when evaluatin is made by outsiders. The temptation is great to impose objectives and evaluate the programme in terms of them. An outside evaluation can have validity only insofar as it is made in complete harmony with the objectives held by the participants.

The authority of the teacher is further reduced because, we are told, the type of objective tests used in schools cannot be used in adult education:

> To most adults the words "test," "quiz," and "examination" call forth such unpleasant memories that it is often difficult to use them in voluntary adult groups. We have not yet been able to develop satisfactory substitute methods for measuring some kinds of learning.

In most noncredit programmes, thus, no attempt is made to measure learning, though sometimes the difficulty has been overcome by calling a spade a shovel: "We find some adult groups filling out 'inventories' or writing 'summaries' or solving 'case problems.' " We doubt whether it is necessary even to disguise a quize under another name. In a nation where quiz programmes are (or were!) used to sell a variety of commercial products, where puzzles are a feature of many newspapers and magazines, we need not take too seriously the dictum that the very word "quiz" turns potential participants away from education.

As examples of both the difficulties and the possibilities in measuring the change in knowledge or attitudes resulting from adult-education programmes, several studies can be cited.

Four evening classes were evaluated in terms of "the way in which...teachers dealt with the motives of [their] students." While over two-thirds of the students attended the courses for reasons other than content, the teachers apparently ignored these motives. "Although a majority had wanted to learn things about themselves, make new friends or escape their mundane daily life,...by the end of the semester they were thinking primarily in terms of the information they had obtained." Similarly, of the agencies that conduct world-affairs programmes "expressed a desire to provide their clients with opportunities for companionship and self-expression," even though they knew that this was at least in part what participants had come for. "Many agencies sought to 'change attitudes,' but the respondents did not indicate that many of the clients wanted their attitudes changed." From the point of view of the participants' expectations, such programmes must clearly be evaluated as failures. In an educational rather than "democratic" frame of reference, however, the conclusion might well be precisely the opposite.

About twenty-five years ago, Lorimer compared the occupations and certain leisure-time activities of two Brooklyn samples paired for equivalent juvenile education, one of which had and the other had not taken formal adult courses since leaving school. The differences that this continuing education apparently made in the type of jobs held, recent pay increases, and job satisfaction were significant among grammar school graduates, but less so among high school graduates. For both groups the completion of vocational courses since leaving school was significantly correlated with reading of superior newspapers and magazines and with the use of libraries. Liberal arts courses were also positively correlated with these habits, as well as with interest in the theatre and arts. The correlation does not, of course, indicate the direction of the assumed cause-effect relation: we still do not know whether adult courses had subsidiary effects; or whether a larger proportion of persons who, for example, read better newspapers, also enrolled in courses; or both.

After it was discovered that about 30 per cent of Cincinnati's population knew nothing about "the main purpose of the United Nations", all the city's educational agencies, newspapers, business groups, civic organizations, and church groups cooperated in a concentrated six-month effort to educate the city. Ostensibly the programe was intended not to influence opinion but only to present facts, though both aims seem to have influenced some of the campaign's features. In all, 59,588 brochures and throwaways were distributed; 2,800·clubs were "reached" with speakers or written material; club women sent 1,000 letters and 1,350 telegrams; one radio station scheduled spot programmes on the United Nations 150 times a week; an archbishop addressed 10,000 members of the Catholic PTA. "Peace Begins with the United Nations—the United Nations Begins with You", the slogan of the campaign, was ubiquitous, printed on trolley cards, on matchbooks, on blotters. The objective was to "reach" every adult among the 1,155,703 residents of Cincinnati and its environs. At the end of this massive effort, the percentage of persons totally unacquainted with the main purpose of the international organization was reduced from 30 to 28. Some adult educators found cause for rejoicing even in this dismal failure (it happened; therefore it was good): "While follow-up studies have found little lasting effect of these efforts in mass understanding of the United Nations, the cooperating educational agencies have learned valuable lessons in discovery and interpretation of new needs that call for educational attention". The fact that these newly discovered needs remained unmet in spite of the agencies' best efforts is apparently irrelevant.

In contrast to these two evaluations of a whole city's adult-education facilities, the following relates to one effort of a single small institution. This school had a parent-education programme for members of its mothers' club. Its attempt to measure the effectiveness of the programme moved gradually through several of the types of evaluation discussed above. It started with consumer research: end-of-term questionnaires were given to the participants to find out whether they thought the course had been valuable and the leaders good, and what other problems should be considered in future series. Next it devised an end-of-term "attitude-and-practice test"—a type of self-evaluation. Then one test was given at the beginning and another at the end of the programme, in order to measure changes in attitudes as perceived by the individuals themselves. The staff then constructed an anonymous questionnaire for the fathers, in order to find out from a possibly more objective source whether there had been any changes in their wives' behaviour toward the children. Results were encouraging, but tne staff feared that, as representatives of the sponsoring agency, they were receiving biased answers from the fathers. They then circulated an attitude-and-practice questionnaire among all mothers of the two grades involved in the programme, and found significant differences between member and nonmember mothers; but they recognized that the mothers following the more desirable practices might also have been the ones who most frequently joined the clubs. At the time the evaluation was described, they were continuing to experiment with still other methods.

A more complex evaluation was that of an experimental course in social psychology designed especially for adults by the Center for the Study of Liberal Education for Adults. The goals set for the course were: (1) to "sensitize students to the significance of their participating in groups"; (2) to "lead students to understand the base of effective small group action and increase their skill of working in a group"; (3) to "increase their insight into social problems which relate to the interaction of people and groups". Through the use of interviews, a thematic apperception test, and a specially designed problem-solving test, the instructor discovered that the course had produced no change with respect to these three aims. The students, they told him, had enjoyed the course; but one of them, who had "talked enthusiastically to the instructor", when reinterviewed by an outside evaluator said he actually considered the discussion method "a waste of time."

Several studies have been made of participants in packaged programmes. One of the stated aims of the World Politics Programme, for instance, was "the improvement of critical thinking", and one analyst concluded from various before-and-after tests administered to some Los Angeles discussants and a control group that such an improvement had indeed taken place. However, the sample on which the study was based was not only very small but entirely self-selected, and if only for this reason the significance of the results is questionable. Similarly, an earlier study of participants in the Great Books programme "demonstrated a positive relationship between the increase in [their] capacity [to think logically] and length of participation in the course", but according to Houle this relation may not be statistically significant, chiefly because the study was limited to the first year's programme.

As several of these examples indicate, it is possible to make some evaluation, even if not a wholly satisfactory one, of changes more complex than the mere acquisition of new facts. However, when adult educators try to "measure intangibles such as growth of understanding, insight, 'broadness', etc.," many "have substituted a kind of intuition as a basis for judging whether a course is effective or not, which means that they have no concrete means of evaluation left at all". "Indeed, most organizations that emphasize... indirect services seem to live mostly on faith that their work is producing results". For example, in a survey of 54 communities served by ten general-extension divisions, when some activities proved to have been in existence for too short a time to measure their effects, Thompson concluded with typical optimism that "we may assume some good was performed in each instance". To many adult educators, any attempt to implement the lip service they pay to evaluation is unwelcome, especially if it *is* possible really to measure accurately a programme's educational effect. For those who perceive themselves as missionaries, engaged in furthering world peace or mitigating human alienation, an assessment of this effort is "a kind of academic impertinence verging on sacrilege".

Summary

Perhaps the most pernicious doctrine in adult education

is the notion that "democracy" demands that the educator abdicate his professional authority.

Education is not democratic. It must be directed by those who are already educated, and it is based on the fundamentally antidemocratic notion that some people know better than others what should be done. Student self-government can never be extended to an equal voice in educational policy.

The "right" of participants to dictate educational policy contradicts the efforts of adult educators to maintain control over programmes they administer. This conflict is half-disguised by a remarkably ambiguous language, which can be illustrated especially in the multiple meanings given the word *need.*

An educator who attempts to manipulate students rather than teach them cannot stop with this initial hypocrisy, for every facet of adult education becomes infected as a consequence of his refusal to accept full professional responsibility. "Democracy" demands that the content of programmes be set, at least allegedly, by the "felt needs" of those to be educated. By a "democratic" fetish, the discussion group is designed as *the* method in adult education. Evaluation of programmes is principally in terms of consumer satisfaction.

Nothing could be of greater significance to adult education than a method of evaluation of its offerings by which their many deficiencies could be defined, analyzed and possibly eliminated. Most programmes are never appraised, whether in this or in any other sense. The aura of good will that befogs adult education is nowhere more evident than in the implicit axiom that all existent programmes are good. Some, of course, are "better", but the criteria by which they are so designated more often reinforce consumer supremacy than help establish relevant educational standards.

"Evaluation" of adult education is ordinarily based on one of the following:

1. Questionnaires, interviews and less directly, enrolment figures, can give an administrator an idea of students' opinions about adult-education services. While students' satisfaction might well be one factor to be considered in judging administrative practices (registration procedure, library hours) or the physical plant (light, janitorial services), teaching

methods and the educational content of courses are not within participants' legitimate province.

2. Are community "needs" met? A survey to determine this may, similarly, be used to judge what people say they want and whether this is available to them, but not to set educational policy.

3. Participants' self-evaluations may serve not to set policy but to point up misconceptions about the programmes purpose. If a student enrolls, say, in a course in literature and is disappointed in the programme because he is no less lonely than before, he might well be advised to join a social club.

4. The increase in knowledge or skill, or the change in attitudes or values, can be measured, and usually is in credit and vocational courses. Noncredit programmes, however, generally have no evaluation of this type. Notwithstanding the frequently expressed opinion to the contrary, most adults would probably welcome an objective measure of what they have actually learned, rather than a subjective one of—what they already know—the amount of pleasure they derived from a programme.

3

University Adult Education : General Principles

Adult education in universities has grown haphazardly, with little consideration given to underlying principles, with each problem met *ad hoc* when it arose. University adult education, thus, is at least as heterogeneous as American higher education itself; and just as there are few statements that would apply without qualification to Harvard and the University of California, and to small independent liberal arts colleges, and to denominational schools and junior colleges, so also there are few generalizations about university adult education that could not be challenged by citing this or that exception. Since this diversity is combined with a paucity of statistical or other objective data, any analysis of university adult education necessarily reflects, at least in its emphases and overtones, the point of view of the analyst. The reader of this look will not, we think, be troubled by any reticence in our statement of the position we try to defend. Whether or not he agrees with the policy recommendations we offer, we hope at least to be able to convince him that *a* policy is necessary. University adult education "must not be an administrative inadvertance or after-thought".

Ideally, the administrator of university adult education ought to be able to start from a consensus on basic policy. Unfortunately, however, there is little agreement on even the most basic questions. What is "college-level" education? Should the university restrict its extension services to this level, or even to education altogether? Or, most fundamentally, what are the functions of university adult education? Are they the same as those on the main campus, applied to a different population? What is the relevance of the fact that the participants are adults to the kind of programme offered, its standards, and so on? Questions of this order of generality, which are dealt with in this chapter, must be answered before we consider the more specific problems of educational and administrative policy.

The Place of the University in Adult Education

University adult education stands with one foot in the university and one in adult education, and many of its administrative problems exemplify the difficulty of maintaining a balance between these two quite different worlds. To understand university adult education, then, we must begin by studying the influences impinging on it from the two larger institutions of which it forms a part.

As was indicated in the last chapter, the number of agencies, institutions, and associations active in adult education is very great indeed. The point is important enough to be emphasized by listing here some of the typical organizations or programmes that often have this as one of their major interests. The categories are not, of course, mutually exclusive; and in particular the university frequently overlaps with some of the other agencies.

Educational institutions

- public schools
- colleges and universities
- Cooperative Extension Service
- business, technical, and special-interest schools
- private correspondence schools
- private adult schools
- libraries
- museums

Government agencies and departments

- U.S. Department of Agriculture
- U.S. Department of State

U.S. Office of Education
miscellaneous federal agencies that information the public on their specific fields
state departments of education
health departments and institutions
armed-forces programmes
prison education
in-service training of government employees

Private health, welfare, and recreation agencies

health-education agencies
family counselling and guidance agencies
community-welfare organizations
recreation and youth (Y's, settlement houses, etc.)
civic-improvement groups
adult-education councils and associations

Business and industry

trade associations and business organizations
education of the public about specific commodities and business goals
in-service training of employees
labour unions
professional organizations
farm groups

Miscellaneous organizations

women's groups
service clubs
fraternal organizations
parent-teacher associations
alumni groups
veterans and patriotic organizations
political associations
churches and religious groups

Mass media

newspapers and magazines
radio and television
motion pictures and theater

How many persons take part in all these programmes? Estimates are difficult to make, for several reasons: (1) Differences are great among programmes—in level, in duration, in purpose, in cost, in the work required of registrants; and to add the number of persons attending a single talk on cancer detection, for example, to that occasionally participating in PTA projects, to that receiving some instruction on their job, to that taking a correspondence course for credit over a period of months or years, does not result in a very meaningful sum. (2) Radio and television audiences, and even newspaper and magazines readers, are sometimes defined as participants in adult education; and estimates of their number, even after agreement is reached on which programmes are deemed educational, can be no more than loose approximations. (3) Some institutions total *students* enrolled and others *enrolments* in courses (without, that is, taking into account the fact that some students take more than one course); and when it is possible to compare registration figures by both procedures, as of the member institutions of the National University Extension Association according to its annual *Proceedings,* the latter figure is frequently more than double the former.

Estimates of the numbers in adult-education programmes in the country, therefore, have a wide range. The most restrictive count was by the Census Bureau, which included persons (rather than enrolments) who had met with a group at least three times. Those taking private courses or correspondence courses or on-the-job training were not counted. By this definition, there are some 9.2 million participants in adult education. According to more inclusive estimates, the figure is between 30 million and 50 million. Of a total somewhere in this range, perhaps two or three per cent, or four at the most, take part in university programmes. Whatever figures are accepted, it is clear that university adult education constitutes no more than a small fraction of the total effort to educate adults.

Adult education in universities, then, can hardly encompass its whole range and operate effectively. When its special skills are relevent, the university has something that only it can offer; but when they are not, the service to the community might better be given by other agencies, which have both different functions and sometimes easier access to funds. That there should be a rational division of labour in adult education is a dictum most general-extension administrators would support in principle. While all of the general-extension divisions surveyed by Morton, for instance, believed that their programmes should be of "significance to 'the public interest'," there was also "substantial agreement that these services should be of 'college grade.' " Differences are likely to arise not over the principle but over its interpretation.

In screening adult-education programmes, the university ought to use a fine mesh. If it exercises a particular, perhaps even an exaggerated, care in maintaining high standards, the consequent level of its offerings for adults will also facilitate another administrative goal, the closer integration of adult with regular university education.

The central functions of the university have been established by a long tradition and maintained by a relatively rigid institutional structure. These functions are, in brief, to educate a segment of the nation's youth in programmes leading to one or another academic degree, and to furnish to the faculty and students the facilities necessary for scholarly research. It is true that the charters of many public universities, and even of some private ones, include a vaguely worded clause enjoining the institution to render service to the people, and that the public obligation of land-grant institutions are specified in various acts of Congress. While this may mean that in some senses public universities have a greater responsibility to the people than private ones, it does not mean that they have a greater duty to respond to any demand from the community. Even the first portion of the statement might be challenged: private universities also receive public support. The foundations and individuals that contribute to them, as well as the institutions themselves, enjoy tax exemptions representing in effect substantial donations out of the public treasury; and many research projects at private universities are financed through grants from government agencies. In any case, it is poor policy to control a public institution in such a way as to induce it to waste its resources on tasks that, however important, do not lie within its proper function. On the contrary, the "peculiar duty" that publicly financed universities owe the people is to avoid accepting too broad a definition of their role. "Always the obligation must be understood within a complex of limitations as to provision of facilities, funds, staff-time, scope of curriculum and relative urgency of needs, and in the light of what the university can do well."

The Meaning of "Extension"

None of the important institutions of higher learning in the United States, one can safely say, presently restricts itself to activities precisely defined by the two functions of (1) daytime education toward a degree and (2) research. The supplementary educational effort may now include credit or non credit courses, in the evening or off campus; lecture series or casual lectures, by faculty or visiting personages, or conferences of various types, on campus or off; mass media and publications; information services; contract research and other aids to business, agriculture, and government; and so on.

The total extension function of the university, thus, is something considerably larger and more complex than what laymen often assume it to be, and this complexity is increased by the facts that the allocation of administrative responsibility varies greatly from one campus to another, and that no standard usage has developed for distinguishing the whole miscellany of extension activities from various portions of it. In this work, we shall use there arbitrary terms to denote successively smaller areas of meaning.

1. The whole of the variegated increment to the university's two basic tasks of education in day sessions and scholarly research (except for Cooperative Extention), we define as its *total extension function.* Cooperative Extension, or the activities of the Agricultural Extension Service, constitutes a special category, which differs so greatly in—among other respects—its legal back-ground, financing, and type and level of education, that we have omitted it altogether from the main text. It is discussed separately in Appendix 1.

2. That portion of the total extension function that is both education and at a college level we term *university adult education.* As will be detailed in ensuring chapters, the university has often taken on functions inappropriate to an educational institution, and within the educational function has often sunk below the standard proper to an institution of higher

learning. The term "university adult education," thus, separates out the major portion of what we deem to be legitimate within the total extension function.

3. By *general-extension division,* finally, we mean the formal unit of the university assigned to administer its adult education, or rather a portion of it. Roughly synonymous terms are "division of continuing education," "division of university extension," "evening college," "university college," "community college," and (in England) "extramural department," which are some of the official designations used by various institutions. The fact that a university does not have a separate general-extension division does not mean, of course, that it does not extension work as we use the term. And when an extension division exists, it is never in charge of the total extension function, and sometimes of no more than half of it. Typically it administers the extension of liberal arts courses but often not those of professional schools nor, for instance, the use of the library by the general public, information services, publications, or contract research.

A mere list of universities with general-extension divisions, thus, would tell us little about how much adult education, or what kind, each university offers; and in any case no complete list is available. Most studies of university adult education are limited either to descriptions of so-called representative programmes, "with very little statistical information to show how representative these institutions are and how they compare with other institutions and programmes," or to an examination of the members of one of the two professional associations. These are the National University Extension Association (or NUEA), which in 1959 had 81 members, most of them state universities; and the Association of University Evening Colleges (or AUEC), which in 1959 had 134 members, predominantly private urban institutions but including 34 NUEA members. According to Crimi's study of the 427 accredited private liberal arts colleges in the United States in 1953, slightly more than half (233) engaged in at least some adult education. A survey of all institutions of higher education conducted in 1958 by the United States Office of Education, finally, lists 593 that offered programmes other than resident degree-credit work. Combining the data from these several surveys gives a total of 752 institutions of higher education (or 748 if the four Canadian members of AUEC are omitted) known to offer programmes for adults. This is more than half of all such institutions in the country. This proportion can reasonably be taken as a minimum, for several reasons: (1) some universities with programmes for adults are not members of either NUEA or AUEC; (2) some liberal arts colleges were not included in Crimi's survey, a few of those to which he sent his questionnaire did not reply, and the number with adult education may well have increased in the interim; (3) the United States Office of Education survey did not distinguish between day and evening degree-credit work, so that, for example, 35 AUEC members, 2 NUEA members, and 140 of Crimi's respondents are shown to offer only resident degree-credit work; and (4) many other institutions sponsor activities such as concerts, lectures, etc., that they do not classify as adult education, while we do.

Though the statistics available constitute no more than rough approximations, they certainly warrant the conclusion that programmes for adults are a significant and growing element of American higher education. The extension has taken place in several senses.

The first and most obvious one *in time and place.* In 1906, when President Charles Van Hise of the University of Wisconsin organized its pioneering extension division, he intended to make "the boundaries of the University campus coterminous with the boundaries of the state." The means of reaching the social classes unable to attend the regular sessions have varied according to the circumstances. Courses for adults are now conducted (1) on the main campus, usually in the evening; (2) in extension centers (also called evening or university colleges, or resident centers); (3) in schools, libraries, and other widely dispersed public buildings, usually in the evening; and (4) by correspondence, radio, or television.

An extension in time and place does not imply in itself any change in curriculum or standards. An adaptation of courses or methods to the special demands of particular sectors of the population, but still without lowering the standards of higher education, can be termed a *functional* extension.

When the latter change *is* made, in order to carry "knowledge to the masses rather than [extend] the scope of the university along traditional lines," this can only be termed a *substandard* extension.

In some of the activities in which universities are now engaged, finally, the adaptation to new purposes has been so substantial that the term "extension" seems inappropriate. When only lip service is paid to education or research, so that these purposes are in effect supplanted by others—social welfare, public relations, commercial profit, for example—we can more aptly speak of a *conversion* of the university's function.

Some state universities, believing that they are morally bound to serve all the people of the state, have followed the "Wisconsin pattern" in sacrificing educational standards to this end. Private universities, on the other hand, have tended more toward what has been designated the "University of Chicago pattern" of university adult education: "emphasis seems to be upon academic and cultural subjects and the shaping of adult curricula at the highest university level". These alternative terms, however, are not wholly accurate even of the two institutions chosen as the contrasting types, and we think our designations are preferable. The important thing is to differentiate, in one way or another, university adult education from extension activities that are either nonuniversity or noneducation.

What is "College Level"?

Every discussion of this important question seems to reach the same conclusion: "a set of specific criteria... for determining the kinds of services appropriate for inclusion in extension programmes...[has] yet to be defined." There are several, not necessary mutually exclusive, ways by which the standards appropriate to an institution of higher learning can be indicated approximately.

1. What is meant by the phrase "college level" can be spelled out at greater length. University adult education, thus, "should concentrate on the qualitative and relatively complex, on programmes and courses that emphasize ideas and provide intellectual stimulation," those "requiring familiarity with broad fields of knowledge and the exercise of mature judgment in their organization and interpretation." These paraphrases of "college

level" are useful to some degree; but since they also have to be interpreted, there must still be an administrative policy to implement the intent of the expanded definition.

2. By rigorous admission requirements and/or by stipulating a general examination as a prerequisite to graduation, the university as a whole can maintain at least a partial control over standards. When it exists, this is usually confined to credit courses.

3. Entrance requirements may be set for particular programmes. Certain credit courses, thus, typically are restricted to students with a given number of completed credits, and sometimes certain other courses are prerequisites. Similarly, many conferences and other noncredit programmes are so specialized or at so high a level that they appeal only to those with an appropriate background.

4. The various academic departments on the home campus can be made responsible for curricula, texts and other reading material, teaching personnel, and academic standards generally.

Most university extension directors [surveyed by Morton] believed that "college level" courses are those (1) "equivalent to resident courses offered for credit", (2) "with standards of information and attainment and inclusion of subject material fully equal to resident courses and would be so recognized by 'usual catalogue descriptions of universities'," or (3) "which colleges and universities usually provide and which would be recognized by university faculties as being of college grade".

The control by the faculty that these recommendations imply has the obvious advantage of vesting the discretionary power in the carriers of the academic tradition, who have themselves undergone the discipline of attaining advanced degrees. To point out that standards on the home campus are not very high, while often true, enough, is not too relevant; it would be utopian in most institutions to expect the quality of extension programmes to be higher than that in the university as a whole. Some degree of faculty control is usual, and is especially appropriate, over credit courses. For it to be effective, however, it has to be part of an administrative arrangement by which faculty members become fully involved in the general-extension division's welfare. And their intrinsic competence to determine the content of the much more heterogeneous noncredit programme is not so obvious.

5. The dean of extension can be given full control. This system, which has the advantage of focusing responsibility on the one person most directly associated with the programme, is that most used with noncredit programmes. "That responsibility for non-credit courses rests solidly in the hands of evening college deans is apparent from the fact that of the 82 schools offering such work, only seven place the responsibility elsewhere." Similarly, in 33 out of 39 general-extension divisions surveyed by Dugan, the deans exercised "complete administrative control over non-credit classes." General-extension administrators, however, cannot be expected to have subject-matter competence in all areas of their programmes; and many of them are under heavy financial pressure to increase enrolment. If some deans have used their discretionary power to improve on the curriculum of the day campus, others have perpetrated courses in driver-training, conversation, and so on.

6. The extension dean and the appropriate academic department can be given joint responsibility. Such a system is apparently seldom used, though when either the dean or the department has sole control, this is usually exercised after consultation with the other.

7. One way of setting standards for noncredit programmes, finally, is to maintain that all courses, credit or noncredit, should be of equal equality and that the same control should apply to both. If "universities will husband their resources for education that comes within the meaning of the term 'higher,'...there is no good reason why anything that a university is willing to offer at all should not carry credit if students wish it."

In sum, we must distinguish both between worthless and worthwhile activities and between the broad genus constituting the second group and, within it, that smaller species appropriate to a university. To do this, we must ask several questions:

1. Is it education or research?
2. Is it at college level?
3. If so, would the programme duplicate activities that either are already in existence or could be undertaken by other institutions?

4. Within the class of nonduplicating college-level programmes, is this one more significant than alternative ways of using the money, personnel and facilities it will require?

The principal difficulty in defining "college level" is not in saying *what* it is—there is really no great mystery here—but in designating *who* shall decide in doubtful cases. So long as the responsibility is left vague, it helps little to specify criteria. As we have seen in the preceding paragraphs, different universities have established a number of administrative structures by which the responsibility for quality has been specified. Which arrangement is most likely to continue from the nineteenth century the tradition of democratizing educational opportunities without vulgarizing this mission? In abstract terms, that which combines real control over academic standards with an incentive to use it in order to establish and maintain a high level. What particular division of responsibility will lead to this end in any particular case would depend in part on local circumstances, but we believe that an arrangement that encourages the executive, administrative, and teaching personnel to cooperate is usually better than full control by any one of these.

Since the matter is of considerable importance, the reader may find it useful to compare this set of guides to programming in university adult education with one other that has been drawn up. According to Kidd, five criteria have won general acceptance among Canadian universities, several of which believe that "every course offered should be subjected to this kind of enquiry by some committee once every year".

1. Will the programme meet the demonstrated demand of a sizable number of people? (Our comment is that this seems to smack too much of customer sovereignty, by which "felt needs" take precedence over educational policy. Even if an administrator is limited by his budget, as he almost always, should his creativity be restricted to programmes for which there is not a probable, but an already "demonstrated" demand?)

2. Will it contribute to the "economic, social or cultural well-being of the people?" (Our comment is that if the programme is educational in a true sense, the answer to this question is Yes in all instances; and if the programme is not educational, then the university has no business in it, whether or not other benefits might ensue.)

3. Do participants care enough to "support it with intellectual effort as well as with fees?"

4. "Is the subject matter of the course on a level that is suitable for the university?" (These two questions, we feel, might be improved by specifying how, and by whom, the answers would be given.)

5. "Is any other agency in a position to provide the service at least as well as is the university?" (This is one of the best ways, though not sufficient in itself, of specifying "college level".)

The Teaching of Adults

One excuse frequently offered for the low level of university adult education is that the participants constitute, in one sense or another, so special a group that ordinary standards do not apply. It is true that students in extension differ in some respects from their regular-session counterparts, but there are no intrinsic reasons excusing systematically lower standards.

First of all, by definition, participants in adult education are considerably older on the average than those in the regular day session. The physiological relevance of this age difference, however, can easily be exaggerated. While it is true that the ability to learn—particularly if "learning" is defined as memorizing—reaches a peak before thirty, deterioration thereafter is very gradual, so that "at least well beyond the age of fifty there is ample ability to learn far exceeding the limits attempted by most individuals". Though not for physiological reasons, adult students do have certain special handicaps. If they have been out of school for a long period, they may well have lost the habits of study established there. Adults are less malleable than adolescents; they tend to be more set in their ways, less inclined to assimilate new theories and abstractions. While such an "attitude is often a serious limitation, it is also their great strength, for it disciplines any instructor who would move their minds with a jejune preoccupation with a fact or a principle. They insist, to the perpetual vexation of teachers and the eternal enrichment of subjects, upon wedding their own knowledge of things to the generalizations of learning". Among the adults who are likely to take courses, moreover, such a resistance to instructors' generalizations is likely to be based on at least as sound a general factual background as the average day undergraduate has mastered. Groups of day and evening students matched for sex, high-school scholastic record, and the number of college credits completed, were given three-hour tests in history and social studies, fine arts, and science and mathematics; and the evening students did as well as the day students in one case, and better in another.

The one really significant deficiency of adult students derives not from their age but from the related fact that education is for them a secondary part-time activity, undertaken usually after a day's work. In that case, they may well be less able to concentrate on a lecture or discussion than when they are fresh, and they generally have less time to study at home. Their education is usually spread over many years, often with long gaps and little continuity from one course to the next.

The point is often made that such handicaps are offset by the generally high level of motivation of extension students. They demonstrate by their very presence in the programme that they are willing to work hard to learn what they deem to be useful or necessary. That they are highly motivated is patent, but motivated in what sense? According to the studies summarized in Table 1, two-thirds to four-fifths attend classes, whether for credit or not, mainly in order to improve their occupational efficiency.

Table 1. Proportion of Extension Students taking classes in order to improve their occupational efficiency

Date	Sample	Percentage vocationally motivated
1956	University College, Syracuse University	75
1953	8 universities in the Chicago area	78
1951-1952	57 NUEA member institutions	More than 80
1951	University of California at Los Angeles	66
1948	Rochester Institute of Technology	73
1939	10 NUEA member institutions	63
1937	6 universities	about 75

Certainly a much smaller proportion of the students in regular daytime classes are so directly focused on future professional needs. The reasons for taking extension classes are often compelling, if not coercive. Not only do degrees lead to better jobs, but in a number of professions the accumulation of college credits (not necessarily degree-credits) is required even in order to maintain one's present status. According to one survey, many of those in credit classes had enrolled because their employers (who occasionally also paid the fees) urged them to do so or even set studying as a prerequisite to promotion. Extension students, then, are very often a captive audience in almost the same sense that school children are; and the frequent statements to the contrary hardly apply to credit courses and are not wholly valid concerning noncredit programmes. Many extension students, on the contrary, are in a hurry to acquire credits, or at least to master a technical field; and very often the instructor will need to make a particular effort to explain why the seemingly extraneous liberal arts courses required for a degree are also useful to them.

It is true that some participants in noncredit programmes are not captive, but it does not follow from this fact that academic standards ought to be lowered, not even if the administrator's main desideratum is to maintain a large enrolment. Take a noncredit class, say, in American history. Some joined it out of what we have termed an "interest" in the subject—that is, either partly or wholly for social or other noneducational reasons. Others joined it out of a "concern" with American history; they are serious in their intent to learn something of this field. So long as both types of motivation are called "felt needs", one cannot distinguish between them; but now that a distinction has been made, what follows from it? To some degree, a choice must be made between the "interested" and the "concerned": the same course will not necessary appeal to both. If some of the "interested" drop out, this may be all to the good; they may not have belonged in a college programme altogether. Others, if they have the ability, may be stimulated by a good course. Though they joined it for reasons irrelevant to the function of the university, they stay in it in order to get an education. A person "concerned" with the subject, on the other hand, will drop out of a programme if it is watered down; having come for bread, he will not be satisfied with pap. The irregular attendance, the high drop-out rate in some non-credit programmes, thus, are not—what they are too often taken to be—compelling arguments to reduce the academic level. It may be that some participants had a "felt need" for high standards and therefore quit a programme conceived in the "philosophy" that no adult can become seriously involved with truly intellectual questions.

Summary

University adult education constitutes no more than about 4 per cent of the whole adult-education movement. This fact reinforces what would be true in any case: the proper role of the university in adult education, no less than in any of its other activities, is to educate by standards appropriate to an institution of higher learning.

The prerequisite to intelligent administrative policy is a precise definition of the organization's purpose. The purpose of a university's adult-education programme, we believe, should be to conduct college-level education. Of the four types of extension that we have defined, that in time and place generally and correctly forms the basic fare. Given a population of potential participants much more heterogeneous than college students, however, the administrator of university adult education ordinarily seeks a greater variety of content and method than on the day campus—what we have termed functional extension. While this is usually a smaller element than the first type of extension, it is no less important for that reason. What we have termed substandard extension and conversion, we deem to be illegitimate—not because high-school education, recreation, and social welfare, for example, are reprehensible in themselves, but because the university's reservoir of scarce skills and facilities should be used exclusively for the highly important tasks that only the university can perform.

Many adult-education programmes lack a traditional guide to either content or method, and thus offer the university administrator the opportunity either to experiment truly creatively, or to sacrifice educational quality to commercialism, public relations, or social welfare. If he is to distinguish between novelties that are appropriate to an institution of higher learning and those that break completely with the scholarly tradition, the administrator must be very precisely aware of what he means by "college level". Ideally, noncredit courses in particular ought to have as their primary function the education of adults seeking learning for its own sake, helping them find new meaning in life after they have been jolted out of their routine sufficiently to go back to school. If this ideal has sometimes been approached, in many programmes the content has been set without any regard for this or any other educational goal, simply in response to the "demonstrated needs" of the participants.

Adult students are different in several important respects from their counterparts on day campuses. Their participation is ordinarily a part-time venture, secondary to other activities. They are more mature, and thus more critical and less flexible. About three-quarters attend general-extension courses in order to improve their earning capacity, and they are thus hardly less a captive audience than regular daytime undergraduates. Those who stray into university programmes with no understanding of their purpose ought to be seduced, if they have the ability, into learning something at college level, but they should not be permitted to pervert the programme.

4

Educational Policy

The first two types in our proposed classification, extension in time and place and functional extension, might appear to be paraphrases of the more usual designations, credit and noncredit programmes. While there would be some truth in this supposition, it is better to restrict "credit" and "noncredit"—like "general-extension division"—to formal descriptions of actual programmes, and substitute other terms in an abstract analysis of university adult education. Moreover, practice varies so much that the meaning of "credit", even in this limited sense, is somewhat ambiguous.

At one time courses accepted toward a higher degree were "credit", and all others were not. Today, this dichotomy has spread out into a continuum, with a variety of intermediate types between the extremes. Often no more than a stipulated proportion of the semester-hours required for a degree may be taken in extension, and sometimes extension credits add up only to an Associate degree or a certificate rather than an A.B. Some credit courses can also be taken without credit, though often the fee and requirements are then lower. And sometimes no credit is offered for the most advanced programmes, such as a review of recent developments in a professional field for persons with graduate degrees, for whom more academic credits would be pointless. Yet while there is a large overlap in all respects, the typical participant, his motives for enrolling, the subject matter and teaching method, the maintenance of standards, all still differ to some degree between credit and noncredit programmes. Most obviously, the student in a credit course wants some formal recognition of the work he has completed, while in a noncredit programme the participant may not. This means that those who attend for no credit are sometimes more interested in the content itself, rather than in pursuing a course of study for its instrumental value; sometimes they are interested only or mainly in meeting people. It means, that better records are ordinarily kept of credit courses and that more studies have been made of credit students; and much of the discussion in this chapter, willy-nilly, will reflect this imbalance.

'Credit' and 'Noncredit' Courses

There is a broad consensus among university administrators that both credit and noncredit offerings are appropriate to its adult programme, though some exceptions to this rule can be noted. In 1958, a faculty committee at Columbia University recommended that all students in its School of General Studies "be required to take full programmes leading to a degree of Bachelor of Science," and when the administration put this new policy into effect, Dean Louis Hacker resigned his post in protest. The contrary position, that credit work be abandoned, has seldom been defended, except by indirection:

> [A] director of an extension organization offered the opinion that the real purpose of a university programme is to provide opportunities for any learning important to the problems and the lives of people. He expressed the belief that the greatest opportunities are in the area of non-degree-credit specialized college level courses and that these should be offered whenever and wherever a real need and demand exist.

Given the typical shortage of funds, personnel and facilities, setting this priority would probably lead to skimping degree credit courses.

In any case, in view of the varying proportions of the total extension function that are defined by different universities as "extension", it is difficult to say what the relation between credit and noncredit work is in actual practice, as opposed to stated policy. While a few universities in addition to Columbia, as well as a larger number of liberal arts colleges, restrict their general-extension *course* work to degree-credit classes, probably all also sponsor some sort of noncredit or "informal" activities.

Responsibility for the content and teaching of degree-credit courses usually but not always rests with the corresponding subject-matter department of the university, either directly or through a committee. Which courses are offered is usually determined by student demand, the requirements of the various degree-curricula, and the availability of teachers, rather than by any policy of the administration.

As can be seen from Table 2, over the past two decades the increase in general-extension activities for degree-credit has been very much faster than that in day colleges, rapid as their growth has been. Whether one compares the number of institutions or the enrolments, the contrast is striking. If one could include in extension the university credit courses over radio and television, for which no separate data are available, the difference would be still greater.

One step below degree-credit courses are the so-called certificate programmes. The number of institutions offering this kind of credit has risen markedly in recent years; among NUEA members, for instance, there was an increase from twelve in 1951-1952 to 23 in 1956-1957. The meaning of "certificate", however, varies considerably from one university to another. The 642 certificate programmes at 66 AUEC institutions in 1952 ranged over the following areas : business administration (most frequent), liberal arts, science-technical, home economics and agriculture. Of the sixty AUEC members that responded to Neuffer's, questionnaire on this point, seven required a minimum of 16 to 30 credit hours for a certificate, eight 30 to 40, and ten 40 to 50; the maximum was 90.

One meaning of a certificate, thus, relates to technical, business, and professional education. If a person follows courses in a well defined technical subject such as air-conditioner installation, or a similarly narrow area of business administration, the university gives him a formal certificate upon their completion. The distinction between this and a degree is feasible in such fields, because one can specify with equal precision what an electrical engineer, for instance, should know at one level and a television repairman at another. Certificates in liberal arts, on the other hand, are in principle more dubious.

Table 1. Degree-Credit Courses in Some General-Extension Divisions and Daytime Colleges, 1930–1952.

Activity		Number of Institutions				Students Enrolled				
		Increase		Increase		Inrease		Increase		
	1930	1940	over 1930	1951-1951	over 1940	1930	1940	over 1930	1951-1952	over 1940
Extension classes.	18	23	28%	57	148%	50,558	53,140	5%	325,220	512%
Extension centers.	7	9	29	23	156	28,758	34,185	19	480,506	1,306
Cores-pondence	27	33	22	44	33	36,826	53,887	46	133,223	147
High-school correspondence.	12	23	92	27	18	2,005	11,037	450	22,666	105
Regular Daytime Courses	Public Colleges					532,647	796,531	50	1,155,557*	45
		1,708		1,832*	7					
	Private Colleges					568,090	697,672	23	1,146,327*	64

*1952.

Sources: Calculated from Morton, *University Extension,* Table 25, p. 46; and from U.S. Census Bureau, *Statistical Abstract, 1955,* Table 145, p.124, and Table 147, p.125.

The education that one receives through four years in a liberal arts college cannot so easily be divided into parts that are meaningful in themselves. To what degree do the first two years of college (the portion taught in junior college) constitute more than preparation for the upper-division courses?

Among certificate programmes in liberal arts, perhaps the best known is the one at New York University. The course of study leading to the certificate in general education "offers the mature student an opportunity to develop his educational talent and interests under the guidance of the faculty of the Division of General Education." All courses are open to the general public with no prerequisites, and none carry degree-credit. To obtain a certificate the student must have worked out a programme approved by a faculty representative and the administrator of the certificate programme, but there are no required courses. He must complete 48 semester-hours with a grade of "C" or better and complete a personal project, which is understood as the "directive goal in planning the student's individual programme."

The College of General Education of Boston University, to cite another example, has developed a two-year curriculum taught off campus. If the student goes no further, he is given an Associate in Arts degree, but he may also transfer with junior standing to any one of the other colleges of the university. This policy, thus, sets half as the maximum number of extension courses that may be applied toward a bachelor's degree, and it also gives formal recognition for the successful completion of the first two years of college work. In both respects, this extension division is analogous to a junior college.

Brooklyn College has gone farther. Under a programme established in 1953 with a grant from the Center for the Study of Liberal Education for Adults, mature persons are permitted to obtain college credit for equivalent experience outside the formal academic environment. Many of the goals of a liberal education, according to the assumptions underlying the programme, "can be so defined" as to make them equivalent to informal nonacademic experience. It is still too early to judge this programme in terms of its results: the first bachelor's degree under it was granted in 1956, and there were only sixteen by 1958. An average of 32 hours, and a maximum of 68 hours, were granted toward a degree. Up to 1958, 1,100 persons had applied for admission to the prgramme, and of these some 200 had been evaluated with oral and written examinations. Credit for "adult experience" is given in humanities (English, art, music, philosophy) and social sciences (economics and sociology), but not in physical sciences, and the various professional schools have not accepted the programme at all.

The value of such a programme must be judged principally in terms of how it is administered. If an adult is able to demonstrate by a test the equivalent ability in a clearly defined subject matter such as a foreign language, it is at least arguable that he should be exempted not only from the ordinary requirement in this subject but also from the number of credits toward a degree that it represents—in effect, the same as advanced placement of freshmen in daytime colleges. If this equivalence in competence capable of gross abuse.

Included in the usual adult-education programme, finally, is a large number of noncredit offerings. An illustrative list, quoted from Morton, suggests their diversity better than could any description.

Air Condititioning and Heating
American Foreign Policy and the Far East
Art Appreciation
Meaning of Atomic Energy
Cost Accounting
Creative Writing
Current Affairs
Economics of Collective Bargaining
Employee Selection
Engineering Mechanics Review
Family Life Problems
Geology of our National Parks
Health problems for Social Worker
Income Tax Changes
Industrial Safety
Insurance
International Relations
Interior Decoration
Landscape Gardening
Management of a Small Business Merchandising
Problems of the Small Investor
Retail Sales
Soviet Imperialism

Conferences

The university frequently acts as host to what are variously known as conferences, institutes, short courses, lecture series, clinics, forums, seminars, panel sessions, round tables, work conferences, or workshops. While there are slight differences in meaning among these terms, they are generally used as alternative designations for the same type of activity, often approximating what we have termed a functional extension. Perhaps the most common term is *conferences,* which are defined as "short periods of study on questions of importance to the participants at the university campus or at other suitable locations, arranged for the purpose of using university facilities and staff and other appropriate leadership to gain new insights or skills". It is usually difficult to differentiate sharply between "conferences" and "noncredit courses," or even courses for credit. Participation may bring credit toward a degree, "professional-advancement" credit, a special certificate, or no credit, depending on the circumstances or on someone's arbitrary decision.

Conferences are usually set up on request from a particular group or groups, especially such professional societies as those in business administration, engineering, medicine, dentistry, industrial relations, law, education, public health, social welfare, public administration. The task of arranging a conference may be undertaken by either the appropriate academic department or the extension staff, or the two in combination. During the academic year 1951-1952, 38 of the institutions included in Morton's survey acted as hosts to some 3,500 conferences on 300 topics ranging from aeronautics to wild life, and attended by a total of 402,848 persons.

More than fifteen years ago, the University of Minnesota set aside for resident conferences a special building, complete with its own seminar and classrooms, library, dormitory, dining hall, and chapel. "In its first 12 ½ years, the ...department conducted 812 'schools' or courses for a total of 40,252 persons. The courses varied in length from two years to a month, with the average seven days." The participants were educators, physicians and surgeons, public employees of professional standing, engineers, social welfare workers, dentists, pharmacists, lawyers. Civic or cultural courses, "although they have been conducted upon a professional level, have been attended by many who took them less from a professional interest than from the equally keen interest of the enlightened amateur." In recent years, several other universities have set up similar centers, most notably Michigan State University and the University of Georgia.

According to a 1958 survey of NUEA institutions, there were sixteen continuation centers in operation and eleven more planned.

A common educational device, perhaps better classified under conferences than anywhere else, is the special "courses" or "institutes" established to refresh professionals' knowledge of their field and to keep them abreast of new developments. Examples of such programmes are the Continuing Education of the Bar, at the University of California; the Conferences on Business and Tax Policy, originally offered jointly by the University of Miami and New York University; the Advanced Management Programme, at Harvard; and similar programmes for physicians, engineers, social workers, nurses, librarians and other professional groups.

A more recent trend has been to establish liberal arts programmes for professionals and businessmen. The fees and expenses in most of these programmes are paid by the employers, for according to the view of a number of large corporations, their executives need an understanding of society and skills in human relations beyond those provided by the technical and professional curricula they followed in college. The first firm to set up a programme to repair these deficiencies was the Bell Telephone Company, and its resident Institutes of Humanistic Studies for Executives for one academic year at the University of Pennsylvania, one semester at Swarthmore, or eight weeks at Dartmouth, Williams, or North-western, are still the most ambitious. Some other examples are the one-semester Institute of Liberal Studies for Executives at Clark University, a nonresident programme; the two-week resident institute for professional secretaries at Vassar College; various part-time programmes at the Universities of Akron and Denver and Southwestern University; and the International Harvester Corporation programme offered in cooperation with the University of Chicago.

A special type of composite university activity—part conference, part course, and part institute—is related to business and trade unions Programmes in industrial relations, which began to be set up in the mid-1930's, are now fairly we establi-shed. Their purpose has been to provide for the joint training of labour and management representatives, so as to facilitate cooperation and reduce industrial strife. Institutes of Industrial Relations are usually associated with one or more of the departments in social sciences (political science, economics, sociology); in some cases, especially at state universities, they have extension programmes either of their own or as part of the general-extension division. At Cornell University, for example, the New York State School of Industrial and Labour Relations has offered both undergraduate and graduate resident courses and, through its own extension division, tuition-free noncredit courses to members of labour, management, government and civic groups. At the University of Illinois, as an example of a different pattern, the extension division of the Institute of Labour and Industrial Relations, operating through general extension, has offered credit and noncredit courses and administered such services as conferences and libraries.

While these programmes in industrial relations were obtensibly planned as much on behalf of labour as of management, trade unions were generally suspicious of them and demanded special programmes in workers' education parallel to those provided for management in schools of business administration. Among the twelve university programmes in workers' education that could be cited in 1951, the best known was at the School for Workers of the University of Wisconsin. In October 1957, L.H. Adolfson of Wisconsin's general-extension division was listed as one of the directors of the newly established National Institute of Labour Education, "a national vehicle for labour-university cooperation" with headquarters in Madison. Among other functions, the institute was to solicit funds from foundations, unions, and business, and to make grants to nonlabour educational agencies.

When a university enters the field of workers's education, how should it avoid duplicating the educational functions of the trade unions themselves? The education that ought to be available to workers can be divided into the following four categories:

1. "Bread-and-butter" union courses, such as shop-steward training, grievance procedures, contract negotiations, union administration, etc. This type of training ought to be undertaken by the union's own educational department.

2. Remedial, in the usual limited sense of this term. Since

remedial courses are ordinarily in subjects taught in primary or high school, in accordance with our proposed rule that the university restrict itself to college-level material, the adult-education programme of the public school system should offer them.

3. Professional—time and motion studies, job evaluation, economics, health and welfare, journalism, etc. Courses in these two categories might well be provided level; but in that case there would seem to be no good reason for segregating union members in special courses.

The NUEA has attempted to establish more general standards for deciding whether a university ought to sponsor any given conference. In 1951, a committee of this organization proposed the following criteria:

1. Sponsorship that cannot be better done by nonuniversity agencies.
2. Sponsorship or cooperation with related academic departments.
3. Must be educational.
4. Universities must play active role in planning the conference or institute, not just provide facilities and prestige for "canned" programme.
5. University must have financial control of institute.

Two years later, most of the member institutions indicated that they generally used such standards to decide on conferences, though some also accepted canned programmes under pressure. In 1957, the NUEA's Division of Conferences and Institutes set "appropriate procedural channels" for the "three major categories of programmes"—"Institution Sponsored", "Request from Within or from Outside the University," and "Programmes without Formal University Sponsorship". The proposed rule against providing university facilities for canned programmes had apparently been abandoned.

The relevance of a campus setting lies mainly in the easier contact it provides between faculty (together with advanced students) and the outside world. At these conferences, not all learning is in one direction; in Dean McGhee's words—

> Consider the most modern developments, new techniques and problems arising in manufacturing, in management and in

legislation. Perhaps General Electric and I.B.M., the American Management Association and the American Law Institute *would* do the job better. But how does that benefit the Colleges of Engineering, Business and Law? Where is the feedback into the curricula for preparing tomorrow's engineers, businessmen and lawyers?

In setting policy concerning conferences, thus, the university ought to consider carefully their educational value in either direction. In particular, it ought to make sure that its facilities are not being used as a cheaper and more convenient substitute for a hotel or other meeting place.

Methods and Technical Facilities

The developing shortage of even regular university instructors means that those available for university adult education will increasingly be too few in number to enable it to fulfil its task satisfactorily. Against this background, the experimentation with various methods and supposed aids to teaching acquires especial importance. The effects of most of these on the learning process have not been adequately tested, and no implication is intended here that they are, or are not, suitable to university adult education. This is merely a list (and not an exhaustive one) to exemplify what has been done in either credit or informal programmes of various types.

As we have pointed out at length, we do not agree with those devotees of group discussion who regard the absence of a subject-matter expert as a good thing in itself. But it is reasonable to suppose that if, say, several persons read a number of college-level assignments and come together regularly to discuss them following a discussion guide, they will learn more than from reading on their own; and in many situations this is the realistic alternative to no programme at all. Given adequate controls and tests, such teacherless courses might even be offered for credit.

Regular discussion groups are frequently based on so-called *packaged programmes,* or selected readings on a specific topic, usually but not always from previously published sources, assembled into a series of pamphlets or a book. Before each session the participants read one assignment and then convene in one of their homes or at a public building. Sometimes films or records are then used to supplement the readings. Discussion is led by one or two participants, who in some cases have been briefly trained in discussion techniques but not in the subject-matter. A few of the better known programmes of this type are the "Great Books" courses of the Great Books Foundation; "Economic Reasoning", "Ways of Mankind", "Introduction to the Humanities" of the Fund for Adult Education; "World Politics", "American Foreign Policy", and "Russian Foreign Policy" of the former American Foundation for Political Education; "The American Heritage" of the American Library Association; and "Freedom Agenda" of the League of Women Voters. The "Great Decisions" of the Foreign Policy Association and "Challenge to Iowa" of Iowa State University combine packaged readings and discussion guides with a correlated information campaign in the mass media.

Over the past several decades the development of new communication media has made possible a still greater proliferation of adult-education programmes. Teaching by *correspondence,* one of the oldest activities of universities, has remained an important and growing part of their extension programmes. Most correspondence courses attempt to duplicate for individual students some of the regular campus offerings. Of the 76 member institutions of the NUEA in 1957-1958, 45 reported that in the preceding year they had correspondence courses, of which 42 carried degree-credit, 10 certificate-credit, 34 high-school credit and 23 no credit.

Teaching by mail was supplemented by *radio courses* shortly after this became technically possible. As early as 1924, about half a million adults were participating in educational programmes over the radio. Some twenty-five years later there were more than two dozen university radio stations broadcasting both regular classes and many more informal courses and public-service programmes. By 1956, 99 institutions of higher education, including 39 state colleges and universities, held licenses to operate educational radio stations. Some broadcast over both AM and FM, or from several locations in the state. One license is held by the general-extension division of a state university (South Carolima).

The Canadian Farm Radio Forum consists of weekly *radio* broadcasts of panel *discussions* by experts on issues of current interest to rural audiences. Participants are organized into discussion groups, which meet at the home of one of them. All are sent a discussion guide and supplementary facts. After listening to the panel, each group discusses the issue, and at the end of the session a secretary records its decision on a Findings Sheet and mails it to the provincial Farm Forum office. There all opinions are collated and summarized, and eventually reported back to the participants.

The considerable experience with correspondence and radio courses laid a base for teaching by *television.* With this new medium, some of the advantages of classroom teaching can be made available to a mass audience. Though it has developed rapidly during the past several years, television teaching is still in an experimental stage, and current practices are only indicative of probable future developments. In 1959, New York University used a grant from RCA to institute a Center for Instructional Television, whose purpose it is "to develop effective techniques for television teaching."

At present, closed-circuit television is used by some 93 universities, including 43 state institutions, mainly in order to pipe lectures by master teachers to several daytime classes, which sometimes also have junior faculty members to direct the discussion developing out of each lecture. The Oregon State System of Higher Education, with a grant from the Fund for the Advancement of Education, is experimenting with closed-circuit television over several campuses. In 1957-1958, courses in history, chemistry and education taught at the University of Oregon, Oregon State College, and Oregon College of Education were broadcast to students at the other two institutions and at Willamette, a private university. Starting in the fall semester of 1957-1958, the University of New Mexico has offered courses in biology, anthropology, English and mathematics to evening students over closed-circuit television. The same courses on 16-mm. *film* are made available off campus in eight New Mexico communities, where students can attend them and earn residence credits.

Television classes are presently given over both commercial stations and educational channels. As early as 1951-1952, Western Reserve University had degree-credit offerings in psychology, child psychology (with elementary psychology a prerequisite for enrolment), elementary economics, geography, and comparative literature. Of the 46 educational television stations on the air in January 1960 (four of them on non-reserved channels), 15 were operated by universities, of which 14 were state institutions. In addition, commercial stations were operated by one private and there land-grant universities. Educational stations licensed to councils, associations, or foundations, moreover, often have one or more universities as participating agencies. By fall of 1957, 77 universities, including 34 state institutions, were offering or planning to offer "telecourses" for credit in a great variety of subjects.

In the fall of 1957, when New York University introduced a television course in comparative literature at the rather discouraging hour of 6:30 A.M., the bookstores and libraries of this metropolis were unable to meet the extraordinary demand for Stendhal's *The Red and the Black,* the first work the instructor discussed. There were 177 enrolled for degree-credit in this course, and the total audience was estimated at 120,000. In early February, 142 of the former took a final examination at the university, and all but 10 per cent passed the course and gained three credits toward a college degree. By the instructor's estimate, the final showing of his television students was as good as that of the campus students, if not better.

The major advantage of television instruction is, of course, that the number of potential participants is large, particularly if it is supplemented by the use of kinescopes, which make it possible to serve areas not reached by the station's own transmitters. It is possible to follow a course at any one of three levels. To take a course for degree-credit, the student enrolls with the university, pays a fee, and purchases the syllabus and texts; he sends in periodic examination papers for correction, and comes to campus at the end of the course for his final examination. (Given the demand for such an arrangement, it would be possible to have student's final examinations administered throughout a large area by various cooperating institutions, as is sometimes done with final examinations in correspondence courses.) Those with a high level of interest but no desire for college credits can purchase the syllabus and texts but need not submit examination papers. A much larger audience can follow the course at the level of observers. This combination of audiences, however, suggests an implicit invitation to try to appeal to the largest one.

There is a danger of becoming so fascinated with the medium as such that we might be trapped into becoming pseudo- or semi-television-professionals and forget our goals and missions as educators. Our role in television is that of the educator.

Audio-visual kits were originally developed by Dr. Robert S.Warmer, with a grant from the Kellogg Foundation, as part of a programme of postgraduate medical education. Each of his kits consists of a recorded discussion on one of a number of medical topics, a set of 35-mm. slides correlated with the discussion, a viewer and a script. The kit can be used by one isolated physician or by a group with a projector. Dr. Warner later developed a similar kit for the American Heart Association, and this "Cardiac Clinic" is used by local branches of the association in their programme of professional education.

In sum, recent experimentation in teaching methods in adult education has been even more striking than the great variety in subject matter. Supplementing classroom lectures, and discussion groups, and correspondence courses, there are now radio, television and film programmes; audio-visual aids; and various combinations of these. With these methods, faculty participation in the programme is reduced or even, in some cases, dispensed with altogether. Unfortunately, the educational effects of most of these methods have never to our knowledge been adequately tested, and before adopting them it would be important to know how much is lost by the attempt to preserve faculty time.

Standards in Degree-Credit Courses

There is no reason, apart from the lack of data, why a discussion of standards should be limited to those in credit courses. High quality, we feel, should be a routine characteristic of every university product; and if more university administrators agreed with this dictum, in fact as well as in principle, recommendations for experimentation in methods and techniques would more frequently include some evidence of their educational value.

However, even the relatively simple case of credit courses, which are closest to traditional disciplines in content and are controlled by regular examinations, must be examined with care if we are to judge their standards accurately. There is, it is true, a general feeling among university faculties and administrators that credit courses in general extension, no matter in what subject, are not typically at the level maintained on the home campus.

Many sincere and dedicated university leaders... regard adult education with uneasy suspicion. They dread the possibility that the hordes of new claimants on their time and service may finally destroy the university itself. The university, such observers fear, may grow to be like the lumbering behemoths of prehistoric time, whose bodies grew too large for their brains to integrate and who thereby failed in the struggle for survival. This fear of size is paralleled by a fear of cheapness and vulgarization.

In order to refute such sentiments, several studies have been made comparing extension and day students. Dugan, for example, compared the grades *in the same courses,* taught by the same instructors, earned by 499 extension and 2,330 resident students at the University of Wyoming, and on this basis concluded that extension students did better. From this finding, one might conclude (1) that, indeed, extension students do better work, or (2) that instructors find extension teaching more stimulating and consequently do a better job of teaching, or (3), most plausibly, that grading in extension is more lenient. Dugan's study does not refute this third alternative and several others confirm it.

McMichael, for instance, compared the grades earned at the University of New Mexico by *the same students* who had taken courses both on campus and in extension (either by correspondence or in extension classes, or both). The mean grades earned by this sample of 380 students were 1.41 in residence courses, 1.65 through correspondence, and 1.70 in extension courses. From a number of studies at several other universities, Sorenson concluded that instructors generally mark extension students a half to a full grade higher than their regular campus students, and he concluded that "it is therefore unsound to evaluate the quality of extension work by comparing extension and residence marks". Instructors in extension are under pressure to be generous to their highly motivated students, who are often in a minority ethnic group, or who depend on the credits earned to keep their jobs. They "seem to grade with their hearts rather than with their heads, ... [and this] soft grading practice... is one way by which an objective observer can detect dissimilar standards".

The lower standards in extension, whether or not they are admitted in words, are often given at least informal recognition in a number of administrative procedures. For example, admission requirements for evening students are sometimes lower; and on some campus students who flunk out of the regular day college are permitted to make up the courses in extension. Or, most strikingly, only a certain proportion of the credits required for a degree may generally be earned in extension. It would seem logical to allow a student to earn a degree in extension if the courses are at the same level as those on the home campus; and, if they are not, not to permit *any* extension credits toward a degree. If the lower quality of extension courses is not frankly admitted, and the number of extension credits acceptable toward a degree is nonetheless limited, what reason can be cited for this differentiation? It may be, for example, that certain required courses cannot be given in extension because of the lack of library or laboratory facilities, or of qualified teachers; but such a limitation, while it would force the student to take a required course given only in the regular day session on campus, would not justify a residence requirement as such. Or the point is made that extension students lack counselling; but "mature persons ... would greatly resent a requirement that they interview a counsellor at periodic intervals." The occasional problem that really requires special attention, particularly at registration time, is often given it no less in the case of extension than of regular campus students. Arguments about counselling, thus, "often fall very flat", especially with students who have attended both regular and extension classes and can compare them in this respect. Or the point is made that the informal life on the campus—for example, clubs and bull sessions—is as educational as classes; but even if this unproved thesis were to be accepted, it would hardly apply to the older, often married, sometimes commuting, *part-time* student, whether he attends classes in extension or on the regular campus. Setting an arbitrary limit to the number of extension credits that may be applied toward a degree, thus, can reasonably be interpreted as a covert recognition that standards in extension classes are generally lower.

How prevalently is this differentiation made? In extension *centers,* "usually no distinction is made between the degree credits earned in their programmes and in campus classes," and this seems also to be so of independent liberal arts colleges that offer degree-credit extension courses and the evening colleges of urban universities. However, university extension *courses,* including those by correspondence, usually have a lower status than nominally equivalent ones on the home campus. Among the members of the NUEA who replied on this point to Dugan's questionnaire, thus, the maximum credits that might be earned in extension toward a bachelor's degree ranged from 20 to 100 per cent, with the median at 42 per cent. Similarly, of the 46 universities that replied to this question in Morton's survey, all set a limit on the number of extension credits toward a degree except two, which took.

> the position that provision of any courses by them was a guarantee, at least insofar as an institution can guarantee quality, of the worth of these offerings, and that if a high quality of educational service could not be maintained, none would be offered. These institutions make no distinctions between "residence" and "extension" credits.

This, we believe, is the correct policy.

The same difficulties as in extension generally have been encountered in setting criteria for degree-credit in telecourses. At a 1955 meeting of universities offering such courses, one participant maintained that the credit that can be earned should be limited to a maximum of twenty-five hours, while others declared that no courses should be offered for credit over television unless approved by the faculty and administered in such a way as to be acceptable without limitation.

Community Services

Universities perform a great many services for the community, often though not necessarily always through their general-extension divisions. The diversity of these services, which vary considerably from one university to another, can be indicated by an illustrative list:

The broadcasting of cultural and scientific programmes by radio or television; or the maintenance of an educational station.

Lectures open to the public, on or off campus.

Concerts, plays, motion pictures, art exhibits, readings of poetry, etc., open to the public.

A speakers bureau.

The printing of publications for use also off campus.

A lending service of library materials, to individuals or groups off campus.

The circulation of audio-visual aids.

Consulting services to business, industry, municipal or state governments, public schools.

Social welfare services.

Placement services for persons other than students and graduates.

Testing services for persons other than students.

Participation in community improvement projects.

Information services to the general public or to special groups.

Recreation, sports, etc.

Some of these types of services—lecture tours, library extension, etc.—Are obviously educational; others have only a remote relation (if indeed any at all) to the main functions of an institution of higher learning. All reflect the alleged duty that universities owe the community, but we fell that this is a somewhat overworked theme, and that it would be well if administrators tock a long, hard book at this shibboleth. Fifty or seventy-five years ago, in a near-frontier area like the Middle West, the state university was *the* harbinger of urban culture; and if the people there were to hear concerts and lectures, or have access to adequate libraries, it usually had to be as a consequence of the university's effort to provide them. Today, the situation is reversed. As we pointed out in the introductory chapter, we are now faced with a tragic paradox: a great, rich nation is skimping badly on its educational system, one of the important historical bases of its greatness and wealth. The main problem has become how to induce the community to serve the university.

In terms of this perspective, what criteria can be set for judging which community services are *now* suitable, and which not, for an institution of higher learning? Let us begin by classifying some of the activites according to the amount of additional money, time and personnel they are likely to cost.

1. The first and simplest type of community service is rendered when the general public is given access, at no great additional cost to the university, to an existent facility or to a special event planned primarily for the student body. For example, university *libraries* may often be used by local residents; and *television* courses, as was noted in an earlier section of this chapter, are usually followed by a very much larger audience than those who enroll.

2. It is often difficult to draw the line between such instances, where the public is permitted access to university facilities, and those where the extension administration has planned for a joint student-public participation. For example, most of the universities surveyed by Morton declared that the purpose of their *broadcasting* facilities is "to allow the university to contribute directly and continuously to adult education", and this vague formulation permits them to avoid setting a clear policy on how far into the community this service should reach, and at what level. *Concerts, recitals,* and *special lectures,* similarly, are ordinarily not merely open to members of the community, but also organized, at least in terms of the size of the hall and publicity, with both the campus and the general audience in mind. *University presses,* as another example, publish not only the works of their own faculties but also those of other scholars, and also books of a broader appeal.

3. Certain university facilities are not merely made accessible to the public but taken to it. *Library services*—not only books and periodicals but also pamphlets, clippings, plays, art exhibits, etc.—Are often made available throughout the state, either through a special division in the library or through the general-extension division. The university assists public schools, organizations, and individuals with programming, book lists and bibliogaraphies, specially prepared packets of

materials, etc. At the University of Wisconsin, for example, the Bureau of Information and Programme Services has a special staff and separate collections of materials, including plays, reproductions, music, and magazines. *Art exhibits, theater* productions, and *concert* groups are taken to rural areas of Nebraska, Washington and North Carolina, for example, by the general-extension divisions of these state universities.

In many localities, *audio-visual teaching aids* are regularly distributed to schools, organizations, and individuals; and sometimes instruction is given to educators on how to prepare and use them. Some audio-visual departments make their own films. Among the institutions surveyed by Morton, the 25 audio-visual departments serviced nearly 28 million people, principally through public schools. According to a 1956-1957 survey of these institutions, audio-visual services of one kind or another were offered by 53 members of the NUEA.

4. The faculty of a university is often approached by business firms, private organizations, and government bureaus; and professors are usually expected to respond to such requests for *consultation* or *lectures* in their spare time and frequently without remuneration. In some universities the general-extension division has acted as liaison between the public and the faculty, channelling inquiries to the appropriate department, institute, or person. We have no information on how well this system works.

These four types of community services—university facilities and special events (1) made accessible to the public, (2) set up in part for public use, or (3) distributed to the public; and (4) consultations and lectures—are in principle unexceptional but secondary to the university's main functions of teaching and research. Several guide lines are suggested to define which services are suitable:

1. They should be related to college-level education or research. To sponsor a concert series, for example, would be appropriate, but not to set up a mimeographing service for the community.

2. The university should not compete with other agencies in providing services. It "should confine its activities to those for which it has *unique* resources". In particular, it should not do gratis what commerical firms do for a charge. Here is an

especially striking instance of what in our opinion is illegitimate:

> A member of the staff of the Department of Physical Education at Massachusetts State College has given valuable service to communities throughout the State by giving information on the construction, cost, and maintenance of swimming pools. The College, largely through the work of another member of the Department's staff, has given outstanding services in the field of winter sports.

On the other hand, university presses, which perform a unique and valuable service by printing nonprofitable scholarly books, complement rather than compete with the commercial publishers. The distinction is in many cases a fine one, but we believe that usually any doubt should be resolved by restricting the university's role. Such a rule of thumb would counteract to some degree the bureaucratic expansionism of the ambitious administrators who in universities, as in other types of institutions, tend to confuse increase in size with progress. And as we pointed out, it is an especially fit rule at the present time: since the university' resources will be increasingly strained in carrying out its main functions, subsidiary tasks should not be undertaken unless these cannot reasonably be avoided.

3. To the degree that it is feasible, community services should pay their own way. A counter argument is often made that fees discourage community groups and individuals from turning to the university for such services. Though there is little evidence to support this contention, it seems reasonable and we can accept it as at least probable. The question still remains, however, whether the money spent on free services is better so used than for the education of students and for research. Finances are never adequate to provide for *these* services, and in principle money should not be spent freely on peripheral matters, however useful they may be. Thus, it is quite reasonable for even a public university to charge a fee of towns people or organizations for the use of the library or other facilities, or for a lecture or concert. Or, as another instance, it is neither reasonable nor just that university faculties, an occupational group grossly underpaid for performing essential services, should be expected to respond gratis to taxpayers' requests for consultation. Nor should they

be paid for such services out of the university's own budget or—what in monetary terms is the same thing—be excused from regular duties in order to do research for other on university time.

Summary

Just as the available data make it necessary to analyze university adult education largely in terms of what general-extension divisions actually do, even though the portion of the total extension function that they administer varies greatly from one institution to another, so it is necessary in a discussion of the educational range of the offerings to retain the ambiguous, and partly obsolescent, distinction between "credit" and "noncredit" programmes. Since on the daytime campus, academic credits are one important means of maintaining academic standards, the blurring of this distinction in extension is an important. What are the reasons for it?

1. In extension courses (though not usually in extension centers), credit is generally rated lower than that for ostensibly equivalent courses in the regular curriculum. That is to say, even within the class of degree-credits, those earned in extension are typically one step down, one step closer to no credit.

2. On the other hand, there has been a contrary, upward trend, in response to the demand that formal recognition be granted for completion of a programme of less than the four years ordinarily required for a degree. Thus, we have "associate degrees", "certificate-credit", credit for "nonacademic experience," "professional-advancement credit", "alertness credit", and so on.

3. The subject matter of adult-education programmes ranges widely over areas too new or recondite, or sometimes too peripheral or insignificant, to have been included in the regular curriculum; and in such cases there is no precedent to denote what credit is appropriate.

4. The range of participants, similarly, includes persons who have no interest in credit—because they are looking mainly for social contacts, because they are interested in the content of the programme *per se*, because they already have an advanced degree and need no further formal recognition.

While credit courses do not necessarily impose higher

standards than informal programmes, the fact that some control in exercised is important. Probably the best and the worst in university adult education are to be found among the noncredit programmes, the lively innovations that are the product of true creativity and, at the other extreme, the flagrant caricatures of education, devoid of content, sometimes of taste, in fact of anything except commercial profit. Between these extremes lies the credit programme, solidly based on academic tradition but often taught with no hint of how exciting learning can be.

During the past several decades, educators and particularly adult educators have become increasingly aware of "the community". That the university should serve its community in an appropriate fashion is axiomatic. "But where does a reasonable recognition of the claims of the community end and community-worship, a fetishism as disastrous as state-worship, begin?"

The extension of the university has made available to a larger sector of the population not only courses but also such other facilities and services as, among other, radio and television programmes, concerts and lectures, library facilities, audio-visual aids and faculty consultation. Conferences are arranged for a wide variety of professional, business, labour and other groups. With no principle to guide in their selection, such activities can be almost indefinitely expansible. We hold that university services ought to be related to college-level education or research and ought not to overlap with other agencies' programmes.

Parallel with the experimentation in content there has been one in methods. In an earlier chapter, we tried to deflate those enthusiasts who hold that the discussion group is the best, or even the only valid, medium of education. But if competent subject-matter experts are not available as instructors, then a self-administered discussion group that reads significant works and talks over their implications may be an acceptable substitute in noncredit programmes and possibly even in credit courses. Discussion groups based on packaged reading programmes, the mass media, or a combination of the two, have been sponsored by a number of adult-education organizations, often in collaboration with a university. New methods of teaching have been made possible by various technical developments over the past several decades. Of these, the most important are educational films, audio-visual aids and, of course, television, whose potentialities for education have hardly begun to be exploited.

If it is true that the level in extension classes is lower than on the main campus, one reason is the distinction between residence and extension credits, for such a compromise helps to maintain the difference in standards by recognizing it as quasi-legitimate. The administrative structure, which half isolates the general-extension division from the rest of the university and forces it to pay its own way in a unique proportion, has of course an important effect on educational standards. Under the usual financial arrangements, it is inevitable that general-extension administrators should constantly be tempted to lower standards—either to branch out into popular and therefore profitable fields, or to ignore educationally valuable new programmes because they will not pay for themselves, and in both cases with little regard to what activities are appropriate to an institution of higher learning. Unfortunately, this temptation may sometimes be encouraged by the main-campus administrators, who too often believe that the university's public reputation can be improved if general extension caters to every "felt need", however irresponsibly. These are some of the topics that we will discuss in the next chapter.

5

On University Non-Education For Adults

The term "community services" is ambiguous. We have used it to designate a great number of extension activities, useful in themselves, that are only loosely related to the education of students or research. Our contention is that the greatest service a university can offer to the community is to perform these limited tasks well. That some of the peripheral activities are worthwhile in themselves is true—and irrelevant. The university, to repeat, is a reservoir of rare and expensive resources, assembled to perform a crucial function. Particularly in the years before us, with the already great strain on institutions of higher education bound to get worse, increasing the burden still more is socially irresponsible. It is as though in the middle of an epidemic the ground floor of a hospital were cleared to make room for fire engines. An argument that the community needs fire-fighting equipment, though often made in the context of university adult education, is not convincing. And it is even less so if not fire engines but gambling tables are substituted for the hospital beds. Our partial, contingent rejection becomes a total one with respect to those "services" devoid of educational content. The distinction must be made sharply, particularly since the terminology is not consistent and "community services" are not always differentiated from "community development."

Community Development

Community development is the attempt on the part of universities—

> to discover ways for helping communities to help themselves through the study and efforts of their citizens. The projects...point in the direction of a new kind of extension education—education for all, education for action on a wide front, education that is democratic in nature and education that comes to grips with the realities that people have to face daily in the homes and communities in which they live.

In other words, community development is an attempt to make over the community and the people in it; to seek out and eliminate any and every deficiency from inadequate sewers to juvenile delinquency, from unemployment to a lack of square dancing; and thus to strengthen again the social cohesion of the citizenry and promote personal and community "growth." In greater detail, the aims of community development can be spelled out as follows:

1. The first goal is to strengthen the "community," identified by some community developers as the village or small town, by others as the neighborhood in a larger city. In either case, the community is a group of persons who interact on the basis of personal, familylike knowledge and sentiments, rather than the businesslike relations of the metropolis. The community, this "backbone of American democracy," has been markedly wakened by the migration of America's population to the anonymous city; and the university, instead of doing something to improve "the quality of living in the small towns and communities from which many of their students are taken," has actually been one of the main offenders in furthering this shift. "The general effect of college life is to withdraw American youth from their home communities, train them for a specialized, individual-centered career as contrasted to a family-centered or community-centered life, and send them off into the impersonal crowds of a great city." One of the main objectives of the Montana Study thus, was to inhibit the migration of young people from small towns to the city, and this is presently one of the aims of the Department of Community Development at Southern Illinois University.

2. In order to reduce the incentive to leave small towns or

in order to convert areas of a city into real neighbourhoods, one must improve their physical facilities and social life. The community's problems are discussed in an open meeting, which decides which "needs" are most pressing. This very discussion, culminating in a community decision to act, is seen as an enhancement of the democratic process. In the words of the Ogdens, pioneer community developers in Virginia, "the philosophy on which the programme was based was an honest belief in the democratic way of life". Or, in more effulgent prose:

> The community organization movement...is the sole, indispensable, not-to-be-escaped, channel through which freedom of the individual and the "right to life, liberty and the pursuit of happiness" can be realized.

3. Following the decision to act, the "action-solution" can consist in almost anything. Community developers:

> Focus directly on the improvement of the immediate conditions of community life. The citizenry must be aided to achieve anything it thinks it needs: a sounder economic structure, health, better sanitation or schools or recreation, a deeper appreciation of the arts, or a more effective political structure.

The way these goals are sought by community developers can be described most effectively in terms of an example, and our choice to illustrate the pattern is the well publicized Montana Study. In 1944, the Humanities Division of the Rockefeller Foundation made a $25,000 grant to initiate this programme and to support it on a decreasing scale for three years, with the University of Montana providing the balance of the budget each year. According to the application to the foundation, the Montana Study was to be a "research programme to determine the contribution of the humanities to a programme of higher education designed to improve the quality of living in the State of Montana". Its director was Baker Brownell, whom Poston describes as "the father" of the best type of community development.

The staff began by preparing a discussion outline listing ten topics, one for each meeting, with detailed suggestions and discussion questions; and each meeting of each group was usually led by a member of the staff. "Brownell said he wanted the group to be completely informal, so they refrained from a regular election of officers and everyone just decided to make Free Halverson chairman". The meetings supposedly enable the participants to get to know their community and to identify its most pressing problem or problems.

After their use in the application to the Rockefeller Foundation, the words "higher education" do not appear again in Poston's book, which has Brownell's endorsement. The "humanities" are mentioned frequently, in the sense of "everything from having a good time to making a living". A tentative programme for "one year's community cultural events" was drawn up as part of the "renaissance":

January—New Year's Celebration and Winter Sports Day

February—Washington-Lincoln Dinner and Home Orchestra Concert

March—Community Drama Day

April—Singing Night

May—Garden Day

June—Graduation Day and Chorus

July—Community Picnic

August—Ice Cream Night

September—School and Teachers' Night

October—Hunter's Day and Game Dinner

November—Harvest Festival and Thanksgiving Dinner

December—Christmas Chorus and Community Tree.

The accomplishments claimed for the Montana Study include fourteen discussion groups set up in three years, several recreational programmes, new small business, health services—even one small library, as though as a partial concession to learning, if not to higher education.

While the Montata Study has had an important influence, there have been various patterns of community development. In the early days the extension division "offered its services rather insistently" to communities considered by the staff to be in need of improvement; and once a programme was started the professional organizers also carried the major responsibility for its continuation. While the extension division now usually waits until the community invites it in, this invitation is frequently solicited or contrived. "Sometimes it is hard to find a felt need for the community to rally round." Extension personnel call the first meeting, or are present at one organized by a community group. They encourage more meetings, with if possible more participants, who discuss the problem and decide what needs to be done about it, under the "nondirective" guidance of the general-extension division.

What has been accomplished by community-development programmes? To what degree were the stated goals achieved? Most of the reports have been written while the programmes were still in progress, or shortly after their completion; and they overflow with optimistic statements about "new creative relationships", "growth", "added insight", "action programmes for better living," and sometimes even the expectation of new interest in educational activities. In the large literature on community development there appears to be no mention of a discussion that, at least after the first warming up, did not go well. There is no suggestion that some discussion may be nonproductive or that any action programme resulting from such discussions may not always be an unqualified success.

The universal approbation with which its proponents view community development suggests that they have no standards by which to judge what is worthwhile. Any programme that materializes is *ipso facto* good. One reason a more critical evaluation is not attempted is that so many of the goals of community development are defined too vaguely to be measured. Its proponents generally maintain, for example, that they are more interested in the "personal growth" of the individual participants and in "community growth" than in the achievement of material goals. This disclaimer of interest in the physical results of action programmes, however, is neither consistent nor unanimous. While all the university consultants on community development that Orcutt interviewed agreed that "working together has an impact upon the community and individuals that is more important than any other results", they all also said that the problem picked by the group must not be too difficult, for otherwise the resulting action will not be successful. "The ultimate test of discussion which focuses upon devising action-solutions to problems always lies beyond the process of discussion itself in the consequences of action undertaken".

Even when a goal is one that can be precisely defined,

success in reaching it is not necessarily evaluated. For example, one of the objectives of the Montana Study, as has been noted above, was to halt the cityward migration of young people; but apparently none of the many works appraising this programme—neither Poston's book-length study nor several articles by Brownell and members of his staff—ever state whether this goal was attained nor even refer to it in the so-called evaluations.

Long before community development was established in university adult education, innumerable agencies existed whose specific function it was—and is—to encourage citizen groups to cooperate in getting better community services, or a library, or folk-dance groups, or whatever. Many such programmes have been carried out by social welfare agencies, both private and public; industrial concerns; chambers of commerce; various government bureaus and the Cooperative Extension Service. None of these agencies, it should be noted, have as their primary function college-level education and research. This includes even the Cooperative Extension Service, though it is attached to universities. Under the various laws by which it was established and defined, it has a specific mandate both to convert the findings of university research into education assimilable by the whole of the general public, and to assist the people of the area in many other ways. Neither function can be properly ascribed to the university itself. Cooperative Extension, moreover, is financed not out of the university budget, but out of federal, state and county appropriations.

The dimensions of the work done by these various agencies can be illustrated by discussing very briefly some of the activities of the Cooperative Extension Service. Many of its 9,000 county agents and some of its state specialists, assisted by many more volunteers, are engaged in various community-improvement programmes. "Throughout the country, extension agents assisted 34,100 communities with their recreational facilities, 57,600 community group with organisation problems, nearly 7,000 communities in obtaining library facilities, and 2,266 commu-nities in building community houses." Together with other federal and state agencies, the Cooperative Extension Service is currently expanding a federally financed "rural development" programme on a community, county and regional basis.

It would be impossible to maintain realistically that community development is a neglected field, or even that the particular emphasis of university community developers has been bypassed. It is simply not true that "unless adult educators see to it that it happens, there will not be citizen participation in community development programmes". In replying to this allegation, one social worker referred to his own profession, which "over a period of decades has developed the professional practice of 'community organization for social welfare'. " Nor have adult educators brought a higher level of competence to the well staffed field of community development. And it has even happened that citizen groups have accomplished a limited objective without outside organizational help.

Many adult educators are neither for nor against including community development in their field, but merely skeptical: the effectiveness of action projects and "the extent to which the university should participate in them are still open to discussion". Others, however, deny the relevance of community development to adult education. At the 1955 national meeting of the Adult Education Association, according to Powell, "a threatened split over 'community development' and 'education' was averted... by the statesmanlike persuasions of Cryril Houle, Kenneth Benne and Howard McCluskly." In reply to strong statements denying that community development is a legitimate function of adult education, its advocates assert their cause with the fervour of missionaries. Democracy, they say, is doomed unless adult education comes to its rescue. A university-inspired, locally implemented revival of the neighbourhood is urgently needed to counteract the "malevolent influences of rampant urbanism". Community development, according to one community developer, "has the potential to bring a rebirth of spirit in America and to eliminate war and starvation from the earth". "Survival of the university depends upon survival of the community. Unless the university dedicates itself to the support of the community, both with perish".

The disagreement over the propriety of including community development in a university's programme has not, however, prevented its expansion. Whether one measures the influence of community development by the number of universities with such programmes, by the recognition of the professional societies of adult education, or by its literature, it is manifest that this field has grown rapidly during the past two decades. According to a 1956 survey of community-development programmes in NUEA institutions, most of them were less than ten years old. As far back as 1951-1952, Morton found that 43 per cent among his sample of NUEA general-extension divisions were engaged in community development. In 1955, the NUEA replaced its *Committee* on Community Organization, which for some years had been at least partly concerned with community development, with a *Division* of Community Development. Michigan State University has recently appropriated $1.5 million for a community-development programme in suburban areas. Among 2,000 members of the Adult Education Association, almost a third denote community development as one of their three major areas of interest within adult education.

There are various indications that this rapid growth will continue. "At least one major university is now planning to establish a five-year degree programme in this field". Professor Poston sees it as his function as chairman of the Division of Community Development of the NUEA to spread this type of programme as widely as possible through universities. He succeeded in getting the Sears Roebuck Foundation to finance a two-year project in which NUEA universities will cooperate in training members of the General Federal of Women's Clubs. As he put it—

> I was impressed by the almost unlimited potential for community development throughout the world if these 11,000,000 women [the world membership of the Federation] could have the benefit of the necessary training and field consultation that could be provided through university extension if our NUEA member institutions either could or would see fit to equip themselves to provide such training and field consultation. And, in this possibility, I saw that I believe could be one of the greatest opportunities of this century for university extension to contribute toward the enrichment of American life and the preservation of free society.

A meeting held to plan further steps in this project included representatives of the following universities: New York State,

Utah, Washington, Virginia, Maryland, Kansas State, California and, of course, Poston's own bailiwick, Southern Illinois. Not all of these institutions had the necessary staff, but this lack could be remedied.

In our opinion, community development is not only not college-level education or research; it is not these at any level. It is not research: community developers do not even pretend that they go into a community, as anthropologists or sociologists would, in order to study its workings; and in any case it would be an empty pretence, for they are not trained to make empirical studies of any scientific value. And it is not education. Indeed, some of the attacks on education that community developers have made are as strong and as Philistine as one is likely to find in print. A commentary on a group sitting around exchanging funny stories, for example:

> Lonepine was participating in a form of culture that certain intellectuals might not appreciate, but to these people it meant more than tea at the Metropolitan or a course in the classical works of art.

Or, as another instance:

> Teaching, particularly at the university level, has emphasized the giving of information. The man whose gizzard is chock full of facts and who scratches diligently for more facts is honoured; the practitioner is not...To talk learnedly about juvenile delinquency in a class or institute on the campus is easy compared to helping John Doe and Rachel Roe do something about juvenile delinquency in the town of Crossroads. There the scholar is often at a discount and what counts is know-how in human relations,... and may be a good hand at poker or a guitar.

Community development is a social-welfare—or, better, a social-reform—movement. That its aims may be worthy is not relevant. There are many other institutions designed and financed to perform these functions; and the fact that even Cooperative Extension engages in community development is another good reason why general extension should not. A university's decision to use money for community development means, in effect, a decision that in some way, in quality or quantity, the adult education offered shall be less. Community development does not come "anywhere near paying for itself" in any part of the country. Writing about the Department of Community Development at Southern Illinois University and similar activities at the University of Washington, Poston asserted that their "increase in budget and the spread of the work have been effected in the face of economy measures in virtually every other area of adult education". This boasting is particularly distasteful when we contrast this "increase in budget" with the finances of other extension activities.

Extension as a Money-Maker

Too many universities regard their general-extension divisions as commercial rather than educational ventures. Among the evening colleges surveyed by Neuffer, only 11 per cent were permitted to retain any excess of income over expenses; that is, 89 per cent of these evening colleges refund to their parent institutions a part of the funds allocated to them, whenever they show a profit. About three-quarters of the independent liberal arts colleges with adult programmes studied by Crimi said "that they are realizing a direct financial surplus from their adult work", "Because of the complexities of accounting systems it is difficult to estimate the amount of this contribution but in many institutions it will range as high as 40 per cent of the evening college's income". In Canada, "in all but a few universities, the entire service 'pays its way' and in some it turns back a substantial cash surplus into the general revenues of the university".

Where does extension income come from? Miscellaneous sources do not ordinary amount to much. Some general-extension divisions have a small profit from the sale of materials and of tickets to lectures and similar events. Services to industry, government agencies, other colleges, hospitals, voluntary health agencies, and miscellaneous organizations are sometimes the source of a substantial income; but this is the exceptional case. Conferences, on the other hand, are run at a loss: of the annual average of $50,000 spent on them, the participants furnished only $46,000. Libraries incur a much greater deficit: total library income from fees ranged from $325 to $4,000 per year, as compared with library expenditures of from $2,000 to $55,000. Film and audio-visual services are given at a deficit of between 25 and 60 per cent. Funds for university broadcasting come almost entirely from state and institutional appropriations, except for a few intermittent and occasional gifts. Community development, as we have pointed out, is an expensive boondoggle.

The major source of extension income is student fees, as can be seen from the data compiled in Table 3. Since no two of the studies cited include the same institutions, the figures are not wholly comparable. The range is wide: in 1954, four general-extension divisions were *wholly* supported by student fees, and three not at all. Nevertheless, there is in general a sharp contrast with both Cooperative Extension and regular daytime sessions. If we take 60 per cent as the average proportion of general-extension income derived from student fees, this is more than three times the comparable figure for the regular campus. Most of the balance is allocated—at least in bookkeeping terms—from the over-all university budget, only about 4 per cent of which goes to support the general-extension division.

Table 1. Median percentage of general-extension division income derived from student fees

Sample	Year	Media Percentage
8 land-grand colleges[1]	1954	52-58
7 state universities[1]	1954	57
22 land-grant colleges combined with state universities[1]	1954	73-75
47 NUEA members[2]	1952	78
46 NUEA members[3]	1951-52	61-70
7 state universities[4]	1949	45
36 NUEA members[3]	1940	71-80
10 universities[5]	1939	50*
28 NUEA members[3]	1930	51-60

* Average rather than median.

1 Association of Land-Grant Colleges and Universities, *A Study of Problems;* calculated from Tables II, III, and V, pp. 33-36.

2 Dugan, "An Extension Class Programme," p.88.

3 Morton, *University Extension,* Table 57, p.98.

4 Quoted in Sheats et al., *Adult Education,* p.435, n.

5 Thompson, *University Extension,* p.245.

An unofficial but important source of income is the preposterously low salaries paid to general-extension faculties. Some universities do not pay faculty members at all for participating in their conferences or giving evening or off-campus lectures as part of the general-extension division's programme. And whatever the rank of those who teach in extension, they usually get paid for this less than the lowest rank of instructor on their home campus. A disproportionate number of extension teachers are either full professors, who can lay claim to a greater share of the small plums that become available, or beginning instructors who must take these assignments if no one else wants them. This bimodal distribution may be one reason for the sharply opposed views about extension teachers. According to one survey, they are "somewhat above the average of the faculty in their respective departments both in scholarship and in teaching ability"; according to another, "in general, an insufficient number of instructors, poorly qualified instructors, and a limitation of the extension class programme tended to be the consequence of low stipends".

The rank of extension teachers is in any case less important than the quality of extension teaching. Faculty members who receive their status and income from their position on the main campus understandably expend most of their thought and effort in their teaching, research, and writing there; and if because of their low salaries they are induced to teach also in general extension, many do this reluctantly and undoubtedly devote less effort to what is—according to the catalogue listing—an identical course. Where the income of part-time faculty depends on the number of students in their classes, as it still did in nearly one-fourth of the extension centers surveyed by Morton, the instructors are given a direct money incentive to make their courses popular. A popular course may be one in which the teacher makes a special effort to be well prepared, to make his classes meaningful; and in that case teaching can "evoke the highest level of his abilities as a teacher". Or, it may mean a class whose teacher goes "overboard in the direction of showmanship and cheapens the experience for himself and for his students". In abstract, one might say that either possibility is equally likely; but under the actual administrative conditions that generally prevail in extension courses (though not in evening colleges), it is more probable, as Sorenson indicates, that academic standards are sacrificed to the customers' satisfaction.

Many spokesmen for general extension have deplored the fact that it is required to be self-supporting to so great a degree. Indeed, as extension divisions are presently financed, the inadequacy of funds affects everything in university adult education, from organization and administration to faculty and courses.

In some institutions, the criterion of financial success appears to be more highly regarded than is the principle of educational effectiveness. This emphasis on profit is typically imposed upon, rather than willingly accepted by, the dean or director. Regardless of where the responsibility lies within the university, however, it is clear from repeated testimony that many institutions place adult education at a distinct disadvantage in comparison with other university functions, requiring of it a budgetary performance that would be considered an absurd criterion of success if applied to other educational activities. To the extent that money-making becomes paramount, education must become subordinate.

Extension as a Public-Relations Activity

The debasement of extension prevails also in another sense. From the point of view of the president's office, one of the important functions of the division is to develop a positive attitude toward the whole institution among voters and legislators, or among potential donors. By extending itself into the community, in part by welcoming citizens to attend events on campus, the university hopes to establish a greater understanding of both its achievements and its problems. Such a favourable climate of opinion with respect to education is, of course, especially important to public institutions. No reasonable person would challenge this purpose. While in theory all Americans favour a good educational system, in fact they are notoriously penurious whenever they are asked to support it and an effort to bring the fact closer to the ideology is both legitimate and worthwhile.

There is a tendency, however, for universities to equate good public relations with customer sovereignty. The school in educational philosophy that has misinterpreted the meaning of "democracy" has its counterpart in educational administration.

The university wishes to cement the bonds between itself and its public. It therefore—often with the statement that it is "meeting needs"—attempts to enroll as many adults as it can, preferably adults holding some key place in the social hierarchy, in any sort of course of study for which it can find a market... The programmes thus lose all intellectual responsibility, because they are not designed to help adults solve an intellectual problem or explore a new field of interest.

In a recent debate among several deans representing member institutions of the AUEC, John S. Diekhoff, then professor of education at Hunter College, argued that programmes be offered even if "stimulation may be required to attract" participants; while Alfred C. Nelson, dean of Community College, University of Denver, favoured solely those set up in "response to felt needs" and as "a reflection of public demand":

> If institutions did not set out to offer broad offerings in response to demonstrated need, these individuals would be lost to higher education...and ...would consider colleges and universities as available to only the few...[Moreover] taking them where they are and directing them where they should be...[is] far more enjoyable to both students and faculty than the more restricted accomplishments with "captive audiences" fettered by the limitations of credit work.

The moderator of the debate made the peace "by stating that most schools of his acquaintance operated uneasily somewhere between the two standards". According to the editor of the *Proceedings* in which this exchange appears, the audience did not dispute this "no-decision", as he calls it.

The notion that university educators should begin with their charges "where they are" is a recurrent theme; but the road from *Kitsch* to art, from lack of interest to involvement, from lackadaisical pottering to academic disciplines, or, most typically, from noneducation to education, has not been mapped by Dean Nelson or any other ideologue of the "soft pedagogy". "A course in sanitary engineering may finally bring the students to an understanding of the glories of Shakespeare, although I must confess that the intermediate steps are hazy in my mind". Education is a process (the literal meaning is "a bringing forth"); and a good teacher is one who begins—and stays—not where his students are but ahead of them, inducing them to move toward him.

There is no evidence, moreover, to support the notion that abandoning standards *does* improve a university's public relations. Some of the public, on the contrary, might resent paying taxes (or making donations) to help support such courses as one in wrapping Christmas packages, or in "Charm", or in fishing.

A number of...public institutions which formerly felt that political pressure required that they accept all high school graduates have now stiffened their entrance requirements and discovered, to their surprise, that by doing so they have won almost universal approbation. Is there a lesson here for higher adult education?

In other words, the best way for a university to maintain a good reputation is to deserve it. "The first prerequisite for good public relations is to be sure that you have a good product to sell", and the definition of a "good product", while it may be influenced by the public's demands, is in the domain of the professional educator. The legitimate functions of a public relations office are to explain to the people why policies that have been adopted are necessary and in their interest, and thus to develop a greater understanding of the true purpose of a university.

Summary

The extension of the university to other regions of the state or sectors of the population, with new areas of learning and methods of transmitting them, has included also functions—recreation, social welfare and reform, commercialism, and public relations—that do not jibe with the purposes of an institution of higher learning. Community development, a relatively recent interest of universities but one that has grown rapidly in the postwar period, is a prime example of universtiy noneducation. According to a good deal of evidence, the adult educators in community development have gone into an already well staffed field, to which they contribute nothing that is new and little that is useful. We believe that community development has no place in the programme of a university.

A British adult educator, after visiting a number of American campuses and encountering in their general-extension divisions courses in bridge and golf, wrote:

> There seem to be only two major arguments in favour of the practice. One is the hope that a student once attracted to the programme by such an interest will come into contract with more genuinely educational ones, and proceed to take them up. Our own experience is that this hardly ever happens, and that the non-educational activity may even tend to draw students away from educational ones and develop a centrifugal tendency in relation to the educational centre of the programme...The other argument is much more practical: pure entertainment dressed up as classes is a sure money-spinner and provides a welcome subsidy for genuinely educational activities. The question is whether its effect on the rest of the programme and the spirit of the institution is worth risking.

In most cases adult education has the status of a poor relation to other university divisions, "like Lazarus, stand[ing] waiting to catch the crumbs that fall from the degree tables". The share of the university's budget allotted to the general-extension division is ordinarily determined less by its requirements than by what is left over when all other demands have been met. Very often, this arrangement is by the common consent of both university and general-extension adminis-trators. The former too frequently perceive the adult division as a means of buying good will (and perhaps even of making a bit for the university on the side). And the latter so frequently lack a clear idea of either their educational objectives or the organizational means to achieve them that their divisions have been shaped to an inordinate degree by their chronic need to produce income.

Good educational policy cannot be effected merely by reforming the usual financial arrangement, but if this remains the same no other change is likely to be significant. Under the present system, about 60 per cent of extension-divisions income is derived from student fees, a relatively inelastic source. In effect, most of the balance comes from the faculty, who are generally paid less than beginning instructors on the home campus. The only way to meet the problem is to view adult education within the context of an educational institution, and not as a commercial venture, a social gathering, or a general means for doing good, and to bring it meaningfully within the university's organization. This is the subject of the following chapter.

6

Recapitulation : A Guide to Policy

The word *policy* has two meanings, either the sum of administrative decisions or the general principles from which these decisions flow. We use it in the second sense, to denote the relation between abstract statements of what is desirable and the specific applications of these to particular conditions. As we have already noted, policy in the deductive rather than inductive sense is a rather rare commodity in university adult education.

Every college and university in the nation is in one way or another engaged in adult education activities. These activities have grown so rapidly and institutions have been so busy responding to these demands that relatively few have had the time or the resources to examine the implications of this development.

Adult education is at best a poorly charted sea, and the "creative challenge" of unexplored areas has induced many a captain of extension to sail his ship on the reefs of triviality and sloth, where its standards break up one by one and the vessel finally sinks into the murky depths of commercialism.

Setting policy is necessary, but it is not so simple a matter as in what we have termed standard education (that is, all but adult education). Educational philosophies differ, but with respect to the primary and secondary schools or colleges, the framework of the differences is set by the relative homogeneity of a student body of about the same age and with more or less the same educational background and goals. A discussion of standard education can begin, thus, without having first to define the institution, the student, the degree, the period of residence and so on. In adult education, on the contrary, each of these axiomatic categories is an object both of dispute and, more often, of obfuscation. We found it necessary, therefore, to include a section, Chapter 2, in which we attempt to define some of the most important terms used in adult education.

If in this volume we have often taken a negative stance, it is because we accept university adult education as an institution good and valuable in itself. Its functions, in the words of John S.Diekhoff, are as follows:

> 1. The primary aim of evening colleges should be learning, not social reform, recreation, or therapy.
> 2. [Their] objectives should be to offer opportunity to students to acquire new knowledge, new skills and [to] develop the capacity for self-education.
> 3. This kind of learning should be appropriate to the university: intellectual, dignified and leading to interest in the latest research.
> 4. Colleges should thus recognize their special mission and their special clientele; *i.e.*, people of intellectual competence and prior knowledge, and leave the lesser tasks to other agencies.

The reader of this book knows by now that in this statement Diekhoff was not speaking for the whole of his profession and, even more, that much of university adult education deviates greatly from the standards he suggests. For when the intention is to offer programmes of such quality, this high purpose is frequently frustrated by, for example, the necessity of mixing commercialism with education. In short, to be effective policy must guide not only the educational ends but also, and equally, the organizational means by which they are presumably to be achieved.

How are general-extension divisions—or, better, all of the facilities for university adult education—organized; and how does this actual structure compare with one best suited for their purpose? What of their staffs, their administrative rules, their relation with the rest of the university? These are the key questions, and in order to discuss them in full context we shall summarize relevant portions of preceding chapters.

Should the University Engage in Adult Education?

The answer to this question, the most fundamental in setting extension policy, is not obvious. It has become axiomatic in the United States that free public education should be available through high school, and this principle has been extended also to include the regular day curriculum of public colleges. Whether tax money should be used to support adult education, however, is still a moot issue, which includes questions more basic than the manner in which the institution should be financed. Opposition to the general-extension division among main-campus administrators and faculty is often related to their fear that its low level will come to pervade the whole university, but this again does not touch on the most essential question. Supposing an administrative system could be established by which the quality of extension work could be guaranteed, should the university then divert some of its scarce faculty and facilities to the education of adults?

It is arguable that the answer to this question should be No, at least for noncredit. Even those who believe that learning should be a life-long process might well hold that, from a certain point on, organized education is no longer necessary. Should not adults who have been taught to read—particularly those qualified to enroll in a university programme—be able to use, for example, the country's public-library system and thus continue to learn on their own?

> There is something pathetic in the mature adult still dependent on a school for intellectual stimulus and intellectual security...At some point schooling should be terminal. "Terminal schooling" should be a self-explanatory phrase: it is the schooling which leads not to more schooling but to self-education.

We also would disagree with adult educators who believe in life-long enrolment, ranging from programmes in vocational improvement or marriage guidance during early adulthood to, finally, those designed to help one adjust to widowhood or retirement.

This is the perspective, we believe, of one or another type. There is first the "educator" who views education less as a learning process than as a way of combating alienation and loneliness. One can also become a life member of Arthur Murray's dancing schools: the number of dances to be learned each year may be limited, but it is always pleasurable to meet congenial people and do with them the things one enjoys. Then there is, second, the "educator" who refuses on principle to admit that there is a limit to the educability of anyone. Given the very great differences in innate ability, home environment, and interest, such a misconceived "democracy" can be applied only by abolishing standards, catering to those who attend a programme for the wrong reasons.

In spite of these strictures, we believe (as does Professor Diekhoff) that university adult education has an important place in present-day American life, and we devoted the first chapter of this volume to an extended argument for this position. Many adults are less well educated in the formal sense than would be desirable for both their own and society's welfare, and while they may know how to read they have not learned what is worth reading. One reason for this is that public education in the United States has developed over the past generation or two, with the consequence that many gaps have been left. In any case American society is changing so rapidly that even an adequate education can become dated very quickly. Engineers, Physicians, Accountants and other professionals find it convenient to keep up with the latest developments in their specialties through courses, which represent only the most obvious kind of educational adaptation to social change. The American population is highly mobile in every sense. Each year one out of every five persons moves to a different home, and many of these removals are combined with a change of job or even of occupation. This high rate of social mobility is at once one of the most valued features of the democratic system and an important reason for the country's high level of technical and economic efficiency. To move up in the social scale, however, is generally possible only if one is able to acquire basic knowledge in a formal college education, if not as an adolescent then later in life in adult-education programmes. And moving up need not be interpreted merely in occupational or monetary terms; it is no less important that Americans acquire a liberal education—the knowledge and understanding by which their increasing leisure could really enrich their lives.

Ever since the struggle in the last century to establish first free primary, then free secondary schools and colleges, the principal argument in favour of this gradual extension of public education has been that in a democracy, where the people exert an important control over the government, they must understand public issues in order to carry out their civic duties adequately. With the growing complexity of our urban society, the ideal of a town meeting has become more and more a meaningless slogan, but it is still true that a representative government requires an informed citizenry.

For all of these reasons, we believe that a university, if it has or can acquire the necessary facilities, faculty, and other resources, should engage in adult education. We also believe, however, that adult education of poor quality is worse than none, and that the university's decision to extend its services to new age groups, social classes and areas of knowledge should not be taken lightly.

University adult education constitutes no more than about four per cent of adult education as a whole. It is one sector of a vast, amorphous institution, in which universities, junior colleges, public schools, government bureaus, community agencies and private organizations engage in recreational, vocational, remedial, cultural and educational activities of every type, at every level, for every purpose. Within this all but infinite range, university adult education can play a meaningful role only by rigorously defining its distinctive place, by setting a limit to the tasks that it will undertake and an order of priority among them. Thus, many of the current extension activities are out of place in an institution of higher learning, in our opinion, and should be transferred elsewhere or abolished altogether.

The function of university adult education is education (and, legitimately, though usually to a small degree, research); it is not making money or public relations or social service or therapy or recreation. While no one, at least to our knowledge, has challenged in so many words the truism that the university's function is education, many define this term so broadly as to include these other activities, all of which are commonly associated with adult education. Even more frequently, general-extension administrators fail to think through the implications of contradictory purposes. In setting any kind of policy, accepting A means that B is inevitable, M likely, and Σ impossible. A university that tries to be both educational and commercial (with detours, say, into social work) succeeds only in being a monster.

The function of university adult education, to define it more narrowly, is *college-level* education. Once again, the truism that a college should offer college-level programmes is ordinarly disputed not in words but by defining the term so loosely that it lacks any effective meaning. College-level means, very simply, the standard maintained in the traditional academic disciplines of the day campus, or in programmes with a content of comparable or greater difficulty and complexity. Considering the heterogeneity of present-day curricula, such a definition is broader than an educational purist would like, but also certainly broad enough to include all of the legitimate purposes of extension. To designate the persons responsible for maintaing college level and to establish the kind of organizational structure that would motivate them to up-hold standards are more important, we believe, than to attempt to spin out longer paraphrases of this self-explanatory term.

From the very beginning of university adult education in the United States, as in the philosophy and practice of President Van Hise of the University of Wisconsin, the "extension" of the university had several meanings. In order to discuss the issue, we found it useful to designate four types of extension. The simplest type, extension in time and place, consists in making available to persons other than the regular day students catalogue courses and other university services with no change in their content or quality. Since this type is of college level by definition, it is in principle a legitimate activity for the university. A second type of extension, consisting in the adaptation of college work to the particular needs of subgroups in the adult population, we have termed a functional extension. A large portion of noncredit programmes and community services would be included in this class. It gives an opportunity for creative administration, but unless the limitation to college-level education is followed, this deviation from the traditional academic disciplines diverts the university from its proper course. The attempt to take over all of education and to teach subjects below college level, thirdly, we have termed substandard extension. While this may have been a legitimate activity of the university fifty years ago in a semi-frontier state like Wisconsin (we do not think so), it is certainly not so today anywhere in the United States. To undertake an educational task below college level, a dozen agencies are available; for higher education there is only the university. The fourth type, the extension out of education altogether into recreation or social service or whatever, we have termed conversion. We deem this to be an illegitimate practice of the university under all circumstances, though the line may be difficult to draw in particular instances. With a good teacher learning is not a dull experience, but having fun or mitigating alienation should never be more than subsidiary by-products of the essential process of education. Similarly, we judge the main purpose of the community-development movement to be social improvement, and we believe that it has no legitimate place in the university.

The Dimensions of the General-Extension Division

As we have noted, the very concept of "total extension function"—that is, the whole of a university's activities in addition to its two core purposes of scholarly research and the education of young people toward a degree—is not ordinarily to be found either in the minds of university administrators or in abstract discussions of administrative policy, not to say in the records of extension activities as compiled by such an organization as the NUEA. Some elements of the total extension function are typically administered by a general-extension division (for example, correspondence courses) and others more often by a separate office (for example, university presses); but with respect to most activities, practice varies a good bit from one campus to another. No organizational principle seems to be involved, but more probably the interest or ability of one rather than another person in having developed a particular activity some time in the past, or in maintaining it now. Perceiving the total extension function as a unit is important, thus, because it can stimulate thought on questions that to date have generally been settled *ad hoc,* with no consideration of underlying principles: Under what circumstances is a general-extension division useful? When it exists, ought it to administer all or only some of the university's total extension function?

And if the latter, what should be the basis for distinguishing one from the other type of activity?

In any field, a prerequisite to the formulation of intelligent policy is accurate and complete information. Amazing as it may appear, it seems that even top-level university administrators are often not aware of the adult education offered by their own institutions. The dean of faculty of one large state university, for example, stated verbally that unfortunately it had no adult education (apart from that offered by Cooperative Extension); actually, 40,000 persons had attended short courses on his campus during the past several years. At another state university (not a land-grant institution, and thus with no Cooperative Extension), the vice-president recently had a survey made of all extension activities and found, somewhat to his surprise, that the general-extension division administers less than half of the total. We suspect that this ignorance is typical, and wherever it exists it constitutes a block to intelligent policy.

Every institution ought to establish an accounting system capable of measuring the portion of its budget that goes into adult education, as well as the allocation within this among various types of programmes. Unless this is done, there is no possibility of real control, either in the sense of banning unsuitable types of activity or of setting a schedule of priorities among those that are suitable but of greater or lesser importance. The office assigned to maintain such a record could also serve as a central information bureau, both for administrators and those faculty members interested in keeping informed on what is being done supplementary to regular teaching and research. Whether this minimum degree of coordination ought to be exercised by the president's office, the general-extension division, or a special center, is not a principled question. In any case, it would supplement the general-extension division as it is presently constituted.

The actual range of control of general-extension divisions varies greatly. For example, among 51 universities surveyed by Morton, in 10 the responsibility for off-campus work was divided between academic departments and the extension division; in one the faculty of each school could operate any such programme it chose; in 22 all off-campus activities had to be administered by the general-extension division; and 18 had no policy on this matter. Like all such statistics, however, these pertain mainly to formal course work and similar programmes. If we had full information on *all* extension activities, the picture would change considerably.

There is an equally great variety in the organizational relation between general extension and the rest of the university, as can be seen from a few examples:

At the *University of Chicago,* "in addition to Committees, Institutes, Centers, there are eleven divisions and schools. University College is one of these. But unlike the other ten, it is merely an administrative adjunct of the Office of the Chancellor, is not under University Statutes a 'ruling body' and has no relationship to the Faculty policy-making body, the Senate. Hence it is not represented in the Council of the Senate, which legislates academic policy."

The *Pennsylvania State University* has one extension director, who is advised by an administrative committee comprising the assistant deans for continuing education from the undergraduate colleges and the graduate school, representatives of the admissions office, and the director and two associate directors of continuing education. The state is divided into three regions, each with a regional director and assistant director of continuing education as well as district administrators in the principal population areas.

The *University of California's* statewide general-extension division is headed by a university dean of extension, and the Agricultural Extension Service by a director under the university dean of agriculture. All extension activity is coordinated through a university extension advisory board, of which the university dean of extension is chairman. Its members comprise the director of agricultural extension and faculty representatives from the several campuses.

At *Michigan State University,* the various off-campus programmes are coordinated through the provost. The continuing Education Service, the Labour and Industrial Relations Center, and the High-way Traffic Safety Center report directly to his office, and the Cooperative Extension Service to it through the dean of agriculture. As of the beginning of 1960, according to a prior announcement by the presidents of

Michigan's nine state universities and colleges, a coordinated system of extension courses went into effect.

Oregon has a state system of higher education, with the director of the Division of University Extension responsible to the Chancellor. *Florida* also has a unified system of higher education, with the dean of the single general-extension division serving the entire state and responsible to the president of the University of Florida. The Agricultural Extension Service has a separate director responsible to the provost for agriculture.

What impressions do such illustrative organizational systems make on the observer? Within the continuing great variety, there seem to be a great proliferation of titles and a certain tendency toward statewide centralization. Whether these are altogether healthy trends we do not know, and a good case can be made for either side.

The central administration of all off-campus and evening activities seems, at least in the abstract, to be a good thing. It is desirable as a means of "conservation of planning, funds and energy", since the "elimination of conflict and confusion" makes for greater efficiency. There is a "need to coordinate the work...so that the resources of the institution will be used carefully and economically." For example—

> The president of a southern university, on a recent visit to a countyseat town, encountered five members of his staff, each one of whom was working in the community with no knowledge that anyone else had any contact with it. Even worse, five university cars had been used for transportation!

On the other hand, the unified administration of such variegated activities as off-campus courses, noncredit programmes of several types, concerts and lectures, conferences, the university press, and so on and on, is inherently difficult. Centralization of control can result in bureaucratic waste almost as easily as in greater efficiency; and in the best case "efficiency" is perhaps more likely to be defined as carrying out established routines well. This danger is particularly great in university adult education, since its purpose is often ill defined, the means of achieving it are a matter of dispute, and neither administrative structures nor any other variables are generally evaluated for their educational efficacy. If the measure of "efficiency" is to be set in an educational framework, there must be concern for "the careful preservation of the right of the respective departments and schools to establish and maintain...standards". Moreover, "by far the majority of [general-extension] directors expressed themselves as not all alarmed" by the fact that they were not administering all adult-education activities; they had more than enough to do without trying to add to their responsibilities.

We do not believe there is any resolution of this dilemma that will fit every institution. Within the framework set by certain general principles, which we believe to be applicable to all adult education in an institution of higher learning, many different organizational structures are possible. The goals appropriate and the means and personnel available are different for a large or small university, a public or private one, a rural or urban one, and so on. We do think, however, that a good deal of the existent variety is the consequence of historical accident, of irrelevant precedent, or of lack of policy—and that little, if anything, in the typical organization need be regarded as sacrosanct.

Indeed, the crying need for reform is in itself a relevant factor in setting the future organizational structure, and in some instances perhaps a more important one than any other. An attempt to tighten standards would undoubtedly be welcomed by some extension administrators and faculty. But the group therapists, the mongers of better bridge, the community developers, the advocates of the soft pedagogy—these would regard any reform as an attack on themselves, to be answered with a counter-attack. Where such types are well entrenched in a university's adult-education programme, no abstract argument that centralization effects greater educational efficiency would justify bringing a larger share of the total extension function under their control. A university president interested in fostering significant adult education in his institution might be able to do this, at one extreme, by facilitating the work of a competent dean; but at the other extreme he might have to resort to the device (familiar enough in bureaucratic manipulation) of building a second adult-education section of the university, designed eventually to undermine and supplant a general-extension division that he considers beyond repairs.

Relations between Extension and the Main Campus

It is the task of the general-extension division to administer a given portion of the university's total extension function, but what is meant by "administer"? Here, once again, we find no agreement on fundamentals. According to Dean Morton—

> An extension organization...can and should be only an agency for interpreting, promoting, organizing and financing the types of educational services desired by the deans and department heads of the various instructional divisions of an institution of higher learning. It is, however, the duty of the staff of the extension organization to see that the deans and department heads understand the alternatives they face in making these choices.

According to the no less authoritative view of Professor Houle, however, while the general-extension division is in part "a facilitating organization through which the other departments operate in the field"—

> It is not...merely their instrument but attempts to survey the community, organize and develop new programmes of educational activity, call needs to the attention of the regular instructional departments, and, in other ways, see that the community's needs and interests are represented within the institution.

In another publication, Houle goes farther and asks under what conditions the person in charge of extension merits of the title "dean". "Only if", he replies, "in addition to or *in place of* the service functions he may have to perform, he accepts the responsibility for being creative in the construction of ...programmes...appropriate to the mature students he serves... Even if the university has a vice-president in charge of extension, it will still need a special officer acting as dean, to arrange the unique programmes of adult education".

The issue, in other words, is whether the "extension division" ought to be merely an extension or at least in part a division of the university. How one resolves the question affects a wide variety of policy decisions. An extension administrator operating under the first principle is likely to make fewer mistakes. The educational quality will be set, at least in theory, by main-campus faculty, who tend to follow the academic disciplines. If they sometimes perform their role of guardians of traditional standards somewhat stolidly, and if these courses—particularly as presented under the conditions prevalent in extension—are sometimes rather dull, their subject matter nevertheless includes the significant core of our higher culture. Some of the wider-ranging, more experimental extension administrators have deviated from tradition with tawdry programming, but others with true educational creativity.

> The alert extension department will often have organized lectures on Internal Auditing, Electronic Data Processing, and Zen Buddhism long before the "academic department" head has recognized them as proper subjects for inquiry. Again and again, academic departments have to be dragged screaming into the twentieth century—especially into the latter half.

The ideal relation between main-campus faculty and extension administrators would seem to be a dialectical interaction through which both types of virtue could be expressed. Unfortunately, the frequently poor reputation that the extension has in the rest of the university hampers cooperation between the two.

This is an important question, and it is worth citing several, partly conflicting, opinions from a number of authorities. "In most institutions", in Morton's opinion, "the administrative staff members of the extension organization... [have] the same status in the university as other university staff members having similar responsibilities", and Houle believes that the status of general-extension deans has been increasing and is on occasion higher than that of any other dean. According to Neuffer, on the other hand, "evening divisions have not yet reached a position where their status in terms of respect and influence on the campus is equal to that of the day division". One of the major tasks the Center for the Study of Liberal Education for Adults has set itself is "improving relationships between divisions of adult education and their parent institutions". Similarly, according to the executive secretary of the NUEA, this general-extension administrators' association "does not enjoy the eminence...it should have... among educational circles in Washington and perhaps else-where". The difference in opinion may be due to stressing one or another element of that rather vague word "status". In formal terms, as Morton shows, extension staffs usually have equivalent titles, salaries and personnel working under them; but this does not mean that they have an equal voice in determining over-all university policy, nor that day administrators and faculty necessarily regard them as peers. And the differentiation with respect to faculty is much sharper: in extension they have neither the same prestige nor equivalent salaries and prerogatives.

Most main-campus administrators and faculty, if the question were put to them in the abstract, would undoubtedly express themselves as in accord with the democratic principle that educational opportunities should be extended to social classes and age groups not able to attend regular college sessions. In practice, however, they ordinarily want as little as possible to do with extension. Even apart from the quality of adult education, deans and department heads prefer to have their faculty do research in their spare time rather than teach additional courses, so that on principle their cooperation with the general-extension division is reluctant and partial. Many of the regular administrators and faculty are thoroughly hostile. "A number of university men", as Houle has put it, think it "highly appropriate" that *adult education* and *adulteration* are coupled as the heading of one page of the *Encyclopaedia of the Social Sciences.* The main campus acquiesces, therefore, in the isolation of extension, the low salaries, the commercial standards imposed on it by the university—in short, in conditions that reduce still more extension's standards, and thus also their already low estimate of them.

The tendency is to regard extension work as something inferior to, and generally beneath, residence. Since it is so regarded, the result is that it sometimes is inferior work. All of you are acquainted with the department head who has a feeling that anything goes in extension, and who will approve classes and instructors in extension which he would not in residence.

The reputation that extension has and the one it deserves interact, thus, by what Myrdal has termed "the principle of cummulation". In his classic work on the American Negro, he was able to organize a vast mass of data into an easily assimilable narrative by relating them all to this single theme.

White prejudice and discrimination keep the Negro low in standards of living, health, education, manners and morals. This, in its turn, gives support to white prejudice. White prejudice and Negro standards thus mutually "cause" each other. If things remain about as they are and have been, this means that the two forces happen to balance each other...If either of the factors changes, this will cause a change in the other factor, too, and start a process of interaction where the change in one factor will continuously be supported by the reaction of the other factor.

This pattern is commonly called "the vicious circle", but Myrdal preferred the neutral term because he wanted to stress that the interdependence of factors affecting Negro-white relations can work in either direction. If we apply the principle of cumulation to university adult education, however, it suggests also that great improvement is likely only if it initiated from the highest university level. If extension attempts by itself to raise its level, this intent is likely to be frustrated by the discriminatory policies reflecting the negative attitude of the main campus. And if, on the other hand, one or another academic department tries to infuse its higher standards into extension's work, it may well find that the danger of adulteration must be taken seriously. Only an executive with control over both sides of this interacting system can negate the dead weight of the past and begin to turn the vicious circle in the opposite direction.

The changes in the organizational structure the president should effect can be stated simply—the elimination of all of extension's differentiating features that do not follow naturally and inevitably from its special educational functions. This means, on the one hand, the abolition of programmes in social improvement, individual therapy, recreation, and so on, and the maintenance of equal quality in its educational offerings. It means no less, on the other hand, the removal of discriminatory practices, such as the markedly lower salary of extension instructors or its quasi-commercial status altogether. Such a reform would encounter, of course, entrenched prejudice and opposition from vested authority throughout the university.

It would be necessary, in our opinion, to root such reforms as firmly as possible in new administrative rules. The quality of part-time instruction in extension could undoubtedly be greatly improved if it was made an occasional regular portion of *each* faculty member's teaching load (*not* an addition to it), with extra pay only for travel time and expenses. Apparently this system is not followed anywhere. The control that home-campus departments often have over extension courses, usually exercised with listless disinterest, would become more meaningful if all adult courses for "credit" were actually given equivalent credit, and if instructional departments were given a budgetary stake in extension. Full-time instructors, such as are usual in extension centers, would be equally competent if they were hired under the same conditions as their home-campus colleagues and had the same salaries, duties, and prerogatives; and when geography makes it feasible, administrative regulations might also encourage the maximum degree of cooperation and interpenetration between sister departments.

The Financing of Adult Education

In casting the president in the role of adjudicator, we have assumed (for the sake of the argument) that his intent is to foster a significant college-level educational programme for adults. While this is certainly true of some university executives, it is hardly the characteristic attitude. The heaviest responsibility for the failing of university adult education, on the contrary, lies with the president. This is true first of all in a formal sense: he is the superior officer to whom the extension dean or director reports. And it is even more true intrinsically. As we pointed out in the last chapter, the main purposes of the adult-education programme, as seen by all too many presidents, are to supplement the university's public relations office and its fund-raising efforts. No matter what their other faults, extension personnel must reasonably be adjudged innocent of complicity in the vicious system that keeps their budgets so pinched that they are induced, one might almost say forced, to become peddlers of popular commodities. If there were no such financial discrimination, how much would remain, one wonders, of the felt-needs "approach" and the other sops to adult educators' self-respect? In other words, how much responsibility does the president's office have for the whole range of anti-intellectual "philosophies" and practices that we have examined in this book? Most of these originated, it is true, outside the university, in the broader world of adult education; and those in the college community who profess their faith in groupness or pledge allegiance to recreation are undoubtedly sometimes sincere. Yet, if the whole perspective were to be changed, one wonders.

The administrator is... a victim rather than the villain of the piece. As often as not he is under considerable pressure from a university administration which may well force him to try and increase the size, turnover and income of his department at all costs. In any case he must at least balance his budget and this almost necessarily prevents him from balancing his programme...One's immediate and general impression is one of insecurity, despite the exceptions. The dean appears so often to be, or believe himself to be, caught between the upper millstone of the university administration demanding money and numbers regardless of standards, and the neither one of the day faculty who look down, or appear to look down, on his work, with varying degrees of justification.

It is rather easy, the reader may feel, to hit so large and obvious a target as the commercialization of general extension. We deem our reiterated attacks to be useful, even if they indicate no particularly acute perspicacity on our part, since they serve to emphasize a crucial feature that is all too often played down, or even passed over, when the actors in this story drama themselves write of their roles. What should be the financial basis of university adult education?

Since under the present system tuition constitutes so large a proportion of general-extension income, the size of class fees is a matter of unusual importance to the administration. They range from zero to $30 a semester-hour, with most public institutions charging $10 or less. What tuition is just is not a question that can be answered except in terms of a given social philosophy. And what fee is suitable in education terms depends on data that are mostly not available. While no discussion of the issue can pretend to be definitive, it is at least useful to keep the moral question separate from the empirical one.

Let us take the moral issue first. Charging fees, it is sometimes maintained, is undemocratic, because all cannot afford them equally well. Since free public education is available at other levels, it should be made available also for adults. The argument is reinforced by the fact that certain other types of adult education are financed, or at least heavily subsidized, out of public funds: municipal, county, state, and/or federal funds are used to pay for vocations education, various other adult programmes in the public schools, and the entire very large Cooperative Extension programmes. "Should all members, not just farmers and labourers, of a democratic society be given equal adult educational opportunities?"

The arrangement that democracy implies social equality, however, cannot be accepted in *absolute* terms. Having to attend college in the evening after working all day is in itself discriminatory, and if those who argue from the principle of equality were consistent, they would demand that all who want adult education should be subsidized while they attain it during three mornings a week. If absolute equality is rejected as an irrelevant principle, then the question becomes, what is "reasonable", what is "expedient"; and in that case, it is not at all clear whether university adult education should be free. By our interpretation of democratic principles, tuition should never be so high as to prevent a well prepared, highly motivated person from continuing his education. On the other hand, given the grave and increasing short age of funds for all higher education, we must ask whether it is necessary to cut off entirely the largest present source of extension income. Resolving this dilemma is particularly difficult because the relevant data are not only scanty but often also ambiguous.

1. The average adult student has considerably more education than the population as a whole, and therefore also an appreciably higher income. One could argue that tuition is therefore not an unreasonable burden, particularly since most extension students do not take a full programme (and many no more than an occasional course) and their outlay per semester is thus small. But would the higher income of adults be meaningfully so if we were also to compare their financial responsibilities with those of adolescents? And what is the direction of the presumed cause-effect relation: to what degree do adults with lower incomes *therefore* not continue their education, or enroll in fewer courses? Educators are in sharp

disagreement concerning the effect of tuition fees on enrolment figures. Apparently no study has ever been made of this effect in university adult education, but the several studies of this relation in other types of adult-education programmes, while not entirely relevant to general extension, may be indicative. One survey of ninety-five cities in a depression year "showed little difference in the proportion of adults respectively attending free and fee programmes," and a more recent study in six cities confirmed this finding.

2. What effect do fees have on the diligence of students? A number of adult educators, including persons with as wide an experience as Houle, believe that the only argument for tuition is the financial one, that in all educational respects fees are harmful or, at best, irrelevant. However, what little evidence exists suggests the contrary. Lacking data on extension, if we again turn to studies of adult education outside the university, we find that fees do seem to result in better attendance; and this is a reasonable definition of "diligence".

Balancing these several considerations, we make the following proposal as a reasonable compromise:

1. In degree-credit courses, the charge should be precisely the same as for the equivalent courses on the main campus. The democratic impulse that the extension in time and place originally expressed would thus be retained at least for the standard fare of most general-extension divisions.

2. For programes not carrying degree-credit, there should be a charge, ordinarily large enough to cover its cost but with some consideration also to such factors as the ability of the probable participants to pay and the social value of the programme. Non-credit programmes, though they vary widely, often approximate what we have termed a functional extension; and the very fact that many are designed for specific groups reduces the relevance of moral arguments in favour of free adult education. If such programmes pay for themselves, moreover, they permit an imaginative administration really to break new ground.

This discussion of tuition fees, in any case, hardly touches the central problem. Even if the income from course fees were increased, in many universities this would not in itself solve any problems, for the additional funds would be returned in the form of a profit to the over-all budget of the univesity. No other division of the university is expected to support itself; and the partial exception to this rule in the case of general extension, merely an accidental effect of its historical development, few administrators even attempt to justify in terms of organizational principles. The crucial reform would be to eliminate this discrimination, as has been done in a number of evening colleges. Rutgers University Colleges, for example, "is not a revenue-producing but an educational unit, with its budget established and operated like the budget of all other colleges. All costs are paid out of funds allotted by the University; all income goes directly to the University". The Division of General Education at New York University, to take a private institution, is similarly "separately budgeted as one of the 14 schools of the University and 'reports' directly to the central administration as do the other schools and colleges". The division administrators, however, believe that "noncredit activities *should* pay their own way, including allowance for institutional overhead". The fact that these two examples are so large and independent as to be more branches than extensions of the main campus is not relevant to the organizational principle. If anything, one might argue that, on the contrary, the smaller and weaker general-extension divisions (or adult-education programmes altogether) are less able to stand on their own feet than extension centers.

What effect on quality would substantial new sources of income have? We have argued that its commercialization is an important reason for the frequently low standards of adult education; and it is no paradox to hold that, given the present personnel, their "philosophy", and the established routines, additional funds might only furnish a rich breeding ground to anti-intellectual forces. In short, while a reform is urgent in the method by which university adult education is financed, by itself, with no concomitant control over educational policy *per se,* this could do more harm than good.

Summary

Books have been written on higher education, professional and regional organizations established, conferences have met, in which the university's role in adult education was given only a token recognition, or not even that. It is an administrative task of first importance to integrate its adult education with the rest of the university. An institution planning to put its extension activities on a better foundation would do well to recognize the problem and try to cope with it from the very beginning. The optimum organization of university adult education, stated in the broadest terms, is that it should differ from the rest of the university only in those respects that its special function makes necessary. One can compare it with the college education of women. A half century ago, when this was still something of a rarity, the difference between male and female students was very often greatly exaggerated. It was believed that significant adaptations in curriculum and administrative control were necessary, while today relatively slight modifications of standard procedures are seen as appropriate for women's colleges. A similar legend has run the cycle with respect to adults; we have pretty well discarded the myth that there is a substantial physiological basis for the difference between adolescents and mature students, but we have not yet reached the point of recognizing the essential unity of college education irrespective of age. Within this unity there are, indeed, significant differences, but none that warrant the wild aberrations from standards educational aims and methods or, on the other hand, the special and often discriminatory administrative regulations.

In previous chapters, we delineated the main issues in adult education and indicated with respect to each what we deem to be good educational policy. Almost all these questions are relevant to a discussion of the university's role in educating adults. At the most abstract level, as in pronouncements on how "felt needs" should filled, no distinction is ordinarily made between adult education by a university and that by other agencies. The theme of "democracy" appears in a somewhat altered form: universities, and particularly state universities, must "serve" their community. They must maintain good public relations with the voting public, and they ordinarily use their extension function at least in part for this purpose. In a passage that has become deservedly famous, Dean Nolte asked his audience to imagine the figure of the university, holding aloft the flaming beacon of truth and with its ear to the ground to catch from afar the first rumble of the people's will. He did not think it necessary to specify "what part of the anatomy is most prominent to the beholder". When everything else has been sacrificed to this false image of "democracy", it must not be imagined that the educator's dignity has been saved.

University adult education almost always has to pay its own way in an extraordinary proportion, and in some cases it is almost frankly admitted that its purpose is to return a profit to the other, the educational sectors of the university. A fundamental reform from which all kinds of benefits would flow would be to eliminate the prevalent practice by which extension divisions are encouraged to become quasi-commercial enterprises. In our opinion, the fees for at least credit courses should be identical with those on the day campus; all income collected should go into the general university budget, from which allocations should be made to adult education, as to every activity of the university, solely on the basis of educational requirements. Under such a system, the administrator of the university's adult education would have to compete with other sectors of the institution and demonstrate the intellectual worth of his offerings as compared with those in other colleges; thus, not only would the commercial basis of extension curricula be removed, but an educational one would be substituted for it.

Main-campus faculty, like the university administration, tend to regard extension as second-rate, a source of petty increments to their inadequate salaries but also a threat to the quality of higher education generally. Whether originally true or false, such stereotypes are likely to be self-fulfilling prophecies; for the judgment of main-campus administrators and faculty, who held determine the nature and level of general extension, often prove to be correct in the end. Again, there is no valid educational reason for the differences on and off campus in instructors' salary and status, and such invidious distinctions cannot fail to have their effect on the quality of teaching. When extension courses are taught by regular day faculty, we recommend that they be made a regular rotating portion of each faculty member's teaching load, with no extra pay. When there are full-time extension teachers, we recommend that the same professional qualifications be demanded of them, and that they be paid on the same scale as their main-campus colleagues.

The chief administrative officers of adult education more often receive equivalent salaries and have comparable authority in their own domain, but they generally have little or no voice in broader university councils and thus a reduced prestige among their nominal peers. If they are qualified to administer a division of the university, we feel, their participation in setting over-all policy should be taken for granted. And if they are not really qualified by home-campus standards, then giving them the title of "dean" or "director" or even "vice-president" is not defensible.

The standards in ostensibly equivalent courses taught on campus and in extension often differ considerably, and the lower quality of the latter is sometimes half legitimized by such regulations as, for example, that a certain proportoin of the credit toward a degree must be earned in residence. Insofar as it is symptomatic of the lowering of sholastic standards in extension work, this kind of blurring of the distinction between credit and noncredit work is unfortunate. In noncredit programmes it is ordinarily even more difficult to establish and maintain quality. The following quotation from the bulletin of a state university's community college contains in succinct form most of the faults to be found in noncredit adult-education programmes:

> The classes deal with any subject for which there is an expressed interest. Any adult may take these courses regardless of his educational background. Instruction is informal and designed to give each student just what he wants to learn...No listed course will be continued in which the enrolment is less than fifteen.

The courses offered include vocational (acetylene welding, typing, etc.), general (fundamentals of English, etc.), and such miscellaneous items as "self-improvement (charm)", "art of conversation", sewing, gardening and golf.

In contrast, we believe that the content and teaching methods of a university programme should be set by educators in accordance with their professional training. Many adults who attend college programmes do so in order to advance in their vocation, and in that case their course demands are ordinarily quite specific. Adults who return to school seeking a liberal education, however, generally have a vague, unfocused, uninformed notion of what they expect to learn. Those who go to the university rather than to a library or museum need guidance, and not merely the so-called "non-directive guidance" that reflects their own "felt needs". If the university is to perform adequately in adult education, there as in every one of its activities it must set its programme in accordance with its own policy. That it should be necessary to advance such an argument is in itself indicative. Nothing in adult education is responsible for more shoddiness, for greater hypocrisy, than the notion that in a democracy educators must abrogate their professional responsibilities.

No one organizational structure is called for to implement such educational goals; but certain broad principles are universally valid. On every campus, first of all, it would be useful to establish an accounting system from which university administrators could learn what it is doing in adult education, at what cost, with what changes from past years, and so on. It is necessary, in a word, to recognize the total extension function as a meaningful concept, an entity of which the activities of the general-extension division sometimes make up no more than half. The central agency that computes statistics on all extension activities could also carry out two other useful activities. The first is coordination, to reduce undue waste in the use of personnel and facilities. The second is liaison between the university and the public, in order both to mitigate the exploitation of the faculty that is otherwise common, particularly at a public university, and to maintain good public relations.

Without reforms of the type we have advocated here, it can be safely predicted, academic standards in adult education will suffer more and more from the combined effect of inadequate facilities, poorly paid faculties, sharply increasing enrolments, and a "philosophy" of education that makes it easy to interpret chaos as exhilarating. In self-defence, main-campus administrators and faculty will withdraw still farther from interest in and responsibility for general extension, thus increasing its isolation and aggravating its faults. With the pressure on the main campuses, they will inevitably seek ways of getting rid of their marginal students; and what could be more convenient than to dump them on extension, which already has a tradition of accepting students who have flunked out of regular sessions? The worst that can happen, and also perhaps the most probable, is a "success" of overwhelming proportions, with more students than ever before, more instructors (including more "instructors"), more courses, more groups, more conferences, more money for more community development, more self-congratulatory articles on all the felt needs-being met. And the date for this forecast is not 1984 but close to 1964.

7

Agricultural Extension

The Agency commonly referred to as the Agricultural Extension Service has more formal and more accurately descriptive title—the Cooperative Agricultural and Home Economics Extension Service. As this name implies, it is a joint undertaking. Cooperatively administered by federal, state, and local governments, the organization has been so successful in the promotion of its programme that it has gained international recognition me has grown to be the largest tax-supported adult-education institution in the world.

Established in 1914 by the passage of the Smith-Lever Act, the Extension Service has grown rapidly. In 1951 it employed a professional staff totaling 12,642. Approximately 2000 specialists in agriculture and home economics were at work on the campuses of cooperating land-grant colleges and universities preparing materials and rendering specialized help to more than 2500 home-demonstration agents and to nearly 5000 county agents and assistant county agents. Over 95 per cent of the counties in the United States have agricultural agents, and about 70 per cent have home-demonstration agents.

The professional staff, large as it is, shrinks to insignificance as compared with the staff of volunteer workers enrolled in the Extension Service Programme. About 1,000,000 unpaid, voluntary leaders each year give an average of about two weeks each to extension work. This donated time, if calculated at rates paid to unskilled labour, exceeds the amounts of the entire annual budget of the Extension Service.

The scope of the programme is indicated by such statistics as the following, taken from the 1950 annual report.

An estimated 4,661,094 families changed one or more agricultural practices as a result of extension activities. More than 3,300,000 families were influenced to change home practices. Nearly 2,000,000 boys and girls were enrolled in 4-H Club work. Extension agents worked with 339,900 young men and women between the ages of 18 and 30.

It has been stated that nearly 7,000,000 farm families are reached by the Extension programme. In 1951 the appropriation for this programme from all sources was $77,250,000.

The programme of the Agricultural Extension Service is of great significance to the adult-education movement in the United States, not only in its own right but because its record of progress and solid accomplishment over a period of more than a generation is our best demonstration of the fact that the behaviour patterns of adults can be changed in significant ways by a programme of adult education. It has demonstrated, too, that its programme goes beyond changing the behaviour patterns of individuals, because in thousands of communities over the nation groups of people have been stimulated to work together for the solution of their common problems. Its history provides our most convincing evidence that social change toward established goals can be brought about by a programme concentrated on the adult citizens of a community.

The achievements of the Extension Service tend to confirm the faith of many adult educators in the great social and individual values to be derived from programmes of adult education, but there are further reasons for examining the functioning of this agency. It is our best example of an adult-education agency operating with a large professional staff; it is a unique experiment in a cooperative educational programme with federal funds playing an important part in stimulating and supporting programmes initiated and controlled at the state and local level. With its relatively adequate and stable financial base making possible its relatively large and well-trained professional staff, the Extension Service has for many years pioneered with adult-education methods and procedures. No other agency has had the opportunity to try out nearly so thoroughly under field conditions its conceptions of what adult education can and should accomplish.

The remainder of this chapter presents selections chosen to answer the following questions about the Agricultural Extension Service programme:

What is the social setting in which Agricultural extension operates?

What is the basic organization of Agricultural Extension?

What is the content of the Agricultural Extension?

What are the basic methods used by Agricultural Extension?

What are the obstacles and recommended measures for overcoming them?

What is the Social Setting in which Agricultural Extension Operates?

Except for the staff members of the Agricultural Extension Service, few adult-education workers have had first-hand experience with rural American and its problems. The following selection is quoted from material prepared by Charles P. Loomis on "Special Conditions of Rural Adult Education" as part of a committee report resulting from a study sponsored by the Association of Land Grant Colleges and Universities and the Fund for Adult Education established by the Ford Foundation. The selection, which is too brief to do more than suggest some of the disadvantages and advantages for adult education in a rural setting, is well documented in Loomis' original manuscript.

Ecological Factors—Sparsity or Population and Organizational Efficiency

In most respects, rural areas are comparatively disadvantaged in the availability of adult education facilities. One reason for this is related to the problem of space and its effect on communication and organization. Everyone is aware that man is a space-bound creature and that no dreams of magic carpets or supermen change this. However, in an age of supersonic speeds and mass media we may forget that organizations, to function effectively, require a certain minimum number of participants, members or consumers in a relatively small area. ...A large segment of the rural population of the

United States lives in natural service units or trade center communities which have fewer people than these minima. Obviously, the minimum population required for effective service is accessibility, day-to-day interaction and movements of the people. But the disadvantaging factors of low population densities and long distances to services in many rural areas of the United States need no emphasis for adult education workers with experience in the sparsely settled areas. The county agricultural agent, vocational agricultural teacher, extension librarian, and rural minister have very different problems in the Range-Livestock or Wheat Areas of the Great Plains than do adult educators in large cities or thickly settled rural areas. Some of the difficulties of providing services in the most rural parts of the nation could be overcome incomes for all rural section were comparable... However, incomes are generally lower in the more rural and less densely populated areas.

Ecological Factors—Communication Within Informal Groups

Although the most rural areas may have insufficient population and financial support of the formal social systems that provide health, educational, welfare and road services, such areas are not disadvantaged in all the requirements for effective adult education. Thus, in most farming and ranching areas, the family functioning as a unit occupationally is an effective means of communication. Families, as groups usually operate the farms and ranches of the United States. A family enterprise, whether a two-acre truck farm or a 1500-acre cattle ranch, ties the members into a team relationship which no effective adult educator fails to consider in his work...

Outside the immediate family, the kinship or family system is an important communication network and mutual aid system in all rural areas. In many rural areas studied by the author, 80 per cent of the day-to-day contacts off the farm are with relatives. Such communities are rather unusual, being for the most part ethnic groupings, such as the Spanish-Americans in the southwest and Dutch groups in the north. But in the all parts of rural America, particularly in the older settlements, family ties are important—"Blood is thicker than water."

> ... the clique ranks next to the family in the intimacy it provides participating members ... the clique or friendship group is regarded as a small, non-kinship group, consisting of two to about thirty persons, in association and possessing a feeling of unity. Such groups are described as "informal" because there are no formally elected officials, constitutions, by-laws or other formal structuring elements. The intensity, frequency and significance of social interaction of rural people in such groupings is great.

The neighbourhood may be defined as an area in which people "neighbor together." Except in the most sparsely settled areas, rural parts of the nation have the strongest neighbourhoods. This is not the place to discuss the differences between neighbourhoods and trade center communities, but it may be observed that since the invention of the motor car and modern road system, the small neighbourhood of from 15 to 150 families who "neighbor together" is disappearing, whereas the trade center community made up of several to a dozen or so neighbourhoods is becoming more important.

The trend toward the disappearance of the small neighbourhood groups in rural areas and toward much larger trade center communities, noted by Loomis above, has brought with it a demand that Agricultural Extension expand its services to such communities made up largely of non-farm people. There is even some demand for certain types of Agricultural Extension services in urban areas.

Edmund Brunner and E. Hsin Pao Yang call attention to this situation in the following reference:

> ... agents regard urban work as a marginal activity, except of fulfilling an obligation to report to urban taxpayers on what the Service is doing for the general welfare. This obligation, which should include interpreting the farm point of view and farm needs to urban people, is important, and several papers at meetings of the Association of Land-Grant Colleges and Universities in recent years have stressed its value and implied, as did the Joint Committee on Extension Programmes, Policies and Goals, that it should be given more attention. On the home economics side, where cities lack adult education agencies in this supremely important area, Extension may well meet the need when and if asked. Such request are increasing, and in 1948 several states began the process of securing funds to respond to them.

The situation is different with respect to the rural non-farm population. People in such areas are next-door neighbours of the farmers. To an increasing extent rural villages and towns have become centers of rural life. Farmers and their wives in considerable proportions belong to village organizations or community organizations meeting in village or town centers. There they secure many of the services they require, from medical care and banking facilities to education for their children. They comprise an appreciable proportion of the membership of village churches. Social interaction is so frequent and continuous that the village or small town and its rural hinterland are usually two halves of the same community. Village women have the same problems of homemaking as farm women. Village families have gardens or "farmettes", as indeed do many urban workers who can afford to live on the outer fringe of urban commuting zones. Moreover, village business has a lively awareness that its well-being depends upon agricultural prosperity. For that reason village merchants and professional men are keenly interested in farm affairs.

Since centers of this size, if they desire adult education, lack the many agencies which can supply such needs in larger cities, it was natural that Extension should respond to this situation. A vast majority of the million non-farming families changing agricultural practices in 1947 and the equal number changing home economics practices lived in rural non-farm territory. They represented 21 per cent of the families changing agricultural and 35 per cent of those changing home economics practices. The comparable proportions in the peak war year of 1943 were 36 per cent and 40 per cent. The decline from war-stimulated contact with Extension appears to have been halted, and at a level above prewar. If one assumes that practically all non-farm homes reached are in rural territory, then agricultural and home economics agents each reach about one home in six effectively enough to produce actual changes in procedures. The total influence of extension in this area is of course larger than this figure indicates. In any general meeting it is impossible to separate those who attend into farm and non-farm residents. Moreover, many non-farm families send directly to the state Extension office for bulletins and listen to Extension broadcasts without ever entering the agent's offices or attending a meeting.

It would appear that service to this large element in the population should be considerably increased... Nationally speaking, the rural non-farm population is now slightly larger than the farm population. This situation now prevails in exactly half of the states and in the others the trend is in that direction, stimulated in part by the mechanization of agriculture and the steadily increasing size of farms. In the famous dairy state of Wisconsin, in the quarter-century between the two world wars, the farm population declined by about 10 per cent, whereas the rural non-farm population gained about 25 per cent. It is now two-third a large as the farm group. In the 16 to 24-year age group the preponderance of the rural non-farm group is even larger than that for the total population. In about thirty states it exceeds the rural farm population of this age.

It is easy to recommend that Extension greatly increase its service to the rural non-farm population or to criticize it, as some do, for failing in this particular. It must be remembered, however, that any considerable expansion in this admittedly under serviced area would involve either less attention to the farm population or more staff, and therefore larger appropriations.

What is the Basic Organization of Agricultural Extension?

Having noted, though very briefly, some of the conditions peculiar to adult-education activities in rural areas, let us now consider the organizational structure of the Agricultural Extension Service set up to meet these conditions. The Smith-Lever Act, passed by Congress in 1914, established the basic pattern. Brunner, and Yang describe the most significant features of this legislation as follows:

> It provided that extension work in agriculture and home economics should be carried on by the land-grant colleges in cooperation with the United States Department of Agriculture. Cooperation was no empty phrase. The local people acting through their state colleges, initiated the plans for the work in each state. Greater participation and leadership was required to effectuate this cooperation than had been needed in the past. The plans had to be mutually agreed upon.

The extension work, in the language of the Act, was "to aid in diffusing among the people of the United states useful and practical information on subjects relating to agriculture and home economics, and to encourage the application of the same". Practical demonstrations were also provided for, thus perpetuating Dr. Knapp'a major contribution. The audience was to be persons not attending or resident in a land-grant college. The focus was therefore rural adult education, the content of which was very broadly defined in the debates on the Act but not with in its phraseology.

Each state was to receive $10,000 annually from federal funds, and the following year additional amounts, prorated on the basis of rural population, from a féderal fund of $600,000 which should increase by $500,000 annually for seven years and continue thereafter at a total of $4,100,000 making a total of $4,580,000 in 1923 when the maximum was reached.

The additional amounts above the basic grant of $10,000 were prorated among the states in proportion to their rural population and were available only when matched by state or local funds raised or contributed within the state.

This last provision, requiring financial participation, is very important. It is perhaps the secret of the high degree of cooperation which has existed between the counties, state and federal governments in their combined service for farm people. It made the local people regard the service not as something offered to them from outside, which they could take or ignore as they pleased, but as theirs by right of their own support and participation...

Finally ... it is important to note that each college receiving the benefits of the Act was required to send an annual statement to the Secretary of Agriculture covering its use of the funds. This audit was the only control over programme lodged in the federal government. It was simply a device for insuring that the funds granted the states were spent within the purpose of the Act.

From the point of view of programme, the Act provided for the development of Extension through an itinerant agricultural adviser in each county, called in most states a county agent. His responsibility was to give leadership and direction along all lines of rural activity, technical, social and economic. He soon became the voice, the eyes and the ears of the college in his county ... The act also placed work in home economics and with boys and girls on a firm footing...

As launched, then, the Act provided federal assistance to an educational programme that encompassed the whole farm family. It recognized the basic importance of agriculture, of its practitioners and their families, to the nation. It set up a legal mechanism which has stood the test of the intervening years, in large part because its philosophy and provisions were consonant with the value and attitudes of the people, particularly the farm people of the United States.

In order to spell out in greater detail the modes of cooperation provided for in the Smith-Lever Act, a memorandum of Understanding was agreed to by the Secretary of Agriculture and the land-grant colleges. Brunner and Yang summarize the provisions of this memorandum as follows:

(1). To organize and maintain a definite and distinct administrative division for the management and conduct of extension work in agriculture and home economics, with a responsible leader selected by the college and satisfactory to the Department of Agriculture.

(2). To administer through such Extension Division thus organized any and all fund it had or may hereafter receive for such work from appropriations made by Congress or the State Legislature, by allotment from its Board of Trustess, or from any other source.

(3). To cooperate with the United States Department of Agriculture in all extension work in agriculture and home economics which said Department is or shall be authorized by Congress to conduct in the state.

On its part the United States Department of Agriculture agreed to organize and maintain an administrative office to represent the Department in the General supervision of all cooperative extension work in agriculture and home economics and to administer the federal funds granted to the states under the Act. The Department further agreed to carry on all demonstrations and other forms of the extension of work in cooperation with the state agricultural colleges as indicated above.

The memorandum also spelled out certain organizational procedures. Each state college agreed to set up an Extension Division headed by a Director of Extension, appointed by the college and approved by the Secretary of Agriculture. In practice this approval has become practically *pro forma.* Individual project agreements for special activities were provided for. Both the colleges and the Department gave official status to all agents appointed for any sphere of Extension work. These agents, down to and including those in the counties, are hence joint representatives. All publications are plainly marked to indicate their cooperative nature. Finally, provision was made for abrogating the agreement by either cooperating body.

The organizational structure provided by the Smith-Lever Act and by the Memorandum of Agreement noted above provides for operational programmes on three levels—the federal, the state and the county. Operations on the federal level have been described as follows by Brunner in the *Handbook of Adult Education:*

> The federal office has no power to dictate to the states. Its leadership is by indirection, but its functions are manifold. It audits the state accounts to certify that the federal funds are being spent for the purposes for which they were appropriated. It maintains liaison field workers, each assigned to a regional group of states, and has also a small staff of specialists. It issues bulletins and suggestions; conducts research as requested; and cooperates in training the professional staff through summer schools, workshops and institutes. The federal staff is made up of less than 250 persons, a number of whom are part time advisers. Since the Extension Service is the educational arm of the United States Department of Agriculture, one of its functions is to bring to the States news of national developments of importance to their work.

The following selection from Brunner describes the programme on the state level.

> The administration of the Service heads up in each state college of agriculture under a Director of Extension. Under him there is often an assistant director, and always there are two state leaders, one for the county agricultural field workers, called agents, and another for the home demonstration agents. Each state college also has a staff of subject-matter specialists, who are, as the name implies, concerned with the various phases of

the programme; such as marketing, animal husbandry, dairying, poultry, clothing, canning. The duty of each specialist is to keep abreast of research and experimentation in his area; to interpret the results in teachable, readable terms; to develop programmes in the subjects called for by the counties; and to train the agents and local leaders. This training is mostly concerned with methods to be used in teaching the subjects to members of local groups in the various counties of the state.

Well over half of the specialists are concentrated in about ten subject areas similar to those mentioned above. The rest cover a wide variety of areas of interest, such as housing, rural community organization and recreation. The Home Economics branch of the Service deals chiefly with the selection, preparation and preservation of food; the provision of proper clothing for all members of the family; home decoration, sanitation, household budgeting, etc.; child care and training.

On the county level the work has been described as follows by Joseph : L. Matthews. This material is part of the report sponsored by the Association of Land Grant Colleges and Universities and the Fund for Adult Education.

The basic unit of the Cooperative Extension Service is in the County, for it is here that programmes are made and extension teaching is done. County programme grow out of the needs and desires of the local people. The Federal and State organizations are designed to give the maximum help to county extension agents and local volunteer leaders to enable them to give the greatest aid to the people in the counties.

A typical county is served by a county agricultural agent and usually by a woman home demonstration agent. In many States, especially in the East, the county has one and frequently two 4-H Club agents. In many states there are assistant county agricultural agents and assistant home demonstration agents. In many states 4-H Club work is done by the county agent and home demonstration agent or by assistant county agents or home demonstration agents. The average is about three professional workers per county. In some counties with highly specialized types of agriculture and where the financial resources permit there are assistant agents and subject-matter specialists on the county staff.

The county extension service offices generally are located

in the county-seat town. The county staff is responsible for conducting effective educational programmes which are related to problems affecting the welfare of the people in the county. They are aided by volunteer local leaders, adult men and women, and the young people with some training who help the county agents develop programmes, conduct meetings, hold demonstrations, and who help to get information to their neighbours in every possible way.

Country extension workers as representatives of the State Land-Grant college of Agriculture and the United States Department of Agriculture are responsible to both. In addition, the county workers are employees of the county government, and their tenure in the county is subject to the approval of the sponsoring organizations or the county governing bodies and the State extension administration. One of the important characteristics of the Extension Service arises out of this trinity which with its local ties are said to give the people in the county a feeling that the professional workers in the county are one of them.

Thus far in this chapter we have presented material calling attention to some special condition in rural areas affecting adult education, and to the organizational structure set up to function under the conditions described. It is our purpose now to present material indicating in a general way the kind of programme that has been developed by the agricultural Extension Service. We shall concern ourselves here with the objectives of the programme and with the content material designed to achieve these objectives.

What is the Content of the Programme?

The next selection, also from Matthews, calls attention to the basic objectives and the content of programmes.

The first educational responsibility of the Service is to carry to rural people the teaching and the results of research of the state agricultural colleges and experiment stations and United States Department of Agriculture. Its purpose is to help them apply the teaching and research findings in improving the farm, the home, the community and the nation. The Cooperative Extension Service does not operate alone on the knowledge and research of the colleges and the USDA. Long ago it learned that the people, through their own experience and study of their own problems, have much to contribute to the improvement of rural life.

The purpose of cooperative extension, as conceived by its administrators and by its workers, is not so much to make two blades of grass grow where one grew before, but to develop the people into self-confident, effective and understanding men, women, and youth who will have vision and will be capable of meeting leadership responsibilities in the community, state and nation.

* * *

Historically, agricultural production has received the most attention and will continue to receive much attention in the future because it is basic to the welfare of people on farms and to the nation as a whole. Agricultural commodities represent an important part of the national productive capacity. Increasingly higher agricultural production by the most efficient methods is essential to the maintenance of adequate living standards for people living on farms and for their continuing economic and social improvement. During the decade 1940-50, about one-third of the effort of county extension workers were directed toward more efficient production of crops and livestock.

[The graph on the next page shows] that county workers devote about one-fourth of their time to developing and servicing rural organization and voluntary leadership. Much of their effort is directed toward improving social relationships, helping make social adjustments, and developing cultural values among rural people.

Rural organization activities include helping the people to organize themselves for cooperative effort in dealing with their problems in rural living, and in working with established groups to assist in planning and carrying out educational and group action programmes to meet the needs of local people. The most important aspect of working with groups and organizations consists of developing them as a means and an end in programme building.

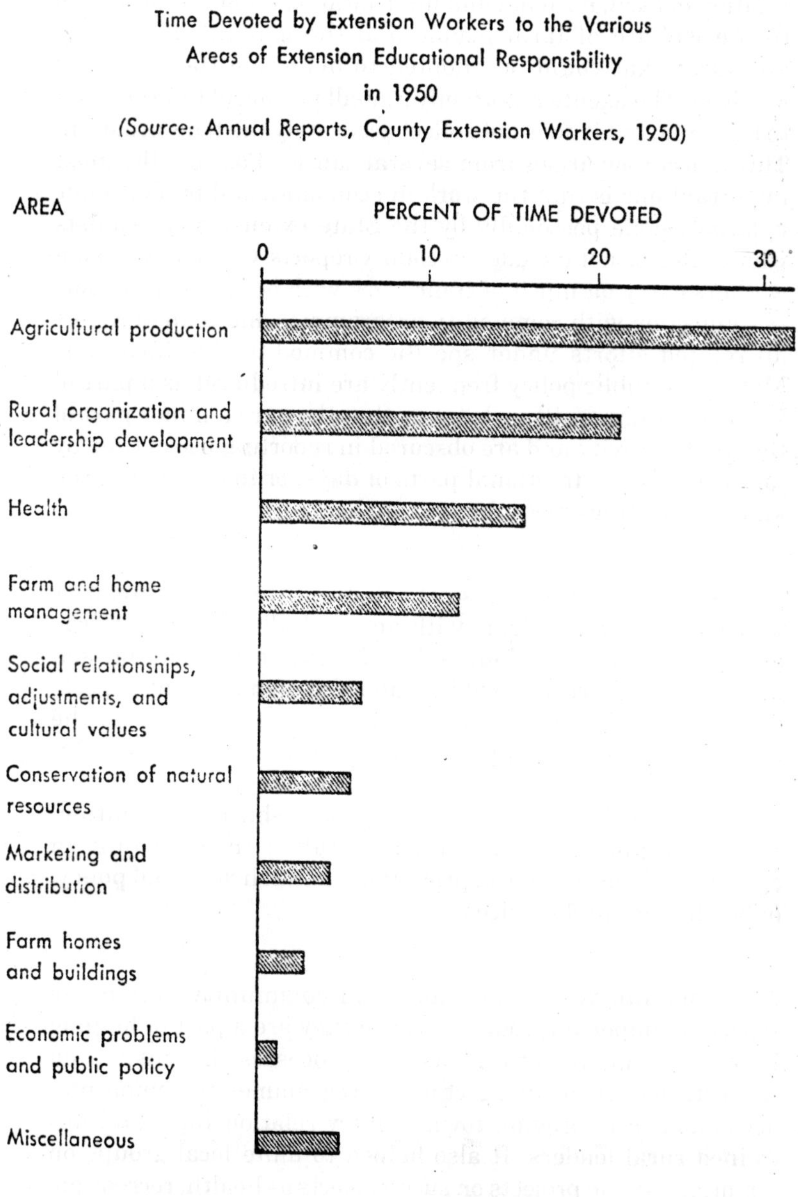
Time Devoted by Extension Workers to the Various
Areas of Extension Educational Responsibility
in 1950
(Source: Annual Reports, County Extension Workers, 1950)
AREA
PERCENT OF TIME DEVOTED
0
10
20
30
Agricultural production
Rural organization and leadership development
Health
Farm and home management
Social relationships, adjustments, and cultural values
Conservation of natural resources
Marketing and distribution
Farm homes and buildings
Economic problems and public policy
Miscellaneous

Fig.

Economic problems and public policies deal with the relation of local, national and international economic problems to the welfare of farm people and the general public and measures that could be adopted to overcome the problems involved. The agents report only a small portion of time devoted to this area, but it does not reflect accurately the true situation. This inaccuracy arises from several causes. Possibly the most important one is that the work in economics and public policy is largely done personally by the State extension economists whose effort is not included in county reports. County extension workers carry on much of their work with economic problems in connection with commodity programmes and tend to report all related efforts under specific commodity classifications. Matters of public policy frequently are introduced as a part of other programmes in such a way that they are a minor part of the whole activity and are obscured in reporting use of time by units of a day or fractional parts of days, or in classifying the kinds of meetings and other events held.

* * *

The agricultural phase of extension work is as broad as agriculture itself. It deals with any and all problems of crop and livestock production, soil and water conservation, soil improvement, forestry, wildlife and the management aspects of farming and rural living. Much attention is given to the business side of farming, including farm accounting, credit, planning, adjustments and tenancy. Marketing and distribution of agricultural products comes in for a share of attention. Economic phases of farming are taken into account in agricultural outlook work, price and trade policies, land policy, public finance and services.

* * *

Community improvement and community action are especially important today, because they are a part of helping to preserve democratic ideas and processes. Extension, on request, helped in fitting church programmes to community needs and in improving town-country relationships, and has trained rural leaders. It also helped to unite local groups on community-wide projects on such subjects as health, recreation, community beautification, conservation and marketing.

Throughout the country extension agents assisted 34,100 communities with their recreational facilities, 57,600 community groups with organization problems, nearly 7,000 communities in obtaining library facilities, and 2,266 communities in building community houses.

Today, 25 states have full-time community-relations specialists, and several other states draw upon teaching and research specialists for extension assistance in this field. In addition to working with communities, these specialists carry on other education activities in the field of organization and rural sociology for improving extension work in the relation to rural life.

The emphasis is on increased community spirit and pride, greater teamwork, stronger feelings of self-reliance on the part of communities in doing things themselves and greater leadership abilities.

* * *

Extension Service administrators feel that the Cooperative Extension Service has made contributions to international understanding for world peace in a number of ways and over a long period of time. About 77 per cent of the county workers in the 263 sample counties have programmes or activities dealing with international understanding for peace, strengthening of democracy, or understanding and strengthening of the economy. On the basis of the survey, an estimated 9 millions of people are reached by such programmes in the United States.

* * *

Ideally cooperative extension work as conceived by the Extension Service is democracy itself. From the beginning its aim has been to improve the people by developing their ability to analyze their problems, decide upon practical solutions, and plan carry out action programmes designed to improve farming and rural living. Extension workers try to implement this philosophy by democratic extension teaching activities conducted with the organization of rural people through which much of its work is done. The county extension services, through their close relationships with the county governing body or other sponsoring organization, are basic part of our system of local government.

Local ties are made even stronger by the men and women on agricultural advisory and planning committees, the home demonstration councils and organizations, young men and women's groups and committees, and the 4-H Club organization and adult advisory committees that work with it. County extension services usually are closely tied to the neighbourhoods and families throughout the county and in its most remote areas by the men, women and youth who are a part of the system of volunteer leaders.

As a result of these relationships and the procedures used in extension work, Extension people believe a large contribution is made to democratic concepts and procedures that are by-product not directly related to the objectives of improving farming and homemaking. This intangible by-product is difficult to measure. It is revealed in growth of leadership and improvement of people in their ability to do for themselves. In this respect a large part of extension teaching activities contributes to the strengthening of democratic ideals and processes.

In addition to the contributions arising out of the procedures used and the organizations with which it works, Extension is making an impressive contribution through activities aimed specifically at democratic objectives. The Extension Service and the home demonstration sponsoring organizations have conducted a four-day annual State conference for officers of the local sponsoring organizations in one State for 13 consecutive years. The conferences deal with the responsibilities of the leaders of extension work and the function of the organization in leadership training.

Another State has held four consecutive two-day citizenship leader-training schools in the last four years. The purpose is to help homemakers become better-informed citizens. Programmes at the school and in the counties deal with such topics as jury systems and the courts, social security insurance, State and Federal taxes, town and county officers, how the government handles your money, voting procedures and assessment. Visitations of both adult and youth groups are made to government institutions like post offices, courthouses, jails, courts and schools. A wide variety of activities are carried on from county to county and State to State, some in all States and in many counties.

Some of the States prepare series of discussion leaflets which are used in local adult and youth group meetings. Leaflets and other duplicated material have been prepared and distributed on such topics as "Group Medical Care", "duties and Privileges of a Voter," "Parents Teach Regard for the Rights of Others," "Training the Child for Good Citizenship," and "Returns from our Taxes." Youth programmes feature such group discussion topics as the philosophical base of democracy; functioning of a democracy; democratic organization; local, State and national government; duties of officers; programme planning; and discussion leadership.

What Are the Basic Methods Used by Agricultural Extension?

We turn now from a consideration of programme content and present material indicating methods which are utilized in the Extension programme. The materials quoted have been selected from Brunner and Yang because they emphasize methods which are basic to the programme of Agricultural Extension but which are not discussed, dealing with methods and materials.

Like all adult education, extension teaching differs from classroom instruction. It grows directly out of the needs and interests of the people. It follows no rigid pattern or curriculum. Participation in its programme is wholly voluntary. It holds its constituents only because of the value of what they receive. Yet almost any extension group will vary in age, educational experience, interests, intensity of need and levels of living. There may also be differences in values and cultural backgrounds. Obviously the productivity of extension education is greatly influenced by the effectiveness of the teaching methods used and the skill with which the agent can fit these methods and the content material to the diverse interests and abilities of each group.

The teaching methods can be grouped in three broad categories. These, as presented below, include not only methods in the usual educational sense of that word, but also the means by which the methods are employed. Thus, a lecture can be given to a meeting in a local hall or it can be a radio presentation.

The first group of teaching methods employs objective illustrations, such as charts and posters, exhibits, slide films, motion pictures, pageants and plays, and, most important, method and result demonstrations. The second group of methods is oral, and includes office calls, farm and home visits, meetings, radio talks, phonograph records and even telephone calls. The third category includes such written and printed materials as bulletins and other publications, circular letters, correspondence and news articles. These different means and methods are used interchangeably to accomplish the same purpose, *i.e.*, to bring about some change in farming or in home or community living. No one method meets all needs.

Demonstration is the foundation stone of extension teaching. Its importance was early recognized by Dr. Seaman A. Knapp. When the Smith-Lever law was enacted this teaching method was specifically written into the act as a means of instruction. Demonstration is based on the "show me" idea. It presents a proved, improved practice in terms of a practical application to a specific situation. Based on the old adage "seeing is believing," it convinces people by what they see rather than by what they hear or read. There are two types of demonstrations, methods and result.

1. Method Demonstration

A method demonstration is one which shows the assembled group how to carry out a given practice. It may be conducted by either an Extension worker or a trained volunteer leader. It deals with actual techniques of farm or home practice, such as culling a poultry flock, pruning or grafting a tree, inoculating legume seed, canning vegetables, building a terrace, picking beans, mixing concrete, constructing a hog or chicken house.

The strong points of the method demonstration are the following:

(a) It teaches skills effectively.
(b) It motivates and stimulates action because seeing, hearing, discussion, and doing are employed.
(c) It provides opportunity for developing leadership.
(d) It builds confidence in the demonstrator, who is often the extension agent.
(e) It promotes personal acquaintance between demonstrator and people.
(f) It serves as a news-creating agency and therefore stimulates publicity.
(g) It yields a high rate or "takes" to "exposures."
(h) It accomplishes changes in practices at low cost.

However, this method also has certain limitations. It is not well adapted to all subject matter. Illustration by performance of a skill or technique is its chief contribution, but even this is dependent upon the demonstrator's skill. A bungled demonstration is bad. It not only confuses the audience, it also suggests that the method has not been perfected. A method demonstration, too, is dependent on adequate facilities at the point where it is given. If only makeshift equipment is available, the demonstration may fail. Where equipment is lacking it is often better to employ another teaching method. Even where the equipment is present, the demonstration can have little effect if comparable equipment is not available or procurable in the community.

* * *

2. Result Demonstration

As the name implies, this teaching method demonstrates the results of a recommended practice, in comparison with a former practice, under actual existing conditions. Result demonstrations are conducted by a farmer, a homemaker, or a 4-H club member under the direct supervision of the Extension agent. Result demonstrations may be used to prove that the application of fertilizer will increase crop yields, that the underweight of certain children can be corrected through proper diet, that the use of certified seed is a good investment.

The principal values of the result demonstration are the following:

(a) It furnishes a local proof of the desirability of establishing a recommended practice.
(b) It is an effective method for introducing a new project.
(c) It appeals to the eye and reaches the "show-me" type of individual.
(d) It provides a good source of information for meetings, news items, pictures, radio talks, etc.
(e) It furnishes cost data and other basic information of use in revising the programme.
(f) It yields a high rate of takes to exposures.
(g) It aids in developing local leadership.
(h) It establishes confidence in the agent and in extension work.

Some interesting and significant research has been reported by Brunner and Yang concerning the relative values of different methods.

In the vocational aspects of its educational programme the immediate objective of Extension teaching is to influence the behaviour of its constituents. Much of this teaching is presented as a suggestion based on research. If the suggestion is adopted, it means that a familiar way of doing something will be changed. In Extension parlance, a changed practice will result from successful teaching. The number of changed practices is therefore one important criterion of good Extension work.

Very early in its history Extension began to study the number of changed practices which the people credited to one or another of teaching methods to which they had been exposed. In 1928-1929 some 27,000 changed practices reported by over 8,700 non-selected farms in twelve states were examined from this point of view. Ten years later a similar study was made in eighteen areas which covered over 34,000 changed practices. The results follow:

Relative Influence of Methods Upon Adoption of Practices

Method	*Percentage of Practices Influenced by methods*	
	about 1929	*1939*
Indirect influence	21.31	19.71
Method demonstrations	15.18	16.41
General meetings	13.80	13.92
Farm or home visits	12.34	12.53
News stories	10.27	9.70
Office calls	6.75	6.58
Bulletins	6.52	6.80
Result demonstrations	6.67	6.58
Circular letters	1.53	2.43
Radio	1.53	1.27
Correspondence	1.23	1.15
Leader-training meetings	.92	1.03
Extension schools	.77	.76
Exhibits	.61	.56
Telephone calls	.38	.37
Study courses	.15	.15
Posters	.04	.04

As these figures show, there was little variation in the effectiveness of the various methods over the decade. This, as will be noted, was in large part the result of the simple research methods employed. The most significant item in both studies is the first-place rank of indirect influence. This is a measure of the changes brought about largely as a result of the teaching, advice, or example of the local lay leaders who assist the professional staff in carrying out the Extension Service programme.

It was quite apparent from this first study that the research should be pushed further. Was the proportion of changed practices resulting from each method worth the cost? For instance, farm and home visits accounted for slightly fewer changed practices than general meetings but were much more expensive. Result demonstrations took 17.2 per cent of the Extension budget but produced only 6.7 per cent of the changed practices. Leader training cost 4.6 per cent of the money, but indirect influence resulting from it accounted for one-fifth of the changed practices. Pursuing this line, H. J. Baker and M. C. Wilson discovered that as of 1928-1929 the situation was as follows:

Type of Teaching	*Share of Agents Time*	*Share of Cost*	*Proportion of Changed Practices*
Objectives methods	42.43	36.42	22.46
Oral methods	35.00	33.78	35.57
Written methods	11.54	16.20	19.70
Leader training and other	11.03	13.60	22.23

On the basis baker and Wilson worked out a ratio or practices to costs. News stories ranked first with a ratio of 2.79; circular letters were second, scoring 1.83, closely followed by general meetings, 1.72; office calls, 1.56; and bulletins, 1.40. Farm and home visits were in sixth place with score of 1.13, method demonstrations next with 1.04, and result demonstrations a bad eighth with 0.47.

Results pointing in the same direction were secured in an intensive investigation in Michigan in 1945. Reporting on sources of useful information about farming, three out of five farmers listed bulletins, four out of five articles in the local paper, but only one out of four mentioned demonstrations. Four out of five also referred to what has been called "indirect influence."

These results would not have pleased Dr. Seaman Knapp. Nor, it is safe to say, would they have been true in his day. But in the intervening years Extension had so demonstrated its value, so gained the confidence of its constituency that they would accept news stories and the advice of circular letters as they would not have done in 1909 or even in 1914. They themselves no longer needed to see a demonstration because they knew that what was written had been demonstrated to the satisfaction of the experiment station staff and extension specialist or it would never have been passed on. In other words, the situation had changed. It has changed further since 1929.

The research results given above are, of course, approximate. Farmers could forget which of several exposures to Extension teaching influenced a change of practice. Further, by mentioning just one they could discount the cumulative effect of other methods. It has now been established that five or six approaches are far more effective than one, and the actual increases in the proportions of the total population accepting a new practice with each added method have been plotted. The proportion of changed practice rises rapidly with each exposure up to the sixth. After that the increase is small.

It has become apparent that research into educational methods as such is not the whole story of why a given method succeeds or fails, why a given practice is or is not adopted. Hence policy based wholly on the implications of such research may not be appropriate in dealing with some situations and groups. The social situation in which a group finds itself conditions its response to a given method. It is a safe hypothesis that in a poverty-stricken area where there are few automobiles, general meetings take a lot of agent time and produce small attendance and few results. Such situations still call for farm visits. Nor will the best of bulletins assist a functionally illiterate adult. Such things are clear without research, but research along these lines, though fairly recent, has uncovered some useful facts and raised significant questions.

In a study made in Maine in 1941 it was found that method demonstrations and bulletins together were responsible for over two-thirds of the changed practices in homemaking, with the former slightly more influential. When, however, the group was studied according to education, it was discovered that the more education a participant had, the greater the degree of preference for bulletins over demonstrations. More than 90% of home-makers with over eighth-grade education had been exposed to Extension and almost four-fifths of them had made practical use of it. The comparable figures for those with less than an eighth-grade education were 70 per cent and 48 per cent respectively. Comparable results have emerged from other studies.

Obstacles and Recommended Measures for Overcoming Them

The final selection in our consideration of the Agricultural Extension Service deals with obstacles and with measures recommended for overcoming them. Personnel and leadership are given much attention in the material which follows. The reader may find it interesting to compare the obstacles recognized by Agricultural Extension workers with the more general discussion of blocks to the development of adult education in general, discussed in Chapter 20. The following selection is taken from prepared by Matthews:

The main obstacles to more effective extension work are related to maintaining a highly trained and efficient staff of professional workers, to the techniques of programme development and execution, and to administrative and supervisory policies and procedures. The obstacles and recommended measures to help overcome them are described in the following paragraphs:

Extension workers need special training because undergraduate education in agriculture or home economics is not enough. Studies of training needs emphasize the social sciences as the area of almost universal training need among extension workers. Extension educational methods, rural sociology and economics, in that order, are indicated by county agricultural agents as their more important training needs. It is recommended that the training of home demonstration agents should include child development and family relationships, psychology, economics, education and sociology. The report of a joint association of Land-Grant Colleges and United States Department of Agriculture committee recommends more emphasis on training in the social sciences.

* * *

More extension workers need to receive advanced study for professional improvement. Institutional facilities of two kinds are available to meet the need. The regional summer schools for extension workers could provide the needed training for the mass of county extension workers. In 1951 about 600 extension workers attended the summer schools which could accommodate about twice that number. In a recent survey of about 2,000 county extension workers 52 per cent of the men and 30 per cent of the women gave financial reasons for not attending summer school. The problem is one of enabling numbers of workers to take advantage of the opportunity for special training in extension. Small scholarships such as were provided by the Farm Foundation for supervisory and administrative personnel in 1950 would stimulate attendance.

High termination of service among extension workers in another obstacle. The rate of turn-over of county agricultural agents in one state averages 12 per cent for 25 years. In another, terminations averaged 15 per cent for home demonstration agents. The rapid turn-over seems to have four main causes. First, the salaries of extension workers usually are less than those of other workers with comparable training, experienc and responsibilities. Second, the high rate of terminations has been attributed by a land-grant college association subcommittee primarily to an inadequate retirement system and disparity in salaries. Unsatisfactory working conditions seem to be an important factor in the high rate of terminations. Third, many men leave county agent work to go into farming and many home demonstration agents leave the service to become homemakers. Others enter commercial employment. Fourth, the Extension Service long has been the source of well-trained and experienced persons to fill position of greater responsibility and higher pay in government, business and industry.

This last cause of termination may be the most serious because it affects the more capable leaders...

* * *

County extension programmes could be improved if more facts were known about the relative effectiveness of the various methods of programme determination. Extension teaching could be improved if more were known about the ways of dealing with objectives related to public policy, social issues, democratic values, and democratic processes. Research is needed to determine the factors that affect the effectiveness of the various methods of programme determination and to develop new and more effective procedures. Investigations in this area are difficult because of the intangible factors and the time interval between programme development processes and accomplishments.

Specific objectives related to international understanding, citizenship and economic processes are needed in extension programmes in order to obtain more results in these areas. Only limited accomplishments can be expected when they are the by-product of programmes based on farming and homemaking objectives.

Wider use should be made of the skills and techniques of working with groups. More information about their application to extension work is needed. Experimental programmes are needed to develop more effective procedures for use in extension educational programmes with intangible objectives of a social nature. This is particularly true of programmes related to economics, public policy and democracy. Recent research in group dynamics can probably be used to advantage in cooperative extension work.

Greater and more skillful use of the media of mass communication in extension teaching are needed in order to maximize the effectiveness of extension workers and provide more assistance to larger numbers of people, both rural and urban. This would initial expanded training of extension workers through summer courses and "schools" and research to throw light on effective information procedures in extension work.

More extensive and intensive use of volunteer leadership is needed in programme execution. More attention should be given to developing leadership and enlisting the aid of leaders in extension teaching activities. Evaluation of extension programmes in terms of the nature and extent of participation by leaders would tend to encourage extension workers to utilize leadership more fully.

Reporting requirements have an important influence on the activities of extension workers: therefore, annual reports should call for information that relates to the desired kinds of programmes. Requiring reports from the agents on results in the nonvocational phases of extension programmes would be likely to result in more effort and accomplishments in that area.

Special effort is needed to reach the low-income groups and the farm labour families with programmes related to their limited interest and resources.

Wider participation of people in cooperative programme development procedures should be obtained. This basic requirement for good extension programmes needs more attention in many areas. The emphasis on this principle tends to reflect the aims and philosophy of the particular extension service.

Improved methods of selecting new extension workers are needed. Studies are under way to develop information about the differential characteristics and competencies needed by extension workers. These studies are designed to develop information which can be used in selecting better qualified workers.

In its quiet way the Cooperative Agricultural and Home Economics Extension Service is one of the outstanding developments in Adult Education. It has demonstrated what can be done through cooperative efforts in developing programmes built around the interests of families and drawing upon the resources of organized knowledge. It has demonstrated the power of the volunteer and the role of the trained worker. It has combined local, state and federal contributions in an interesting illustration of a way of approaching the problem of balancing centralizing and decentralizing forces. It makes no claims to being perfect; one of its outstanding activities is its continuous use of research into its methods of operation. As Adult education moves ahead it is to be hoped that "Extension" will be an increasingly active factor in future organized efforts to promote adequate services for all adults.

8

Public Libraries

The Public Library is one of the major institutions of a democracy. Supported by only a meager budget, it has made available to millions of citizens sources of information regarding current problems and wide range of recreational literature, some of which contributes ideas as well as diversion. Pendleton Herring brings this out in the preface to *The Public Library in the United States.*

The Public Library in the United States is taken for granted. Predominantly local in character, both in support and management, it is deeply rooted in our national heritage. The community's library stands for much that is cherished in our tradition of equal educational opportunity and freedom of thought and communication. It takes its place along with the courthouse, the school, the church, and the town hall as an integral part of the American scene.

The potential power of the library is tremendous. It is well expressed in a message from the American Book Publishers Council on the occasion of the seventy-first annual convention of the American Library Association:

You gave inherited all the learning in the World and your strongbox is at Elm and Main

Your riches are incalculable. They are the accumulation of 4,000 years; they have streamed to you from every corner of the earth. Yours is the wealth of every man who ever committed his knowledge or his dreams to tablet, parchment or to printed page.

You own the mathematics of Euclid, Newton and Einstein. You possess the concepts of Plato and Kant, of Hegel and Berkeley; the ideas of Moses and Jesus, of Franklin, Jefferson and Lincoln. You own the full records of Herodotus and Plutarch, of Gibbon and Carlyle. Sterne and Hugo, Tolstoy and Melville have endowed you with the fruits of their invention. Stevenson and Kingsley, Aesop and Andersen have bequeathed their estates to you and your children.

Your strongbox overflows with the humor of Petronius, Rabelais, Carroll and Twain; with the songs of David and of Shakespeare, of Shelley, Chaucer, Coleridge and Frost.

Your strongbox. Do you know where it is, what it is?

Are your familiar with that dignified building near the center of town; the building with the broad steps, the quiet interior; the building where you can go and thumb through your treasure, using but never diminishing it; the building from which you can remove part of your treasure, take it home with you, enjoy it at your leisure, bring it back again for safekeeping?

Do you know the custodian of your treasure? The librarian whose job it is to keep your holdings diversified and as completed as your town budget permits?

You're the richest man in the world and because your wealth increases day by day, you are richer than any man who ever lived before you. Visit your strongbox and its custodian. Enjoy your wealth.

Imagine what this country would be like if every citizen were to begin using this treasure chest and as a result were to see that funds adequate to the job were available to libraries.

What Services do Public Libraries provide?

The story of the Louisville Library, reported in Chapter 4, illustrates the variety of services which some libraries provide. At present only a small percentage of our citizens get this kind of service, but it does reveal something of the ways in which libraries are trying to make the permanent records of man's experience more available. The concern of librarians that the library work to achieve a wide use of its resources is well expressed in an article by Mrs. Florence Craig, of the Cuyahoga County Public Library in Cleveland.

Why do we are care whether people read more and better books, learn from them and talk about them? Wouldn't it be better to sit in calm seclusion and hand the public what it is accustomed to ask for when—and if—it seeks us out in our sequestered desk chairs? No! We care because self-education is a real necessity for the good life and we'd like to see a greater number of people truly enjoying themselves. Self-education can fill a linely hour, it can solve the problems of a frustrated hour, it can lessen the deadening effect of modern industry and it can teach us how to help the other fellow. Perhaps it seems that this business of richer, more meaningful live for all sounds just too, too platitudinous—but mental illness is increasing, the sound of the divorce court gave practically alternates with the peal of the wedding bell, and the number of people who are ready to fight somebody or hate somebody augurs but poorly for the good life in a peaceful world. Consider the daily losses in happiness and effective living by people who do not know the contents of books! Yes, we certainly care.

* * *

Mr. and Mrs. Public should think of the library not as an institution, but rather as a place where their jolly friend, miss Bookpeddler, is ready to give them useful materials which suit their present needs and point up their future possibilities. There's a very great deal in a name. When Librarians are so good that many patrons know and remember their names, the use of libraries will increase.

Although it would be difficult to do, since for so long libraries have run in the Dewey Decimal groove, it may well be that they can never be personalized until the system of grouping books is changed. Daily there are great issues which the American people need to face squarely and to have bolstered with as many facts as possible. If only libraries could get out of the Dewey Decimal groove and put together books relating to great issues whether they are fiction, history, poetry or sociology!

The library generally has tended to emphasize its custodial functions and has been perhaps too ready to take a passive position regarding the education of adults. At the adult level, education is a voluntary matter but this still leaves broad scope for measures to encourage learning, as many libraries are demonstrating. The matter of just what part the library should play in the community adult-education picture will be the major concern of this chapter.

What has been said of the library is equally true of the museum. Basically the two are identical in their approach—they bring together certain materials in organized form in order to increase the usefulness of these materials to the variety of activities of living. Both the library and the museum are moving out from behind their facades and are ready and eager to work with groups all over the community. For various reasons the book has been the dominant resource unit in our culture and therefore we have more libraries than museums, but there is growing awareness of the values of functional exhibits, and the museum may be expected to take a more prominent place in the coming picture of community education.

It is impossible here to list all the kinds of services that libraries provide. And the headings used below fail to convey the ingenuity and skill which individual librarians have revealed in carrying out some of these activities. In services to groups, a number of libraries, for example, have recognized the growth of workers' education and have set out to work with union groups in their communities. The story of what five libraries (Akron, Boston, Milwaukee, New York and Newark) have done in this area is told in a pamphlet of the American Library Association.

The core of the library's work centers around materials in print—books primarily, pamphlets, magazines, newspapers. As new kinds of materials have been appearing, such as films, film strips and phonograph records, the library has faced its responsibility of adding them. With budgets inadequate for printed materials, many libraries have been understandably hesitant about adding these new materials, but logic is clearly on the side of making the library the source of all these kinds of records.

As a reminder of the kinds of services that libraries are providing, we have listed the kinds of activities found in the descriptions of the work of the library. The list does not attempt to cover everything which is done by some libraries; it includes, rather, the major functions.

Services directed primarily to the Individual Patron

1. Lending books which patrons request.
2. Giving assistance in locating appropriate books. This may be specific or general.
3. Preparing annotated bibliographies.
4. Lending pictures, prints and related materials.
5. Lending phonograph records, including both music and records of speeches, discussions, etc.
6. Lending films and film strips.
7. Giving instruction in use of library.
8. Providing service to outlying areas through branch libraries and the bookmobile.
9. Showing films and television programmes for patrons.

Services directed primarily to Groups

1. Preparing book lists in connection with groups programmes.
2. Arranging book collections at the group meetings or at the library at the time of the meeting.
3. Providing programme services to clubs.
4. Providing films, film strips and recordings (and sometimes projectors) for meetings.
5. Sponsoring groups on current affairs.
6. Sponsoring groups on the American Heritage.
7. Sponsoring Great Book groups.
8. Providing meeting space for groups.
9. Sponsoring film discussion groups.

Services at the Community Level.

1. Serving as a central information service.
2. Serving as consultant to community groups.
3. Cooperating with colleges in providing courses at convenient points throughout the community.
4. Developing special programmes for specific groups, such as Golden Age Clubs, labour unions, etc.
5. Providing headquarters and staff service for an adult-education council.

How much of the library's work is Educational?

Because we have tended to think of the library as a "strongbox", we have tended to emphasize materials rather than users. As long as the emphasis has been on the side of handling materials, there has been an underemphasis on the educational aspects of the work of the librarian. For this reason we believe that librarians have often failed to fulfill their responsibilities in the community picture. The library profession is working hard to change this emphasis, and librarians are doing much to sensitize citizens to participation.

Cyril Houle has made a logical analysis of the work of the library in relation to two conceptions of education. He points out that education can be thought of as synonymous with experience or it can be used in a more restricted sense to mean that part of experience in which there is conscious, deliberate attention to the improvement of learning.

... if we take the first definition of adult education all libraries, inasmuch as they provide the tools of learning for those who wish to use them, are adult educational institutions. Anything which they do to enlarge the number of these tools or make them more widely available is, in a sense, adult education. In such a case, the extension of the library itself is an extension of adult education.

If we take the second definition, we are committed to a more positive programme. We accept the fact that the library must take the lead in stimulating, and helping to shape, the desire to learn on the part of the people of its community. Since only a small percentage of people in the most favoured communities use the facilities of their libraries and since the majority of the people of the world have at best only mediocre library service, librarians must conclude that, if they are to have a greater share in the building of happier individuals and a better society, they must go beyond their role as providers of material into a more active role as adult educators.

After making this decision, librarians ordinarily move in one of two general directions:

The first is to develop a set of special activities, often carried out by a separate division or branch of the library. In the United States adult education has sometimes seemed to be synonymous with readers' advisory services, reading lists for special interest groups, the work of subject-matter specialists, the provision of audio-visual aids, or programmes of public relations designed to persuade people to support and use their libraries. In such an approach , the new service takes its place alongside the old ones. If there is a new department, it exists beside the more traditional ones and makes it own fight for a place in the budgetary sun.

A second approach considers that adult education is not a special emphasis of the library but a central theme running through all aspects of service. Often those who have started with a special department have found that its work, unless it is rigorously limited, spreads out far beyond the original scope of service and creates problems of internal organization. Such libraries have therefore frequently turned from the first to the second approach to adult education.

The implications of this approach for the re-examination of the library's organization and programme of service are of the most far-reading sort. All the parts of the library are drawn into the planning for the accomplishment of the library's educational programme. Specialized departments dealing with such functions as readers' advisory service or extension activities have an important place, but so do all the other sections of the library's organization, staff and programme. Cooperative staff planning becomes essential, as do integration of effort and evaluation of progress and outcomes.

Houle then goes on to point out that the library is a multipurpose agency. He does not believe that adult education covers all the activities in which a library does or should engage. This depends largely upon how on uses terms. Research and reference work we should consider a part of deliberate education as he has defined it above. Recreation certainly is not identical with education, but the careful planning of recreation for adults involves an educational approach on the part of librarians. Houle's statement to which we are referring follows:

> Some librarians feel that adult education is of such great importance that the library should be given over entirely to it. It is hard to agree with this contention.

A library ordinarily exists to serve several functions simultaneously. If one analyzes these functions in terms of the purposes of the borrower, there appear to be at least five major ones. Some people use the library as a tool for research, either contributing to the sum of human knowledge or undertaking some special task required foreign immediate purpose. Some use it for recreation, as they would a park or a theatre. And some use it for education, in the second of the two major meanings of that term. (In the first meaning, all of the functions of the library are educational).

The library must therefore be considered a multi-purpose agency. Only very seldom does it have some one function—research, perhaps, or recreation—as its only goal. As the person who is going on a journey must strike some balance between speed, comfort and economy, so the librarian must think constantly not about some one goal but about many. No matter what emphases he may like to lay upon particular goals, he has a responsibility to serve his community as it wishes to be served. Furthermore, the other four functions are convenient stepping-stones toward education. For education should have a kind of pre-eminent role among the five. Experience which is consciously directed toward the improvement of the individual, the group, or society has a potency for good which is far beyond that which is directed toward other ends.

The reader should note again that this question as to the extent to which librarians should be considered adult educators is a controversial one. The author's position lies further toward making all librarians educators than do most other discussions of this point.

There is much administrative detail in the work of a library. This may not be directly educational in nature, but its purpose is educational. The selection and procurement of books, films, and other durable records of man's ideas (and lack of them), the organization of these to facilitate ready and widespread use, and the steady working with the potential consumer, singly and in groups, to increase his readiness to use these resources are all part of a task that is truly educational: the enrichment of living through ideas. To confine the term "adult education" to the readers' advisor, to leaders of group activities, and to a small number of similar specialists is to underestimate the decisions that have to be made at countless points in the work of the library. Even the children's librarian works with parents.

What is the Role of the Library in the Community Adult-Education Programme?

As adult education comes to assume the responsibilities

which it must in our interdependent industrial democracy, the relations among agencies become more important. Consequently it is important to define as clearly as possible just what services the library should undertake to perform in relation to those provided by other agencies and groups.

Such a definition assumes a democratic way of reaching decisions about function. Some community agencies resist efforts to define functions because of a fear that the scope of their work will be reduced. Actually, the size and scope of the adult-education task are such that more and not less will be required of existing agencies. This, in turn, leads to a fear on the part of some librarians that they may not be adequate to new responsibilities. These fears and resistances need to be recognized and dealt with in the in-service activities for persons with adult-education responsibilities.

One of the most widely discussed and quoted statements on the role of library is Alvin Johnson's *The Public Library—A People's University*. After visiting libraries throughout the United States and talking widely with librarians, users and potential users, Johnson states his conclusions regarding what the library can do as follows:

> There are three possibilities for the development of an effective system of adult education. The first is the extension of the work of the public schools, the colleges and universities, into this field. The second is the development into an independent educational system of the various tentative private or cooperative plans now in operation. The third is to develop the public library into a permanent center of adult education, informally, a people's university.

Johnson agrees that there are certain phases of adult education that schools and colleges can carry on best, but he believes that they are by tradition poorly equipped to do the larger job of working with adults. He then goes on to discuss his second and third alternatives.

Adult education proper involves the application by each individual of the resources of a fairly trained mind to the issues that press in upon his experience. The issues need not be contemporary in their data but they need to be immediate in their bearing, vital to the citizen of the present. Adult education can not thrive under compulsions and rewards. It therefore transcends the experience and rejects the technique of the school and college teacher. Indeed, the adult needs not a teacher but a leader, a leader as the term was understood before the days of Mussolini and Hitler, a person who had experienced the same need and was one lap ahead.

Voluntary organizations for study and discussion come nearer to meeting the requirement of a good adult educational setup. There is no trace of compulsion in them—except in the rare instance of an exclusive organization that by majority vote has decided to go intellectual. Such leadership as there is can not be preceptorial or dictatorial. The one grave weakness of such organizations is their fleeting character. Almost everyone has joined forums, lunch clubs, dinner clubs in high hopes of a continuous experiences of competent discussion, only to find the organization breaking up when every member has said his say often enough to be boring.

There are indeed cases of the continued survival through generations of such organizations as academies of science and political science clubs, as well as instance of long-continued educational programmes under organizations deriving their vitality from noneducational forces. No doubt much might be made of the tendency to organize, even vainly for intellectual purposes. But any progress in this direction involves the right kind of leadership. It is difficult to see where such leadership can come from, except from the public library.

The public library has, as a first requisite of leadership in the adult educational field, control of the supply of books. And books, I may repeat, contain the better part of the essentials of adult education. The public library has built up its scheme of behaviour in relation to a public which, unlike the school population, refuses to submit to compulsion. Adult education can deal only with volunteers. The public library, north of Mason and Dixon's line, is remarkably free from censorship, and the real adult despises censorship, doubts that any honest conclusions can be reached where one side is suppressed. The public library, with its numerous branches, is in a position to reach a larger proportion of the population of a city than any other institution except the public school.

Johnson then discusses the limitations standing in the way of the library's assumption of this leadership: excessive modesty, lack of right kind of books, inadequacy of personnel, inadequacy of financial support. He believes that none of these is impossible to overcome and concludes with this paragraph.

It would be foolish and unjust to fail to acknowledge the fact that the American public library, as its stands today, is a remarkable achievement, indeed, one of the outstanding American contributions to civilization. I know of no department in our national life that exhibits a greater proportion of able and devoted leaders, men and women of outstanding personality whose world will live on beyond them, beneficently. They have laid a broad base for an institution that will have an even greater future when it shall boldly take to itself the leadership in adult education which it alone is capable of developing, and shall make itself over into a people's university, sound bulwark of a democratic state.

The most thoroughgoing study of the public library was one proposed by the American Library Association and carried out by a distinguished research committee of the Social Science Research Council under a grant by the Carnegie Corporation. Robert D. Leigh, Chairman of the committee, wrote the overall report, entitled *The Public Library in the United States.* The report gives a vigorous statement of the underlying faith and objectives of the library:

> Libraries of all kinds during the centuries of their existence have had a common objective—one so generally accepted that it is seldom made explicit. It is the conservation and organization of the world's resources of recorded thought and fact so as to make them available for present and future users. This is an obvious utility for any civilization as soon as it feels the need for something more than oral tradition. And the library, including the public library, has become in most places a kind of symbol as well as servant of culture.

Throughout the years librarians have transformed their concept of function into a dynamic faith. This faith has sustained the men and women who have built and operated American public, as well as university and research, libraries and the men of wealth and political position who have provided for their financial and legal support. It consist of a belief in the virtue of the printed word, especially of the book, the reading of which is held to be good in itself or from its reading flows that which is good.

In order to see to what extent librarians agreed upon the objectives of the public library, the inquiry staff formulated a broad statement which was circulated among librarians. Leigh's report on the reaction to the statement and the text of the statement itself are given in the next selection.

Clearly, although opinion was not unanimous, there was a consensus in approval of the objectives. Only two librarians rejected the whole statement as inadequate or misleading. Concerning four points in the document, however, a minority, each very small numerically, dissented with considerable conviction. ...Making full allowance for them, however, the document may be accepted as setting forth the aims of most public librarians in the United States.

The Statement follows:

A. General Definition of Objectives

1. To assemble, preserve, and administer books and related educational materials in organized collections, in order to promote, through guidance and stimulation, an enlightened citizenship and enriched personal lives.
2. To serve the community as a general center of reliable information.
3. To provide opportunity an encouragement for children, young people, men, and women to educate themselves continuously.

B. Fields of knowledge and interest to which the public Library should devote its resources

1. *Public Affairs; citizenship*

(a) To awaken interest, stimulate reading and discussion on crucial problems;

(b) To improve people's ability to participate usefully in activities in which they are involved as citizens of their communities, the United States, and the world;

(c) To help people develop a constructively critical attitude toward all public issues and to remove ignorance regarding them;

(d) To promote democratic attitudes and values; *i.e.*, sensitivity toward peoples of other backgrounds by knowledge concerning them and by appreciation of the dignity of the individual person; preservation of the

precious heritage of freedom of expression. And understanding of the democratic processes of group life.

2. *Vocations*

To equip persons, and to keep them equipped, for efficient activities in useful occupations and practical affairs (including vocational information, parent and home education, child care, nutrition, physical health, emotional stability and growth, budgeting and consumer information, specialized business and industrial information).

3. *Aesthetic appreciation*

To seek to give people an opportunity to improve their capacity for appreciation and production in cultural fields.

4. *Recreation*

To help people make such use of leisure time as will promote personal happiness and social well-being.

5. *Information*

To help people keep abreast of progress in the sciences and other fields of knowledge, and to finish them with the detailed information required for their personal projects and everyday needs.

6. *Research*

To serve those who are aiding in the advancement of knowledge.

C. Library means for attaining the Library Objectives

1. *Kinds of materials*

Library collections are founded on the printed page, but should be supplemented by films, recordings and radio; also by lectures, forums and discussion groups.

2. *Availability of materials*

By selection and organization libraries should make an educational instrument out of a welter of records; by cooperative acquisition, inter-library loans and book pools they should insure to their patrons accessibility to the world's useful knowledge; their materials should be free to all residents on equal terms; and library service should be established where it is not now available.

3. *Guidance*

Librarians should mediate between seekers for knowledge and the recorded materials which contain and increase knowledge, thus eliminating the gap between the seekers and sources of information and ideas.

4. *Stimulation and leadership*

Libraries should have a positive programme of stimulation in the use of library materials, selecting subjects for emphasis with the view to replacing indifference by interest, and of exercising an influence on what people think about, without attempting to tell them what conclusions they should reach.

The library, in cooperation with all other agencies of education and information, should seek to increase the competence of people to form sound judgments and to realize that they should not only understand about important public problems, but also express their opinions and act in accordance with their judgment. The library should assist in the establishment and improvement of community group programmes, and adapt programmes to the interests of special groups. At the same time, the library's duty remains that of providing reliable information on all sides of controversial questions.

5. *Emphasis*

During the next four year (1948–1952), librarians should change the intensity, the duration, and even the nature of their services so that they will contribute directly to the solution of the crucial problems of our time.

They should make sure that opinion leaders and other citizens have the widest possible range of reliable information on which to base their judgments and action.

Libraries should provide themselves with generous supplies of these materials even if by so doing it means some curtailment of acquisition of popular and general materials.

Setting this current statement of public library objectives alongside the librarian's historic faith reveals a strong family resemblance between the two. The individual and social values which derive from a reading of books is central to both. But in the newer statement of objectives there are significant extensions of the traditional definition of purpose. The public library's function is explicitly broadened to include other materials of communication, including non-print materials. Perhaps more important, the faith in the mere presence of a community book collection as a power to change people's ideas, attitudes and tastes, is now transformed into a positive programme for libraries to guide stimulate and promote public use of public library materials for educational ends.

The inquiry then examined the activities of various other agencies that might be involved in the same area. This study of services now being or likely to be performed was compared with the needs of our society. From this the inquiry derived four functions which it believed were appropriate to noncommercial agencies of communication:

1. To serve as centers for contemporary materials selected from each year's output by the judgment of experts as the most reliable and authoritative, including artistic products of merit as determined by competent critics; and the promotion of the use of such materials by all available means.
2. To serve as centers where materials selected to give adequate and balanced representation to new, critical, often unpopular ideas, and to the pre-classical, contemporary, unusual and experimental in the arts can be brought into full use.
3. To serve as centers for the selection, organization and promotion of the use of materials which are not new, but of great current relevance because of their enduring quality.
4. To serve as centers of selection, collection and organization of the whole range of valuable materials in the form of print, picture, record and film, in such a way as to focus the full resources of record quickly and easily on a particular subject or problem for those seeking such a service.

These four functions are not likely to be performed adequately or at all by the commercial media, characterized as they are by large volume and maximum coverage of the population. It is clear that the functions are not justified by the numbers of people reached so much as by the socially-valuable interests which they serve. They are functions which are made more rather than less necessary by the very flood of materials produced and distributed by commercial means. They seem, moreover, to be functions especially appropriate for performance by the library as a public institution.

The Official Objectives and the Appropriate Services

If we turn back to compare this definition of appropriate function arrived at by our survey of the whole machinery of public communication with the public library's own statements of historic faith and current official objectives, it seems evident that the librarians have been on the right track in describing their purposes. With some differences in phraseology, the librarian's definitions of objectives, with their emphasis on assembling and organizing educational materials, guidance and stimulation in their use, serving as a center of reliable information, freedom of access to reliable information on all sides of controversial questions, and giving people an opportunity to improve their capacity for appreciation and production in cultural fields, are in essential agreement with the four functions deduced from the general analysis of the business of communication. The official library objectives thus seem to mark the almost inevitable road for public libraries to follow if they are to play their appropriate role as a public agency of communication.

The inquiry recognized four institutions as standing out in the total picture of adult education: the Agricultural Extension Service, the services of colleges and universities, the state and local school systems, and the public libraries. It found the libraries generally less developed than the other three, and it raised questions about possible relations among the four whereby the library could provide services to the others:

Naturally the question arises as to whether the public library, with its special skill and resources centered in books and other materials, should not be called upon the serve the other formal adult education agencies, as it now serves the various informal clubs and groups in the community. Only rarely did we find a public library that is recognized as the library of these enterprises in the sense that school, college, or university libraries serve their parent institutions in the instruction of children and young people. There were instances of cooperation between county libraries and county agricultural extension agencies, but not enough so that the county library serves as the materials center for the extension programme. In some cases the city school adult classes leaned heavily on public libraries for class reading materials. The same was true of university adult education classes. But in no place in our sample is the public library clearly recognized as the official library unit for the school, university, or community adult education programme.

The public library, then, has not become either a major center of formally organized adult education under its own initiative, nor does it serve as the officially designated library for the existing major agencies of formal adult education. Nevertheless, to the extent of its means, in terms of materials and skilled personnel, the libraries provide opportunity for many men and women individually or organized into informal groups to continue their education as adults. In this sense it furnishes the essential library service for the host of activities and efforts and which have somewhat romantically been called the people's university.

The inquiry report stirred up considerable discussion among librarians regrading the function of the public library. The March 1950 issue of *Public Libraries* dealt with the general topic "If not the People's University—Then What?" Emerson Greenaway, Director of the Enoch Prat Free Library in Baltimore made the following statement of the library's role:

> I strongly feel, in regard to adult education and the public library, that the following should obtain during the decade to come:
>
> (1) That public libraries accept as their basic objectives the provision and servicing of expertly selected books and other materials which aid the individual in the pursuit of education, information, or research, and in the creative use of leisure time. Since financial limitations generally prevent equal emphasis on all aspect of these objectives, the library should recognize that its *major* concern must be a positive contribution toward the removal of

ignorance, intolerance and indifference.

(2) That we recognize education service to adults as a primary function, and that the library pursue an active programme of stimulation, leadership, and cooperation with other agencies in encouraging the reading of socially significant materials.

(3) That we accept the responsibility for the direct communication of ideas through organization of discussion groups, institutes, film forums and the like, seeking thereby to direct the individual toward a continuous learning process through use of books and related materials.

(4) That we frankly state that in meeting its objective of providing recreational materials, the library encourage such use of leisure time as will promote personal development and social well-being, and tend increasingly to leave to commercial agencies the provision of trivial, purely emphemeral materials.

(5) That our cooperation with other agencies include :

(A) A clearing house to prevent an unnecessary duplication of programmes and provide for the integration of programmes to tackle common problems;

(B) The Provision of expertly selected materials and book lists covering non-teaching or supplementary materials for informal adult education programmes given by any agency;

(C) The recognition of the so-called "text-book problem" by all parties concerned and the possible development of a reserved book service jointly financed by those agencies offering courses requiring the use of such materials. In other words it should *not* be the function of the public library to supply "required" reading materials, as this is a responsibility of the agency giving the course;

(D) The realization that urban and rural problems are so different that separate programmes and policies may have to be set up.

In closing, two more comments seem pertinent. First, we all must remember the phrase "will to do." The human element, that personal something—enthusiasm, faith, institution or an intense belief in the task at hand, may be the determining factor in deciding just what a local public library programme should be. And secondly, let's not forget what Dr. Leigh had to say about popular control and expert direction wherein he cautioned that the exercise of professional judgement is a delegated function, and that in a democracy professional administration will be checked by the lay opinion of the community and will be subject to its ultimate control. Can we as public librarians be smart enough to lay our course, win friends and influence people and achieve a lay opinion that will back our professional judgement? I hope so.

We think it may be desirable to get away from the term "people's university" least it confuse rather than clarify our thinking of the role of the library. We would sum up by noting that through all of these discussions there is a large common core. The library, having major resources in the way of materials, must necessarily work in the closest cooperation with all other groups in adult education. At the same time there will be certain activities which should be conducted directly by the library. The nature of these activities should be determined through a careful study of the community needs by all the agencies offering adult-education services. The decision regarding which of these needs should be met by the library can then be made in relation to its resources. (For a discussion of programme planning and coordination).

Problems and Possibilities

The inquiry clearly indicates the same faith in the potentialities of the library as did Alvin Johnson earlier. Although better financing is crucial to the realization of better services, financing depends, in turn, upon an understanding by citizens generally of the role of the library and the museum in adult education. All persons interested in adult education, therefore, share in the tasks of developing a broad understanding of (1) the role of adult education in a democracy, and (2) the unique services best provided through libraries and museums. We shall leave further discussion of problems of interrelations among agencies, of blocks to action, and of united next steps to the Part of IV of this book. We turn here to some examples of special problems of libraries.

Services to All

The most effective libraries are found chiefly in the larger cities. Although modern transportation makes it possible for persons living at considerable distances outside the cities to come in fairly frequently, the figures show that distance is inversely related to use. Equitable distribution of facilities requires decentralization of services. Within the city, the branch library provides this. Beyond the city limits, regional libraries are an effort in this direction. A number of states have been experimenting with regional libraries. Excerpts from a report by Charles Armstrong describe such as experiment in New York State:

> The Survey of library services in the state showed that about one and one half million people in the state lived in communities that had no public library service. Many more had such poor service that the public libraries were of little value to them. The most serious problems centered in the sparsely settled regions served by small libraries. The State Library and the State Library Extension Division backed up the small libraries by loaning them books and providing some advisory services, but these services were too distant and too meager to offset the inefficiency of the small units. At the same time, the survey found that the small units had great value in their closeness to the community and in the encouragement they have to local initiative and control. The particular scheme proposed for regional service was carefully designed to achieve the needed efficiency while leaving the small libraries independent. The goals set in the survey were as follows:
>
> 1. All citizens of the state should be able to get easily as many books and other library materials as they will use.
> 2. All citizens of the state should be able to get answers to reasonable requests for information submitted through local libraries.
> 3. All children, both in and out of school, should be able to get well-selected library materials.
> 4. All citizens of the state should have the services of professionally trained librarians available as needed.

For reasonable efficiency in achieving the goal of a good book stock, the survey found that at least 20,000 and preferably more than 100,000 persons should be served by a single library unit. Similarly, the efficient purchase and cataloging of books required a minimum population of 40,000 and preferably more than 100,000 persons in a unit. However, the lending and direct public contact function could be efficiently performed in a unit serving 5,000 persons or possibly even fewer, if these outlets were immediately supported by the services of a large unit.

* * *

County-Wide Service

According to the plan, the responsibility for extending the services to the unserved of the area in addition to improving existing library services lay with the local community (school district, village, town, or county), while the state was ready to offer professional advice and encouragement and materials when the localities were prepared to receive them. It was believed that this extension should be planned on a county—or region—wide scale by the local boards described previously.

During the first two years of the experiment there was limited local activity leading toward county-wide local service in the Watertown area. The county boards of supervisors gave the problems some attention, and local library leaders held some meetings. There was undoubtedly considerable hesitation among the county supervisors in undertaking a cooperative programme with the Regional Library Service Center as long as the state assistance was on an experimental and, possibly, temporary basis. They may have been reluctant to form boards to make plans involving expenditure of local funds for projects which could not be carried through unless the state continued to operate center.

* * *

Summary

1. Financial support is increasing more rapidly in this area than in other similar communities selected as a control group. There is local interest in the extension of library service to unserved areas.
2. Library personnel are improving the services offered. In-service training has increased, the morale of the public librarians has risen, and a sense of regional unity has developed among them. There is still a great deal more to be done, however, before they will be making maximum

use of the resources available.

3. Library use has increased much more rapidly in the Watertown region than in the control area. The increase in library use has been largely in the borrowing of adult non-fiction and juvenile books. Thus the character of reading appears to have shifted toward the more serious books for adults and toward greater diversity in the types of books read.

   The proportion of the people using the libraries is small in most communities in the watertown area, but in some communities as many as half the residents have borrowed books within the single year.
4. Unit costs for the library operations performed are about the same as those in the average city library, but considerable reduction appears to be possible as operations are brought into line with more efficient practices. Books have been delivered promptly to the libraries requesting them.
5. Relatively little progress has been made in providing reference service. Attention has been centered on circulation, but reference service will receive more attention in the future.

Libraries and Mass Media

Libraries were established to make books more widely available, and books have naturally dominated the picture. With the rapid development of films, radio and television, our patterns of communication are changing and the responsibilities of libraries and museums will need to be seen in a different perspective. At a UNESCO seminar on Libraries in Adult and Fundamental Education, one of the study groups presented the following points regarding audio-visual materials:

It is too much to say that a library must, of absolute necessity, seize eagerly upon the new communication aids as a *sine qua non* of effective work in the field of adult education, for many libraries are doing dynamic work without the help of the mass media. It may be said, however, that no librarian is adequately prepared for the demands which he or she may be called up on to meet unless there is an awareness of the power and limitations of the new aids, a knowledge of utilization methods and techniques, a working knowledge of the methods of relating the audio-visual aids with established library methods and an ability to judge when local conditions are such as to demand that the facilities of the library to disseminate knowledge and information should be enhanced by the adoption of new materials.

There are a few key ideas ... to discuss ... :

First, audio-visual aids are a logical extension of the informational function of the library and cannot be neglected if end of disseminating knowledge and information is to be adequately served.

Second, because of the physical nature and cost of these aids, and the danger to library standards which springs from their great popular appeal, it is essential that the librarian should consider the over-all effect of their adoption upon his institution. He should above all be satisfied that the community is prepared to use the new tools effectively.

Third, the obvious public-relations value of the films and other audio-visual aids should be placed second to their contribution, through the library, to better human relations within the community.

Fourth, there are minimum, median and maximum programmes of audio-visual work which any librarian should consider thoroughly before making any decision for or against starting a programme.

Fifth, for all but the largest libraries it is essential that there be a willingness on the part of community workers to cooperate with the library in the programme. This brings up the subject of such devices as volunteer, aid, film councils and evaluation panels.

Sixth, the process of film selection differs from that of book selection because the film is seen by a group. Therefore the librarian should make use of expert opinion in the community to an extent never demanded by the book.

Seventh, the physical handling of audio-visual aids raises problems which must be met realistically. It is foolish to labour the idea that because films and other audio-visual aids may serve the same end as books, they should be handled identically. Further, the formula which may suit a large, well-staffed library may be completely unsuited to a smaller library.

Eighth, it is likewise foolish to insist upon the idea of "tying the book to the film" or *vice versa:* the broad view of subject given by a film may, in that it is given to the many, be just as important, from the community standpoint, as is the deeper knowledge gained from the book and given to the few.

Ninth, a knowledge of group techniques on the part of the librarian is just as important as the acquisition of materials for group education, for by this knowledge the true value of all the communication media can be realized. That is, librarians can only play their true role in the adult education programme if they know how the group reacts to books, films filmstrips, radio, television and other media.

Finally, in a large library, in a large community, it may be enough for a librarian to fill the traditional role of custodian of informational materials: books, films, maps, or anything else. But the librarian of today has gained recognition as an educator and this involves an active, not merely a passive participation. In the smaller community, where there may be no other person upon whom the burden of guidance may fall, the librarian may have to recognize that he has no choice but to leave the role of custodian and become an educator in the full sense of the word. We must know the methods of mass education and recognize the signs which indicate that the library may not be doing its part.

Freedom of Access to Information. As the mass media develop, certain problems of balance arise and the relationship of books to other types of communication becomes increasingly important. Luther Evans, Librarian of the Library of Congress and Head of the U. S. Commission for UNESCO, has made an analysis of this problem which points out the vital role of the library in ensuring adequate access to all sides of all questions. He notes that books and pamphlets still require small investments in contrast to the very large investments required for other forms of communication. It is through books and pamphlets that dissenting voices can most certainly be assured of a hearing. But this hearing requires effective libraries, and Evans refers to the library inquiry to indicate the present inadequacy:

> Freedom of speech and freedom of the press we justly prize as among the inalienable rights of the individual. But it is upon the correlatives of these—freedom to hear and freedom to read—

that all our other freedoms rest. For these are not only among the basic rights of society; they are among the necessary conditions of the existence of a free social order. The perpetuation of a free society requires not only that men have the legal right to hear and read the truth, to see information from varied sources, to explore divergent views, to be exposed to new or heretical ideas but that they have the actual opportunity to do so. And the perpetuation of our cultural health similarly requires that men have not only the right but the means to encounter a wide variety of intellectual expression and to share with contemporary creators in the arts their fresh and emerging perceptions of the human experience. Free participation in the state exists only where there is free participation in information; the commonwealth of the human spirit is shared only so widely as the works in which it is embodied are shared.

* * *

The instruments of public information to accomplish that enlightenment are certainly abundant. No people ever spent so many hours of every week reading newspapers and popular magazines, listening to radio comment, observing television programmes, and sitting through movies. At times there seems to exist for us not merely the freedom but the compulsion to read and hear. But all these through which we are so unremittingly approached have on disturbing characteristic; they are instruments through which one or a controllable number of views can simultaneously reach large masses of men. This characteristic lends itself to ideological monopoly. Even where totalitarian usages are not involved, we have seen in our own country the ominous aptitude of the mass media for creating and disseminating one accepted view or a single cultural pattern.

This tenuency is indeed difficult to escape. The economics of the mass media are such as to require a mass market for their support...

This is not to say that the mass media are inherently or usually or even often harmful. On the contrary, they are indispensably useful in purveying the great mass of information and entertainment that is of interest to most people. If the opportunities for recreation given by them were cut off this would be a rear place; and without the flow of news achieved by the mass media the functioning of our society would be impossible. However, the mass media cannot fill one of our great contemporary social needs, and it is highly important that there be other readily available sources of information and means of cultural expression as a corrective to their inherent tendency toward uniformity.

Books are almost the only medium that can fill this need... Even the smallest organization can still afford to publish a book or a pamphlet. Both the specialized learned institution and the small committee with a "cause" find in the book their means of expression.

Moreover, books are the only general medium of communication under the control of the recipient. A man who wants to experience "Hamlet" may have to wait months or even years before he has a chance to see it on the screen or stage or television or hear it over the radio; but he can read it when he chooses. Though the educational potentialities of the other media are enormous, it is only by rare coincidence that a man impelled to find out something about nuclear fission or cancer control will be able to tune in on a programme that will answer his questions; but if he has access to a good collection of books he can get immediately what he wants. A man in the average small city has a choice on a given evening of two or six radio programmes, perhaps half a dozen movies, two or three television programmes, or at least a couple of newspapers. In his public library he may have his choice of tens of thousands of books.

...The mass media have always the menance of becoming the instrument by which the user is controlled, but the book is always and inherently his servant.

An indispensable means is the public library. Though individuals can assemble books that are the working tools of their profession and buy books from time to time that attract them, only the very rich can afford to create private libraries capable of placing at command any considerable portion of available intellectual resources. Even had one the means to buy, only a few bookstores in the largest cities can afford to maintain stocks from which to choose that are at all comparable to those of reasonably good public library. It is of the essence of the book's utility that it gives the user the choice not only among epheremerally appearing products but among the organized accumulation of knowledge and recorded expression; and this only the library can do.

For an institution of such superlative social importance the public library in the United States has faltered alarmingly in support and in accomplishment...

The blunt fact is that almost no Americans living outside rather large cities—and this means most of us—have access to a library capable of giving really good service, as pointed out in Robert D. Leigh's "The Public Library in the United States".

A Living Force

We close this discussion of the library with a manifesto by UNESCO regarding the public library:

UNESCO, The United Nations Educational, Scientific and Cultural Organization, has been created by the will of 46 countries. Its aim is to promote peace and social and spiritual welfare by working through the minds of men. The creative power of UNESCO, is the force of knowledge and international understanding.

This manifesto, by describing the potentialities of the public library, proclaims UNESCO's belief in the public library as a living force for popular education and for the growth of international understanding, and thereby for the promotion of peace.

The public library is a product of modern democracy and a practical demonstration of democracy's faith in universal education as a life-long process.

Though primarily intended to serve the educational needs of adults, the public library should also supplement the work of the schools in developing the reading tastes of children and young people, helping them to become adults who can use books with appreciation and profit.

As a democratic institution, operated by the people for the people, the public library should be:

1. Established and maintained under clear authority of low.
2. Supported wholly or mainly from public funds.
3. Open for free use on equal terms to all members of the community, regardless of occupation, creed, class or race.

The complete library should provide; books, pamphlets, magazines, newspapers, maps, pictures, films, music scores and recordings—and give guidance in their use.

The public library should offer children, young people, men and women, opportunity and encouragement:

1. To educate themselves continuously.
2. To keep abreast of progress in all fields of knowledge.
3. To maintain freedom of expression and a constructively critical attitude toward all public issues.
4. To be better social and political citizens of their country and of the world.
5. To be more efficient in their day-to-day activities.
6. To develop their creative capacities and powers of appreciation in arts and letters.
7. To aid generally in the advancement of knowledge.
8. To use their leisure time to promote personal happiness and social well-being.

The public library should be active and positive in its policy and dynamic part of community life.

It should not tell people what to think, but it should help them to decide what to think about. The spotlight should be thrown on significant issues by exhibition, booklists, discussions, lectures, courses, films and individual reading guidance.

Reading interest should be stimulated and the library's services publicized through a well-planned continuous public-relations programme.

The public library should link its activities with the work of other educational, cultural and social agencies—the schools, universities, museums, labour unions, study clubs, adult education groups, etc. It should also cooperate with other libraries in the loan of publications and with library associations for the advancement of public librarianship.

The books in the library should be made accessible on open shelves and by use of efficient technical processes; and the library's services should be brought close to the homes and work places of the people by means of branches and mobile units.

* * *

What-You Can Do

This manifesto has described the potentialities of the public library as an agency for popular education. Obviously it is to your great personal advantage to have these potentialities realized in your community. What can you do to help?

If your community does not have public library services:

Interest your friends and neighbours and local organizations in obtaining such service.

Ask your national library association or Ministry of Education what steps you should take to get public library service.

Follow through on the action recommended.

If your community now has a public library:

Get acquainted with the librarian.

Find out what services are offered.

Use these services.

Work with the librarian to promote local support and demand the standard of service endorsed in this manifesto.

The picture we have given about the library (and it would apply equally to the museum) in the adult-education picture is admittedly not yet widely achieved. Our descriptions are of best practice, not of modal services. There are large sections of our population that have no library service at all and only a small percentage of citizens that get service that could be considered adequate. The typical library is under supported and lacks the trained staff and equipment necessary to do the job. Loyalty cannot make up for leadership. It is up to all of us to work for what we know is possible and what we believe is vital for adult education.

9

Public Schools

In this Chapter we shall attempt to identify some of the major characteristics and problems of public-school adult-education in the United States. Other descriptive material on public-school programmes will be found in Chapter 4. In Chapter 13, some reference is also made to public-school participation in programme planning and coordination of community resources. In other chapters in Part III, where problems of materials, methods, publicity, professional training, finance and evaluation are treated as they cut across institutional areas, frequent references are made to public-school experience. This leaves for specific consideration in this chapter some of the over-all features of public-school programmes, problems of administration of special concern in the public-school field, and, in a final section, the development of new services under public-school auspices.

Over-all Considerations

In this section we shall examine some of the conceptions which characterize the operation of public-school programmes and some of the differing programme emphases as revealed by a study of the offerings of typical adult schools. First, however, it may be helpful to get some idea of the extent and variety of public-school activities in adult education by quoting the summary paragraphs of a survey report by Homer Kempfer, then of the U. S. Office of Education, on adult-education activities of the public schools during the school year 1947-1948.

An inquiry sent to 3,613 school districts in communities

having a 1940 census population of 2,500 or more brought an 80.8 per cent return. Of 2,922 districts reporting, more than four-fifths claimed to have had educational activities for adults and out-of-school youth in 1947-48, nearly half reported evening and adult schools. An estimated three-fourths of *all* districts above 2,500 population (including those not reporting) provide some kind of education for adults. A minimum of 40 per cent of *all* districts above 2,500 population claim to have evening or adult schools even if nonresponse to the inquiry represents the absence of such schools..

A similar inquiry sent to 1,202 districts in smaller communities thought to have adult education activities brought a 32.5 per cent return. Of 391 smaller districts reporting, over four-fifths claimed to have adult education activities in 1947-48 and nearly two-fifths reported evening or adult schools. Nearly 10,000 other districts with superintendents in communities under 2,500 were not included in this survey.

The evening school is the major type of educational service offered adults by the public school. For every district with an evening of an adult school, however, there are approximately six other types of educational activities provided for adults and out-of-school youth. Adult education activities are relatively widely distributed throughout our public-school system, although a variety of types and fields is more often found in large communities. Among all activities those in the recreational and vocational fields are much more widely distributed than any other. Approximately half of all evening and adult schools offer high-school subjects for adults. Only 1 out of every 8 reporting districts provide elementary education, while 18 per cent with evening or adult schools offer college-level subjects for adults. Slightly less than half of all adult education programmes operate in conjunction with advisory committees.

In this survey 1,951 districts in communities of 2,500 and above reported a total enrolment of 2,104,032 adults and out-of-school youth. Enrolment reported by 135 smaller districts was 72,659. Additional information leads to the estimate that a total of approximately 3,000,000 adults and out-of-school youth were provided some type of organized educational service in 1947-48. Adult education is relatively highly developed in a number of schools and in a few States. The limited number of adults served by most public schools reflected against the widespread and growing interest of adults in further learning leads to the conclusion that a great many districts are providing far too little opportunity for continued education beyond the years of full-time schooling.

It should be remembered that many public-school programmes for adults can trace their beginnings to the period in American life when the influx of large numbers of immigrants from foreign lands created a major need for elementary classes for adults in Americanization and literacy. During this period, it was perfectly logical for communities to turn to their public schools for adult classes through which these needs could be met. Even today, in our large urban school systems particularly, extensive programmes of Americanization and literacy work are still offered.

But the concept of adult education as dominantly a remedial activity on the part of the public schools had long since been superseded by concepts of service much broader in their application to community needs. The perception of adult education as a lifelong process of learning has been characteristic of the literature in adult education and of the thinking among the professional leaders in the field for at least twenty-five years.

Although some vestiges of the earlier remedial emphasis are still to be found among certain lay groups which oppose the extension of tax-supported educational activities, the next four selections indicate how rapidly and drastically the remedial concept of public-school service has been modified. The first is a statement prepared by Thomas A. Van Sant in connection with the survey of the Lincoln, Nebraska, schools.

Public school in a democracy are responsible for meeting the educational needs of all the people of any age group when such needs are consistent with the public interest and the public welfare. This responsibility does not require the duplication of educational facilities controlled by non-public groups already satisfactorily meeting educational needs nor the elimination of such non-public organizations. However, the responsibility requires the public schools to act as the judge of the adequacy of other educational organizations. This latter provision exists in part in the right given most state departments of education to accredit or to refuse to accredit public or private schools within their jurisdiction.

The second selection is from an analysis by Paul H. Sheats.

Thus far in the overwhelming majority of American communities adult education has not been looked upon as an important or even a secondary responsibility of the public educational system. There are today many school administrators and some state superintendents of public instruction who, with complete sincerity, argue that the job of the public educational system is to educate the young and that if it is to do this job well it cannot afford to get mixed up in the rather diversified assortment of activities which go on under the label of adult education. This point of view, no doubt mirroring the opinions of many school board members, dictates all kinds of decisions which drastically affect both the quantity and quality of services rendered to the out-of-school members of the community. The plans and layout of new school buildings, the purchase of equipment, the selection of teachers, the allocation of funds for salaries and supplies, if completely divorced from considerations affecting possible adult use of the school, make an extension of service difficult if not impossible.

Keep in mind that his phrase "extension of educational opportunities to adults" takes in three-fifths of our total population. We are talking about 90,000,000 people most of whom are not now the object of any special educational concern on the part of those who profess statecraft in this business of public education.

* * *

Let us take a closer look at some of the assumptions which lie behind this particular schoolman's insistence that he is a superintendent of schools and not a director of community education. In the first place his view expresses what might be called "the scarcity theory of education" "Education is a good thing for youngsters", he would say. "In fact, in smaller amounts it is even a legitimate charge on the public treasury at the college level but, after all, this sort of thing has to stop somewhere or the school administrator will find himself running an educational programme which stretches 'from the cradle to the grave.' Moreover, if adults want education let them pay for it— the school budget isn't big enough to meet existing needs at the elementary and secondary levels." Finally, our defender of the "schools are intended for children" tradition is likely to point out quite correctly that the school is not the only educational institution in the community and that it is precisely in this area of adult education where civic and private organizations are best fitted to "take over."

These assumptions and arguments must be weighed against the facts of life in these United States...Whether we look at the international or domestic scene, we are faced with a complex of problems which will require intelligent group action based on carefully thought-out, long-range policies if choices are to be made in the interests of the common good. For this task our people are inadequately equipped. The 10,000,000 among us with fourth-grade education attainment or less are only the more obviously underprivileged. The one-third without library service will find this lack a real obstacle to self-enlightenment on the issues of the day. The 54,000,000 adults in the U. S. who according to a recent survey have never heard of or read about the Atlantic Charter face the brave new world beyond the war somewhat inadequately equipped to arrive at an intelligent conclusion regarding its problems.

The people themselves know their needs. A careful block-by-block survey of adult education needs in Denver disclosed what 63 per cent found most lacking —an understanding of what is going on in a world at war. The search for new and improved media of communication, illustrated pamphlets, slide films, film forums, radio forums and discussions is evidence of the need and the desire to learn.

*   *   *

Nor can it be argued that the existing public and private facilities are adequate to meet these needs. Even before the war some 60 to 70 per cent of adults were not identified with any organized community group exclusive of church membership. The same Denver survey already referred to revealed that 85 per cent of the adults in that community had participated in no organized educational activity outside of job training since leaving school. A reliable authority on adult education estimates that existing programmes of adult education are meeting not more than 5 per cent of the need. A survey of a Southern county with a population of 7,000 disclosed 35 active organizations ranging from music study associations to home demonstration clubs. Investigations revealed that less than 200 people comprised the total membership of all these organizations.

The magnitude and nature of the educational task to be done with and for adults requires an extension of publicly supported and school-sponsored programmes. Only through programmes supported by all the members of the community and administered by a staff responsible to them can this task be thoroughly and democratically carried out. We cannot afford in this country the kind of intellectual Brahmanism which assumes that a special brand of educational opportunity should be provided for and by workers, while a different product is offered for and by business men. This conception of islanded adult education with the segments unabridged by common under-standings, purposes, or experiences can be avoided only if the agency charged with responsibility for educating *all* American youth serves also the educational needs of *all* adults. In fact, as the Educational Policies Commission has recently pointed out, the public school cannot adequately discharge its obligations to those for whom it was primarily originally created unless it serves also the needs of out-of-school youth and adults through counselling service, classes, forums, recreation, library service and through its contribution to the efficient planning and direction of community activities.

The Past-President of the Adult Education Association of the U.S.A. Howard Y. McClusky, of the University of Michigan, suggests that the major responsibilities of the public schools for adult education are these:

> To provide such educational facilities and services as it can provide more effectively than any other agency.
> To cooperate with and assist agencies with an educational function to increase the value of their educational services, and
> To take chief responsibility or see that some agency takes chief responsibility for the coordination of the total educational activities of the community unless some other agency is effectively carrying on such leadership.

Robin Maaske, a Past-President of the National Education Association Department of Adult Education says,

> The position of superintendent of schools in these days admittedly is not an easy one, with the many vexing problems of increasing enrolments, costly building programmes, broadened curricular offerings, and limited financial resources, to mention only a few. However, the superintendent who fails to do what he can to provide for the education of adults in the community is neglecting a responsibility and overlooking an opportunity.

It is the purpose of this article to provide specific suggestions for the helpful guidance of superintendents and boards of education in initiating or expanding programmes of adult education in their communities. Since larger cities already have in operation well-organized and well-planned programmes, the suggestions will be aimed principally toward smaller cities and communities.

In building a sound programme of adult education at the community level, it is well to heed certain organization principles which have evolved from the results of experience in communities with successful programmes. These may be summarized as follows:

> There should be local control and planning of the programme. It is axiomatic that people are naturally more interested in anything which they have a hand in planning, and for which they assume some responsibilities. Any superimposed programme is soon likely to fall of its own weight. Hence, the clear need for observing the principle of local control and planning as basic in conceiving the community programme of adult education. Just how this may be done will be told later.

There should be community coordination of the necessary leadership. This principle is highly important. It points to the necessity of bringing together and coordinating the leaders of organizations, agencies and groups in the community. It assures unified backing for the enterprise of starting an organized programme of education for adults. There often exist certain jealousies and assumed prerogatives among organizations and leaders. This makes it desirable that as many as possible be brought cooperatively into the picture at the outset. The situation varies with the community, but the superintendent will usually be cognizant of the sate of affairs.

There should be local participation of financing the

programme. This principle is sound for the same general reasons as the first principle. The extent and manner of financial participation will vary greatly, depending upon such factors as: (a) amount of state aid; (*b*) local public school funds available for adult education; (*c*) ability and willingness of local organizations and agencies to assist financially; and (*d*) sentiment regarding the size of the fees for materials to be paid by local participants in the classes. It is clear, however, that as the local community makes an investment financially in the programme, it stimulates a much greater general interest in the success of the undertaking.

There should be a well-balanced programme of offerings to meet the varying needs and interests of the adults. The ultimate test of the success of the programme depends upon whether it not only meets the felt needs and interests of adults, but stimulates them to want to explore other fields and develop new interests. It is important that the early attempts provide for classes and other learning activities which appeal to variety of the people. It is desirable to build the programme upon ascertained needs and interest of adults. It will have appeal in proportion to the extent to which it meets such needs and interests.

There should be utilized all available community educational resources. Some organizations may already have programmes operating which are not widely known. Others will have leadership or other resources which can contribute to the total programme if they are properly tapped. The superintendent and his aides will have ideas on how these resources may be approached and utilized. One can readily think of the following:

(a) The public school, its staff and facilities.
(b) The public library.
(c) Museum and art institute.
(d) The extension division of the state university, near-by college, or junior college.
(e) State and federal agencies such as agricultural and home extension services.
(f) City health, social and recreational agencies, and similar ones.
(g) Churches and church leaders.

It is at this point that the superintendent who has had but little experience with an adult education programme usually feels quite definitely at a loss. This is not at all surprising. The steps to be taken will require careful planning and clear thinking. Local conditions and circumstances need to be studiously consi-dered. While the superintendent, or a designated staff aid in a adult education, will need to exercise constructive leadership, it should be of a guiding nature rather than a "forcing" process.

It should be stressed that the concepts of service outlined in these selections are not characteristic of practice in most school districts today. Many districts are quite content to leave adult education to other agencies and to limit their activities to vocational classes or to work with parent-teacher associations. Others, as has already been indicated, limit the boundaries of the programme to remedial efforts governed by what Thomas Van Sant calls a "second chance philosophy." Still others operate only in the vocational area, for which community support is likely to be readily forthcoming. The merging of all these and other services in one institution into a fully rounded and carefully planned programme based on the concept of complete service to the adult and the community is still largely in the discussion stage. But, as the materials in subsequent selections in this chapter will indicate, there is growing support for this broader view.

At a 1948 conference of California Adult School Administrators, a statement was formulated which, as reported by Philip M. Ferguson, represents the ideas and opinions of men and women now administering and teaching in the adult programme in the state of California. They are as follows: (1) a public-school adult-education programme is essential to the alert, informed, and active citizenry necessary to carry on and improve our way of life; (2) public-school adult education should be publicly financed in such a way that no one will be denied the opportunity of participation; (3) adult education should be greared to the known and understood needs and interests of the community; (4) the organization of adult education at all levels must be maintained in a state of flexibility which will enable rapid changes in the curriculum to be made as new community needs become evident; (5) adult-education personnel in the public schools should encourage and work with other organizations engaged in desirable adult-education activities; (6) adult education is an integral part of the California framework of education; its leaders must work in close cooperation with all other segments of the schools system; (7) adult-education programmes should provide for the presentation of unbiased information in discussions of controversial issues ; (8) funds provided for an adult-education programme should be spent specifically for adult education rather than for education in general; (9) adult-education administrators must be free to obtain the best teaching personnel available regardless of extent of the formal educational training of the teacher.

One very potent argument which educational administrators are using in promoting public-school adult education deals with the relationship between adult education and the education of youth. An interesting comment on this problem is contained in the following selection, from Leland Bradford's annual report as Director of the Division of Adult Education Services, of the National Education Association.

Educators are gradually realising the importance of adult education to the education of youth. This is in sharp contrast to past attitudes which considered. Adult education a marginal and not too welcome addition to the educational field. This point of view saw adult education merely as a means of making up educational deficiencies. To a certain extent the early development of adult education contributed to this understanding by patterning itself too closely on the content and methods of youth education.

Curiously, it is not so important to adult education whether or not it is a part of the public-school programme, but it is of crucial importance to public education that adult education have a major place in its total programme. First, adult education has the potential of making youth education live in the problems of our time by bringing to it adult-discussion methods, group work, and a more dynamic curriculum. Second, as adult education involves adults in the educational life of the community, so the total educational programme is brought much more closely into the life of the community. The total community becomes part of the educational programme and shares in a combined educational experience for all people. Third, adult education will help in the necessary revitalization of teacher preparation and improvement. Only as training institutions undertake the dynamic training of adult-educators and of community leaders will they realize the inadequacy of their present programme of teacher preparation and bring about a successful balance between realistic teacher preparation and continuous in-serve-ice improvement.

As a result of the partnership of adult and child education, there will come a drastic change in the public attitude toward education. No longer will teaching be the lowest profession in terms of respect and remuneration. The best possible programme of public relations today is that involvement of those who foot the bill for the activity to be supported. Within modern shifting trends the only safeguard for total education is that certainty of complete involvement.

This trend makes it incumbent upon those in adult education to press strongly and fearlessly for real recognition of the importance of adult education to all education by school administrators and boards of education, state departments of public instructions, and teacher-training institutions. In the past, adult education has been sold to school systems as necessary for only one small segment of the population. Now it should be sold as important for all the community.

Adult education needs to be seen by other educators as the way by which adults in the community are trained as leaders and participants in such school oriented groups as the PTA. Only thru the help of adult-educators and adult-education methods will such groups as the PTA reach their effective potential in school improvement.

Finally, educators need to see that adult-educators can materially help in the pre- and in-service training of teachers by aiding them to secure competence in discussion method and group work so needed by all of education today.

What kinds of adult-education programmes are most characteristic of those offered under public-school auspices? As might be expected, there is wide variation from community to community and from state to state. The U. S. office of Education's survey, already referred to, identifies thirty-six categories of activities, ranging all the way from operation of evening school classes to a little-theater programme. There is a range from 13 to 1601 districts reporting activities in one or more of these categories. William P. Wilson, in an unpublished 1947 study of adult-education programmes in selected cities of the United States, received replies from 52 cities broadly representative of geographical sections of the country and from these data identified 604 different titles of courses offered in these cities. Some duplication existed among the course titles, but by classifying titles he found a percentage distribution in the following areas:

Classification	*Percentage*
Art and art craft	8
Better living	23.5
Academic	27
Music	5
Vocational	30
Miscellaneous	6.5

In his study, Wilson identified the following trends: (1) the programmes throughout the country as a whole cover a wide variety of subjects; (2) many cities are giving programmes that are very conventional and academic; (3) the majority of programmes studied schedule four evenings a week for three hours each evening; (4) although English for the foreignborn and citizenship are still being offered in most schools, they no longer constitute the main part of the programme, as they did in the years of high immigration; vocational and academic courses, and courses involving self-expression and development, have been on the increase.

These conclusions should be checked with the results obtained by Kempfer and·Wright in their study of 100 evening schools. Chart I has been adapted from the classification system used by Kempfer and Wright.

These data may become more meaningful if we look at the classification of offerings in specific communities. In his annual report for 1949, Ralph E. Crow, Directing Supervisor of Adult Education in the Cleveland Public Schools, described classes conducted in 76 centers throughout the city. Ninety-five per cent of these classes were held in school buildings, and a total class enrolment of 26,355 was reported. The programme emphasized elementary and Americanization work, classes at the secondary level, vocational and vocational courses, parent education, and classes in homemaking.

Charts II and III describe two other city school programmes in adult education, those in Pasadena and Loss Angeles.

The 1952 survey of public-school adult education conducted by the National Education Association shows a marked increase of offerings in civic and public affairs, world problems, Western economy and society, and the humanities. Although these trends are encouraging, it should be remembered that the data on which these generalizations are based come from urban communities. With fewer than one twentieth of the adults in the United States now being served even partially by public-school programmes, we can hardly call existing programmes adequate to the need.

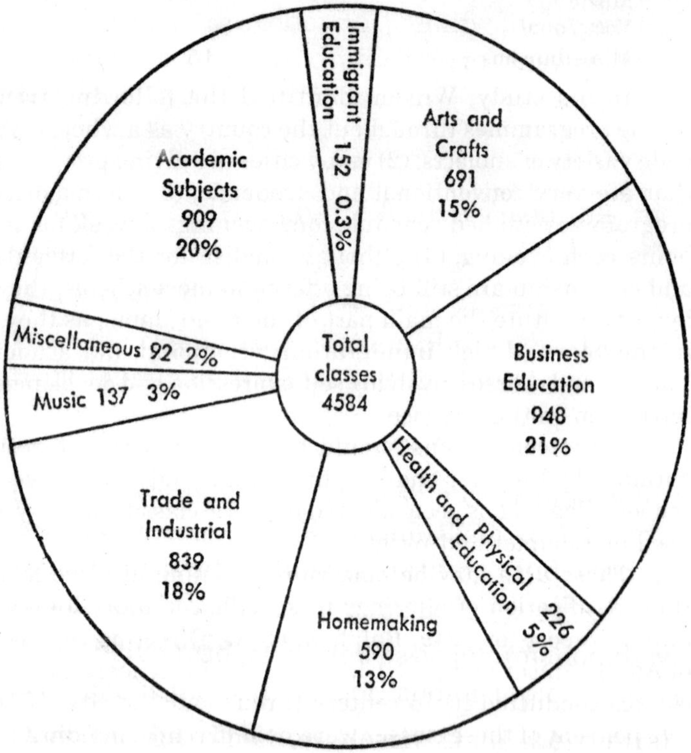

Chart I. Subject distribution in adult education, based on data covering subject offerings of 100 evening schools, 1948-1949, as reported in *100 Evening Schools*, by Homer Kempfer and Grace S. Wright, Federal Security Agency, Office of Education, Bulletin No. 4, 1949.

Administrative Problems Arising from the Operation of Public-school Adult-education Programmes

The success of a public-school adult-education programme depends quite crucially upon the person chosen to administer the programme and upon the way in which it is articulated with the elementary and secondary offerings. Although the assignment of a good administrator will not necessarily guarantee the success of a school-sponsored adult-education programme, instances are rare in which success is achieved without superior leadership. Ralph B. Spence and Benjamin Shangold

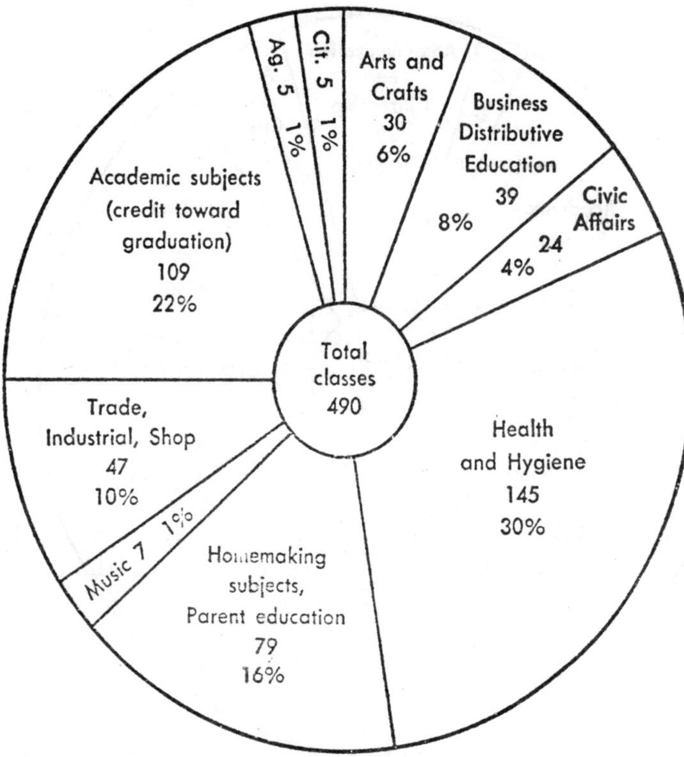

Chart II. Pasadena City College, Percentage of classes for adults assigned by subject fields (day and evening closses combined), Spring semester 1950-1951.

discovered, for example, that leadership by the school administrator, superintendent, or supervising principal was a central factor in determining the quality of programme. The communities which had strong public-school adult-education programmes had administrators that would be rated as "good" to "outstanding", but not all good administrators had strong adult-education programmes.

As long ago as 1943, Andrew Hendrickson, of Ohio State University, noted "a growing tendency to establish under the superintendent of schools a separate administrative head for the adult work called director of adult education or supervisor of adult education". By 1949, when the U. S. office of Education

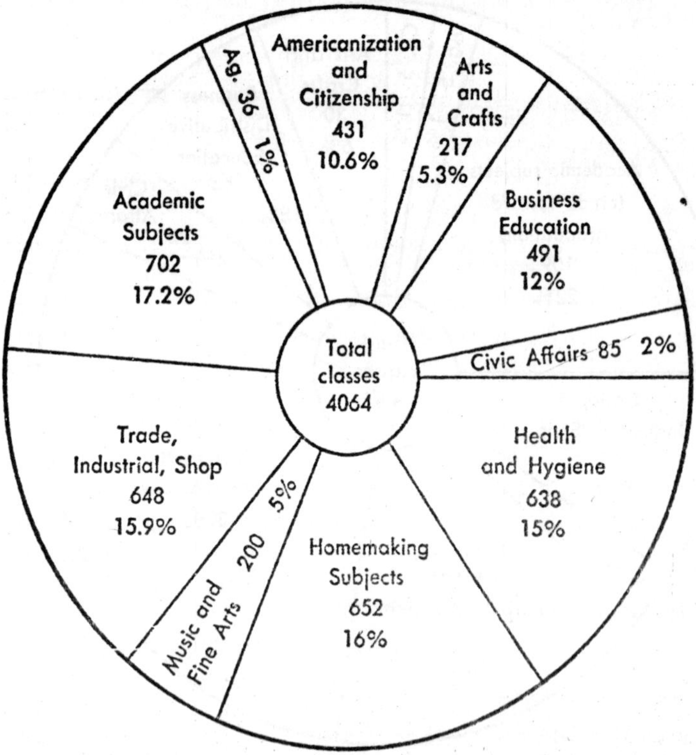

Chart III. Los Angeles City Schools. Percentage of classes for adults assigned by subject fields (including classes for adults in Los Angeles City High School and Junior College districts) day and evening classes (combined), school year 1950-1951, as of March 1, 1951.

report on 100 evening schools was published, 74 of the 98 cities represented in the study had directors of adult education or other persons, whose responsibility included one or more evening schools plus other adult-education activities. Of these directors of adult education, 45 devoted full time or more than half time to their work. Relatively few of these administrators had received any kind of formal training in adult education.

David L. Mackaye,Director of Adult Education at San Jose, California, points out:

> ...As a consequence of this situation a conscious and deliberate struggle has been necessary to maintain the purposes of adult education against a tendency to confine them within the purposes of secondary education in general, thus reducing them to the form of a preparatory form of education. This struggle has been more or less successful and will be increasingly unnecessary.

These general observations are supported by the results of the New York state survey already referred to. A section of that report follows.

The public school programmes of adult education in 1946-47 most frequently were administered by a director of adult education, who reported that he gave from 10 to 15 per cent of his time to this particular task and from 85 to 90 per cent of his time to a variety of other responsibilities. The persons in charge of adult education had a variety of previous experience. Reports on the previous experience of these persons showed that the largest number came from vocational education, several had been school principals, some had been teachers and others had been directors of guidance, veterans' counsellors during the war training, directors of adult immigrant education etc. These persons had little systematic preparation for adult education but considerable experience in some aspects of adult education. Several reported over 20 years of experience. Of 15 persons who reported their academic training, nine had master's degrees, one had a doctor's degree and one was a candidate for a doctor's degree in industrial and labour relations.

The director of the adult programmes generally had a responsibility for planning the programme, securing teachers, organizing schedules, publicizing the programme, keeping records and other similar activities. The amount of responsibility delegated by the superintendent of schools varied, particularly with regard to the budget. Apparently in a number of situations the arrangements with regard to budget were relatively informal with no exact amount allocated to the adult education programme in advance.

The consensus among those reporting was that the administrative responsibilities of a director were comparable to that of an elementary school principal. In practice, however, the position tended to be accorded much less responsibility as measured by the time and salary allocated to it. The attitude seemed to be that the work involved a relatively small number of students and the responsibility was correspondingly small. Relatively little weight was given to the need for intensive promotion of the programme in the community.

An analysis of the administrative duties reported indicates the types of activities carried by some of the directors of adult education:

Survey of existing facilities for adult education in the community to determine needs and the part the school should play in total programme.

Securing of expression of desires of adults for contents of the educational programme

Assistance in securing competent instructors and adequate facilities for the programme

Registration of attendance and enrolment records and of necessary reports to local board of education and State Department.

Making of accurate payroll reports to board of education.

Supervision of building during hours of classes to prevent misuse of facilities by either students or unauthorized persons

Cooperation with instructors in arranging suitable course content for courses to meet expressed needs of students.

Guidance and counselling of veterans and other adults who wish to complete formal high school requirements, which would include checking of previous record, testing of present achievement in some cases and coordination with regular day school programme to supplement it where necessary.

Evaluation of effectiveness of programme through observation, student reactions, further requests, holding power of classes etc.

Follow-up of students to determine reason for drop-outs.

Promotion of desirable cultural as well as vocational activities in the programme.

Study of progressive practices in adult education through the reading of professional literature, visitation of effective programmes elsewhere and attendance at professional meetings concerned with adult education.

Observance of all laws and regulations of the State, the state board of education, the local board of education and the local superintendent of schools and the carrying out of all policies of the local board of education and its executive officer, the superintendent of schools.

As one examines the list of typical activities in which the administrator of public-school programmes engages, it is not surprising that the most urgent problems listed by a group of 61 adult-education administrators in California include a large percentage of what might be called technical and operating difficulties. Although 105 problems were identified in the study just referred to, the top ten in point of urgency will serve to indicate the nature of the administrator's concerns.

1. in-service training and institute programmes for teachers of adults,
2. adequate counselling staff,
3. adequate conference and interview space,
4. teacher's salaries,
5. training regular teachers of adult classes in counselling techniques,
6. registration, display, and exhibit facilities,
7. student news sheet,
8. clerical and secretarial help,
9. filling and storage space,
10. adequate budget for travel to conferences, professional subscriptions, etc.

Two problems will serve to illustrate the kind of leadership called for from the administrator. Let us take, for example, the problem of obtaining adequate facilities for adult-education activities. Ninety-one per cent of the districts reporting in the U. S. office of Education survey indicate activities held in school buildings; thirteen per cent reported activities in other public buildings; seven per cent used factories and stores; six per cent, homes; six per cent, church buildings; four per cent, clubrooms; two per cent, settlement houses; one per cent, museums; and four per cent, other places, such as camps, libraries, parks, playgrounds and swimming pools. In the later survey of 100 evening schools only six schools reported housing of adult-education activities in a separate building. It is little wonder that Bradford, in his annual report for the National Education Association Division of Adult Education Services identifies as a basic problem in adult education the lack of adequate physical facilities.

...Adult education has to long been forced to make use of classrooms designed for children in old buildings which give the impression that adult education is in "rags and tatters". Wise educators, in this day when new school buildings are being planned, should see that such buildings be designed for both youth and adults, and that such schools be constructed as true community centers. Conference rooms should be a normal part of any modern school building, with full facilities for adults. Then, and only then, will adults feel that these buildings are also for them.

On the other hand, many school systems are making every effort to locate and provide convenient and accessible facilities wherever the demand for services exists. The survey of adult education in Pasadena, California, revealed that in the 1950-1951 school year 64 sites were utilized, including nonschool quarters. Out of 428 student respondents to a questionnaire distributed in connection with this survey, 409 expressed themselves as satisfied with the present location of the class they were attending. Fifty-two per cent of the adult-education teachers expressed the belief that classroom facilities in terms of good teaching were either adequate or exceptionally good.

The articulation of secondary and adult education is another matter of major concern to public-school adult-education administrators. Homer Kempfer, of the U. S. Office of Education, has dealt with this problem in the following selection.

Education should be a continuous, life-long process. Educators have said that for years. Yet the attitude and atmosphere around most high schools is that education ends with graduation except for those who go on to college. The "commencement" concept in thinking and behaviour of students, faculty, and community alike marks high school graduation as the sharp terminal point of systematic education for most youth.

Ideally, if principles of growth were followed, transition from full-time school to full occupational life and homemaking would be gradual. The principle of work experience in the late high school years is becoming increasingly accepted. For all youth not continuing their studies full time, whether because of drop-out or graduation, there is every reason for involving them in some systematic out-of-school youth or young adult programme.

Close articulation is the accepted practice between elementary and secondary education. Records move up. High school principals visit elementary schools and visiting days help orient the pupils to the next higher institution. In numerous other ways close liaison is effected. Likewise, college and high school officials spend much time arranging for the transfer of students. Only adult education seems to live apart. There are exceptions, but all too often the director of adult education publicizes and builds his programme without the benefit of close cooperation with the high schools. This is nobody's fault in particular; it is just a condition that has grown up. It remains by tradition and inertia—not reason and logic.

In this situation directors of adult education and elementary and high school principals have a joint responsibility. From their first days in school, children should live in an atmosphere which expects that systematic education will be life long—that they as a matter of course will maintain some part-time connection with the public schools and other sources of intellectual stimulation long after education ceases to be a full-time occupation. Principals are the key people to see that such expectancies are built, although adult directors can do much, too. Here are some things that both can do to bring about a closer articulation:

See that all teachers and other staff personnel are fully acquainted with the local adult education opportunities both in the public school and outside of it. Within the school system this is a public relations job. One way is to involve as many teachers as possible in the adult programme. Let them experience and enjoy it.

Train teachers to develop in youth the concept of life-long education—through precept, example, and an information programme. Develop in every teacher the specific habit of referring youth to adult education activities upon leaving school.

Be especially sure that guidance people know about adult education opportunities and that they habitually guide graduates and drop-outs toward these activities.

Arrange for pertinent data on drop-outs to flow from the guidance department to the director of adult education. Follow up these drop-outs in an effort to draw them into adult programmes.

Encourage seniors to get a taste of adult before graduation by entering also into selected adult activities, provided adults in these groups do not resent the presence of younger people.

Encourage secondary teachers to use adaptations of adult methods whenever feasible—especially discussion group and forum procedures. To acquaint secondary teachers with these methods encourage them to accept responsibility for adult leadership activities. Accompany these assignments with in-service training in the methods and philosophy of adult education. Visible improvement may come in day school methods of teachers who adapt successfully to leadership of adult groups.

Help high school people to develop long-term educational plans which include adult education activities especially when all desired courses cannot be crowded into the schedule before graduation.

Explain to seniors the opportunities in the adult education programme—the richness—the flexibility—the fun. Do a selling job. In cooperation with the guidance department, take an annual spring survey of seniors to determine their interest as a partial basis for programme planning.

Plan the continuation of high school interest groups with a minimum carry-over of traditional secondary school regulations. Develop young adult bands, orchestras, choral groups, science clubs, athletic teams, shop work. Grow these right out of high school with a smooth transition into the young adult groups. Start with activities most liked and with groups giving happiest associations. Isn't it better for young adults to maintain some connection with the school, even though not very academic, than to have them assume a "good-riddance " attitude sometimes encountered?

Design and develop special activities to meet the needs and interests of out-of-school youth—programmes for young adults. Maybe it will be advisable to limit the age of span of these groups. Fields in which activities can be slanted to serve the penduliar needs of young adults including the vocational, civic, family life and parents education recreation, and guidance.

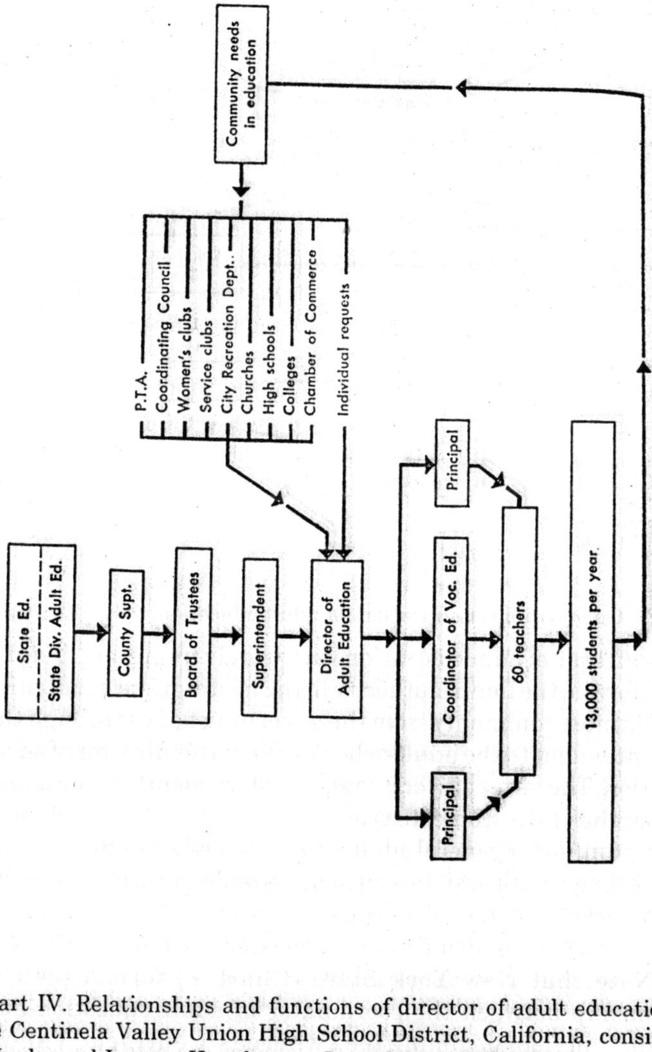

Chart IV. Relationships and functions of director of adult education in the Centinela Valley Union High School District, California, consisting of Inglewood-Lennox-Hawthrone - Lawndale and Wiseburn.

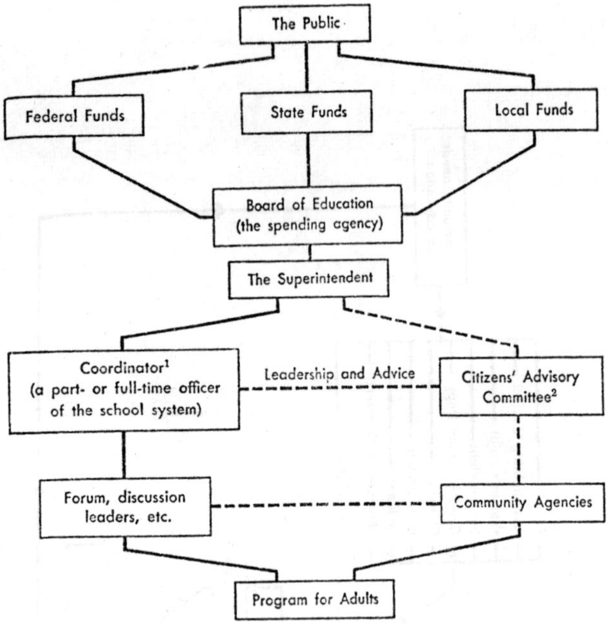

Chart V. One possible organization for adult education.

Patterns of administration vary widely from state to state. In California, the line of authority in the medium and small cities extends most commonly from the governing board through the superintendent to the adult-school principal or director of adult education. The latter officer is found most frequently in the larger cities of the state. Some districts, such as Pasadena and Long Beach, administer general adult-education activities through the junior college, with assistant principals or deans in charge of the community service offerings. Two sample patterns of administrative organization are suggested in Charts IV and V.

Note that New York State (Chart V) formalizes the relationship between the coordinator of adult education and citizens' advisory committee, whereas Centinela Valley, California (Chart IV), maintains community contacts through the director in his relationships with the cooperating agencies of the community.

In the following selection, Homer Kempfer treats the functions of advisory committees in the adult education programme.

To have or not to have an advisory committee—that is the question faced by a great many educators of adults.

Arguments *pro and con* will not be briefed here except to say that any programme attempting to serve the educational needs of the whole community probably can benefit by involving that community in the planning and development of the programme. Good community programmes of adult education can be run without advisory committees, but a great many directors feel that committees help them run better programmes. In a recent nation-wide survey 45.7 per cent of all districts reporting adult education had advisory committees. Of 100 representative evening schools 71 had such committees.

* * *

The advisory committee should be of good working size—10-12-15—maybe 20. It needs to be small enough for each member to speak freely; small enough for efficiency; yet large enough to represent the whole scope of community life. A much larger committee which meets occasionally and a smaller executive committee may be desired in some places.

* * *

No standard pattern exists for the establishment of advisory committees although best practice seems to favour—

(1) formulation of a definite plan specifying purposes, criterion for selection of members, and relationship of the committee to the board, the superintendent, and the director of adult education,
(2) approval of the plan by the board of education,
(3) screening and selection of potential committee members by the director of adult education and the superintendent often with the advice of a committee of the board,
(4) approval of members by the board, and
(5) invitation on behalf of the board by its secretary or the superintendent.

This procedure give the advisory committee a dignity and

standing that it could not have if invited directly by the director or the superintendent. If offers least chance for misunderstandings of relationship; it establishes the channel for the committee to make direct recommendations to the board whenever desirable.

Invitations should clearly—

(1) set forth the relationship of the advisory committee to the board of education, to the superintendent, and to the director of adult education,
(2) state the "assignments"—something of the scope and general methods of operation of the committee, and
(3) specify the term of appointment and method of changing membership.

One of the knottiest problems faced by the adult-school administrator is the relationship between the school programme and the activities of nonschool agencies in the community. A survey of post-high-school and adult education in Montclair, New Jersey, 1948 disclosed at least 110 separate groups, exclusive of private colleges and university extension courses, with programmes of an educational and recreational or civic nature. Sixty-eight groups reported a cumulative total of 13,769 participants. Even allowing for duplications, the authors of the survey estimate that from ten to twelve thousand adults in Montclair participate in some group activity of this type. This figure must be compared with the estimated adult population of 29,000.

If this pattern of participation in nonschool agencies is at all typical of other communities in the United States, important questions of policy face the adult school administrator as he contemplates the kinds of relationship and services which should be established in cooperation with these community groups. Spence and Shangold spell out the nature of this problem in the following selection:

> The general relationship between the public school programmes and other organized programmes in the community as far as this study gathered evidence would best be characterized as "polite." The most general situation in communities in which there were numerous agencies conducting programmes was for the director of the school programme to keep some contact, chiefly by personal

visits or telephone calls, with the persons in charge of the other programmes. In some communities students were referred to other agencies where appropriate. Occasionally there was very active cooperation between the school and some particular agency. An outstanding illustration of this kind of cooperation was between the schools and the libraries or the museums.

In the interviews with community leaders some persons expressed concern over the expansion of the public school adult education programme and possible encroachment upon the programmes of other agencies in the community. More often there was recognition of the scope of the job to be accomplished and the realization that the existing resources of all agencies would not be sufficient to accomplish it.

A number of the persons interviewed raised questions which called for broad community consideration of the role of the various agencies in the total programme. The fact that the school was in a position to get state aid for adult education activities tended to give it a certain priority in the administration of the programme. The questions as to whether agencies which had previously been providing certain offerings should seek to have these activities incorporated into the public school programme and what conditions with regard to a broad policy should be met when the school did accept the responsibility for such activities need very careful analysis so as to avoid later disagreements due to a lack of clarity in the preliminary agreements.

The argument for an expansion of services to nonschool groups is well stated by Homer Kempfer in the following selection:

It is as simple as A, B, C!

Let's divide the total adult population into three parts according to desire for further education. Like this:

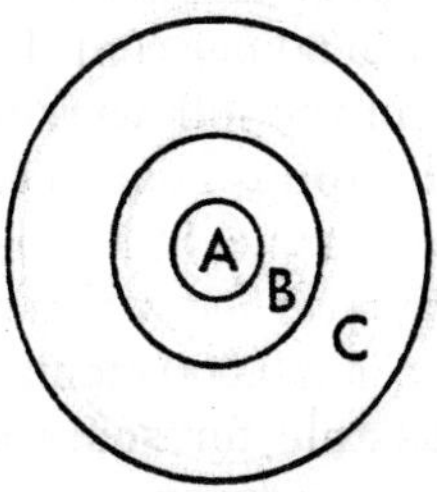

Fig

A is the small fraction who will enroll in an evening school. Their driving ambition will cause them to pull away from all other interesting things they might be doing and join a new group. Their need is so urgent that they will rearrange their schedules and register in your programme. A traditional evening school "offering" with ordinary publicity may enroll one-half to one per cent of the adult population.

A wider list of classes and better publicity may bring in two, five, or even ten per cent of the adult community.

In *B* are those who take some part in the activities of one or more established groups. They may feel a need for continual growth, but they find much of this need can be satisfied by informal interaction groups. Often they feel more comfortable among congenial associates than among strangers in an evening class. While many are interested in further learning, they are not currently in formally organized educational programmes.

Part *C* includes all other adults who do not participate in any organized group. *C* includes many young mothers, many under-educated folk, some old people, non-joiners, stay-at-homes, and others who feel little need or have little opportunity to associate systematically with others for stimulating talk or action. Their stimulation toward learning comes largely from the back fence or front porch, from the local bar, from co-workers or family members returning from work and from the radio, press and movies. Most adult education programmes find ordinary approaches ineffective in reaching people in Part *C* and consequently involve few of them in any systematic programme of growth.

But let us return to Part *B*.

Surveys show that part *B* embraces about half the population—often from 40 to 60 per cent. Here are practically all the leaders and many of the followers in any community. Eighty formally organized groups have been identified in one rural village of 1,000. One county of 800,000 has an estimated minimum of 2,500 groups concerned with some phase of public affairs alone. A community of 100,000 identified 1,100 groups—all meeting on some schedule for some purpose involving interaction of personalities—a primary opportunity for bringing about change in people.

The worth of these groups to the members rests heavily upon the quality of programmes and the richness of human relationships developed. Most groups are led by annually elected lay men and women inexperienced in group leadership and programme building. Many programme chairmen welcome help.

Here is an opportunity for a director of adult education with realistic vision and patience to multiply his area of service several fold. If he knows his community well and will work painstakingly with organization leaders, over a period of years he can build up extensive educational services to community groups. Each group served can retain full autonomy, control its own purposes and programme, and accept only the professional assistance needed. Usually the group continues to meet in its accustomed place on its regular schedule. The school's services can be spread widely and costs of housing, publicity and other overhead can be reduced.

Adult education division of about 100 schools now provide organizations with some or all of these services:

* * *

Training in Discussion Leadership. Through demonstrations, directed observation, analysis of discussion, and guided field practice amateur leaders can grow materially in this major method of democratic adult education.

Officer Training. Job analysis will indicate content for specific groups: A simple, efficient bookkeeping system for treasurers; model minutes, procedures, and practice in secretaries' duties; parliamentary law and discussion leadership for presidents.

Revelation of Programme Resources. After direct mail announcements, programme chairmen and others can preview films, can be acquainted with material and personnel resources of libraries, schools and other community agencies. In one community local authorities on special topics are each introduced for a two minute display of their "wares" while a roomful of club-women evaluate and note any that may interest their groups.

Programme Consultation Services. Individual on-call assistance, in office or field, can help tailor-make one or a series of regular programmes or develop group-sponsored special-study groups. With a file of available experts and materials at hand, programme consultants often can give valuable help. Schenectady, N. Y., has two or three consultants working with 400 groups a year.

* * *

Records and record players, film-strips, films, projectors and projector operator-discussion leaders, charts, study guides and the whole range of effective tools for informal learning can be made available to community groups—often free under a liberal schools-for-community-service policy. Better still can be these when an adult education council arranges for all resources to be tapped through one channel.

* * *

Teachers, discussion leaders, forum moderators, demonstrators, and consultants can be furnished at times and place determined by the groups.

Educational secretaries can be provided to public and qusi-public study commissions. Let the group determine the objectives and outline needs. The secretary can do reference and research work, sift materials, organize, compile and present basic data for group consideration—activities not entirely unlike work done by good teachers.

How is this built up? By starting slowly; by providing helpful service; by publicizing it through mass media, direct mail, meetings of club officers, and by personal contact; by helping groups enrich the educational content of their programmes. As good service is rendered, word gets about; requests for it grow.

Some schools have been providing these services for years. Paid and specialized personnel, by helping leaders inject virile doses of educational vitamins into their programmes, can extend educational services to large segments of the public.

One example of how this type of service operators in a specific community is chosen from many reported by Kempfer and Wright. It deals with the type of services provided by the public schools to community organizations in Schenectady, New York.

In addition to the director of adult education and the regular staff of teachers and leaders, the adult and Extension Division employs a family-life and parent-education specialist, a full-time and a half-time consultant in public-affairs education, 4 part-time specialists assigned by the hour, 2 secretaries, and help as required from the audio-visual office to work with community groups. During 1948-49 services were rendered to approximately 275 different organizations represented by nearly 600 leaders.

Much of this service was advisory and was performed in the field, although after 6 years of operation the office load by telephone and personal call is heavy. Consultative services are provided on content of programmes, educational procedures, educational projects of organizations, resources and personnel. Groups such as the Chamber of Commerce, the Bankers' Association, the Home Bureau, church groups, and social agencies seek counsel and assistance in determining how they may best proceed. This is in addition to the personal guidance services for adults and community clearinghouse functions for information on educational opportunities.

The school provides speakers, forum moderators, discussion leaders, panel and symposium members, and projector operator-discussion leaders from the regular staff and from the special part-time employees in the adult programme. Content areas in public-affairs education included legislative proposals, national problems, international questions, local affairs and intercultural understanding. Family-life problems ran the gamut from budgeting to bed-wetting with some emphasis on human relations. Outside leadership is provided by the resource people in the community and larger region. More than 300 different outside specialists were used last year, some of them several times. Subjects treated by such resource people included UNESCO, race relations, rumor clinics, youth conservation, Japan, atomic energy and numerous others.

Heavy use is made of motion pictures as a foundation for discussion. Movie projectors, a filmstrip projector, filmslide projector, lantern slide projector, portable record player, wire recorder, maps, globes, projection screens, an opaque projector, a portable AM and FM radio, and a set of United Nations Flags are available for use in connection with these programmes,.

Scores of filmstrips, a number of films, and several discussion-recordings were available for use with this equipment. In cooperation with a large electrical manufacturing company, the adult-education programme developed an opinion meter, an electrical device for visually registering composite opinions on dichotomous questions.

During the past 2 years 18 "Guides for Leaders" on "How to plan a programme" have been developed for programme chairmen on such subjects as displaced persons, schools and taxes, UNESCO, civil rights, China, minorities—a national asset, world government, Japan and you and your health. Each guide contains orientation material, programme suggestions, notes on procedures, suggested materials, and a list of suggested resource people who have consented to having their names listed.

Club leaders are trained through a number of specialized short courses in discussion techniques, parliamentary procedure, working with committees, and public speaking; through workshops for programme planners; and through programme aid demonstrations and publications. In addition, a more general leadership-training institute is planned annually. This is usually a 1-day affair beginning about 10 A.M., running through lunch, and ending around mid-afternoon. During this institute round-table discussion are held on conducting business meetings, effectively leading a committee, developing public relations, and conducting group discussions. To provide further help, an attractive booklet has been prepared with suggestions on "wise ways" on planning a meeting, fixing the meeting date, publici-zing the meeting, conducting business sessions, introducing programmes, leading discussion, improving human relations and promoting civic understanding. In each case reference is made to more professional services available from the Adult and Extension Division and other resources in the city.

A monthly bulletin, "Tips and Topics", is mailed free to club leaders. The January 1950 number presented programmes dealing with Federal aid to education, social security, world federalism, the brannan Farm Plan, Taft-Hartley repeal, and Civil Rights Logislation; it listed on one page pertinent filmstrips, films, new personnel resources, new discussion guides, and similar information. The March 1950 issue announced a course in discussion methods, new filmstrips, new pamphlets, and other materials available for club use. Accompanying "Tips and Topics" is "Club Time Calendar," which lists the sequence of programmes presented on Mondays, Wednesdays and Fridays at 11:15 by a clubtime radio news-caster. "Tips for Parents", weekly radio series, discusses home problems. There programmes all tie closely together and help to publicize the activities of clubs and services of the public school.

The above programme services, special programme services available to PTA groups the "Dorp Directory" published by school-sponsored young adult groups for newcomers to Schenectady, participation in the community ambassador project for international understanding, and a forum series are all helpful means of building a sense of community.

A publicity leaflet says *Note These Points:*

1. Programme service is free.
2. You are the boss. We give you help ... *You* make decisions.
3. You can have speakers or discussion leaders from outside your group, or you can use our material to improve member-conducted programmes.
4. You can request a specific programme or general advice from 9 to 1 or 2 to 4 any school day by phoning 6-5248. Our representative will be glad to arrange a conference with you.
5. You can keep informed about new materials and get new ideas by reading "Tips and Topics" (free) each month and by listening to CLUB-TIME on WSNY.

The director of the San Francisco adult programme stated in his report of June 30,1949:

> Any programme of adult education to be worthy of the name must have flexibility. It must be ready to carry on activities of any type which involve a learning situation for adults whether they be organized in terms of the traditional class-room set-up or otherwise. It must be ready to provide its services anywhere and at any time as needed. It must be geared to begin a new activity at a moment's notice and be ready to close one when the need no longer is present. It must be able to furnish teachers experienced in terms of the activity for which they are needed, and because such teachers may not have had the professional educational training which they need it must be ready to give

them the supervision they must have if they are to become good teachers. ... Ours in truly a community enterprise, not just in terms of the breadth of our service or in terms of our meeting the community's needs, but rather because the community had come to think of us whenever it needs a service of an educational nature performed.

One final problem faced by adult-school administrators, among many which might be discussed, deals with the need for providing adequate guidance and counselling services to adults. Klein and Moffit have pointed out "that every man or woman who in response to some urge for self-improvement, seeks the services that an adult-education programme has to offer, is entitled to personal attention sufficient to fit the educational services of that institution to his individual situation".

Results of two surveys are available, one from California and one from New York, the two states that outrank all others in the amount of public money now being spent in support of public-school adult-education programmes. Hence, the services now offered in these states not be considered typical of public-school adult-education elsewhere. Excerpts from the California survey follow:

Findings of The California Survey on Adult Guidance • Services

1. Adult Counselling Personnel

In 70 smaller adult schools the principal does adult counselling assisted by clerks and teachers as requested. Most teachers are limited by time and training to do adequate counselling, although there are many individual exceptions. The large city systems have full-time trained counsellors in nearly all adult centers with regular hours assigned. Where there were Adult Counselling Programmes about 50% of them were coordinated with a total district Guidance Programme.

2. Training and Experience of Adult Counsellors

Most regular counsellors have a M.A. Degree with considerable teaching, counselling, and vocational experience. Others indicated a Bachelor's Degree with considerable experience in Adult Education. A small number had a Doctor's Degree...

3. *Areas of Adult Counselling*

A. *Vocational Counselling*

The following reasons were given for Vocational Counselling in order of preference: (1) Employment and training opportunities, (2) Job preparation, (3) Upgrading, (4) Desire to change occupations, (5) Testing for aptitudes and abilities, (6) Occupational information, (7) Apprentice training.

B. *Educational Counselling*

Educational counselling on evening high school diploma requirements seems to be the starting point and minimum programme for counselling adults in many adult schools. Fifty adult schools indicated that their diploma requirements followed the State Code minimum requirements. Eight had additional requirements, and seven had the same requirements as the day high school. Many small adult schools do not offer credit courses for graduation.

C. *Personal Counselling*

Personal counseling seemed to be limited to the larger systems where phycologists and trained personnel were available, and largely had to do with family problems, self-improvement, personal evaluation, job placement, etc.

4. *Follow-up Plan*

Replies to the questionnaire on this topic indicated that there was considerable interest in this area and desire to know the best methods for follow-up on day school drop-outs and adult school drop-outs. Very few schools indicated any kind of systematic follow-up on adult school attendance or use of the Day School Drop-out List to inform all students over 18 years old of the Adult Education opportunities in their community.

5. *Strong and Weak Points of the Adult Counseling Programme Listed by Administrators*

The best characteristics tabulated in the following order were:

(a) Satisfactory personal interviews, (b) High school diploma requirements, (c) Well-trained counselors, (d)

Educational aspects, (e) Vocational preparations, (f) Testing programme, (g) Occupational information.

The areas which were listed as having the greatest need for improvement were :

(a) Follow-up, (b) How to contact counselees and publicize the programme, (c) More time needed for counselling, (d) Need for trained counsellors, (e) Testing programme, (f) Vocational guidance, (g) Placement.

The following selection, from Spence and Shangold, describes the situation in New York State.

In the interviews regarding adult education needs, the importance of making provision for counseling was frequently stressed. It was pointed out that the field of adult education was new and the range of problems presented by adults was very broad. Many of these were extremely complex and the possible lines of attack were varied. All this stressed the great need for help in providing each adult with the appropriate education.

The counselling task can be thought of as of two types. In the first place there was the problem of finding out through conferences with the persons concerned just what their needs were and devising a programme to meet these particular needs. In the second place there was the individual guidance designed to help the person choose among the particular evening school offerings at the time. A person might wish help, for example, in choosing between the course in dressmaking and that in nutrition, or in choosing from a number of different recreational courses available.

Except for some programmes available for veterans the schools were doing relatively little in the first category. A majority of the schools were making some provisions in the second category. Seventy-six per cent of the schools reported that regular service was available for helping adults choose among the evening school activities.

In general, this counselling was done by the director of adult education and by the evening school principals. A few schools reported that arrangements had been made to have a member of the school's guidance staff available at least one night a week. In such cases presumably more guidance of the first type might be available.

As mentioned above a number of the schools had extensive guidance services available for veterans. The need for careful examination of an individual's qualifications and for the study of possible programmes was recognized. Tests were frequently available and time was provided for extensive personal interviews. Rochester, for example, reported counseling 4515 veterans in 11,096 interviews between 1944 and 1947.

These programmes for veterans were given special financial support from the federal government. When the number of veterans declined and the federal aid was no longer available, the schools did not feel that they could carry the programme in the face of other demands on their local budgets.

The discussions in this chapter point up the growing importance of school-sponsored programmes in the national movement of adult education. Deliberately the emphasis here has been placed upon the issues and policy questions which a growing movement must inevitably face. In spite of its growing pains, however, there are those who predict that the next decade will firmly establish the public school as *the* major agency of adult education in the United States. There is evidence to support this view. No other institution has comparable facilities and resources; no other agency can provide the same potential geographical coverage of the country. Although there are other adult-education agencies supported by public funds, none of them is as close to the taxpayer and therefore as able to convince him of the wisdom of supporting a lifelong educational enterprise.

It may be pointed out that these unique advantages possessed by the public schools have not thus far been adequately capitalized. As is often the case, what the future holds for public-school adult education will depend primarily on the kind of leadership offered by school administrators and boards of education. In turn, the quality of this leadership will depend upon the wider discovery and acceptance of those realities reviewed in Chapter 2, which make expanded programmes of adult education essential whether under public-school auspices or not.

10

Universities And Colleges

Adult Education in universities and colleges is most commonly identified as university extension, and this is the agency that will be the major focus of the materials in this chapter. But many adult-education activities which go on under the auspices of institutions of higher learning are not formally organized as or by university extension. As we shall see in Chapter 10, worker's education programmes sometimes function without benefit of extension sponsorship. The Earlham College programme, described in Chapter 4, is an example of the kind of important adult education that can and often does go on in the small liberal arts college. The evening college, sometimes operated as a "downtown branch" of an accredited four-year institution, may or may not be a full-fleded extension division with field services reaching out of communities in the surrounding area.

A 1948-1949 survey of non-degree programmes in Ohio colleges, for example, disclosed that 25 of 47 colleges and universities in the Ohio College Association reported enrollments totaling 37,707 in non-degree programmes. Eleven of the member colleges provided non-credit courses, most of them apparently geared to the needs of the adults participating.

Another study which reveals possibilities and problems confronting universities and colleges which seek to provide services to community adult-education programmes was made in New York State. About thirty of the institutions of higher learning were involved in the study, and a wide range of existing services was discovered, with opportunities for much-needed expansion and development.

In dealing with college and universities, a distinction should be made between their roles as operating agencies of adult education and their roles as training and research centers. The latter function will be dealt with in Chapter 17. Here we are concerned primarily with problems of organization and administration and with programme trends as these are revealed by materials relating to university extension activities.

University extension, as we know it today in the United States dates back to 1906, when President Charles Van Hise and Extension Director Louis Reber, of the University of Wisconsin, began their now classic effort to make the boundaries of the University campus coterminous with the boundaries of the state of Wisconsin. Prior to that date a number of American universities carried on what we would now call adult-education activities off campus. These activities consisted principally of public lectures, patterned quite literally on the precedents which had been established by English universities. In the earlier period at Yale, at Harvard, and later under President William Rainey Harper at Chicago, these efforts to bring outstanding personalities on the campus to audiences of lay citizens met with wide popular response. The heavily academic content of these lectures and early courses, however, and the failure to adapt offerings and materials to the needs and interests of the lay public led to a gradual decline in popular support and for a time it seemed as though university extension in the United States would lose its force and significance.

The University of Wisconsin idea of extending the resources of the University to meet the needs of citizens groups, whoever they might be and whatever they cared to study, took hold, prospered, and spread. "Between 1906 and 1913, twenty-eight universities organized extension division and twenty-one reorganized departments which during the fifteen lean years had been abandoned or neglected. In 1915, the National University Extension Association was organized and held its first meeting with twenty-two member institutions. By 1950, the membership had expanded to approximately seventy universities and colleges carrying on extension work.

Today, university extension is one of the important adult-education agencies in the United States, encompassing not only classes and lectures but a wide variety of additional services and offerings, including correspondence courses, audio-visual libraries, package libraries, short-term institutes and conferences, residential centers, and community-service activities.

In this chapter we shall attempt to learn something about (1) the unique responsibilities of university extension, the nature of the present programme, and the people who avail themselves of its offerings, (2) the organization and administration of university extension, and (3) programme trends.

The Background

The rationale behind university participation in adult education is well stated in the following excerpts from the report of the President's Commission on Higher Education.

> An expanded programme of adult education must be added to the task of the colleges. This is a vital and immediate need, because the crucial decisions of our time may have to be made in the near future. Education for action that is to be taken, for attitudes that are to be effective, in the next few years must be mainly adult education.
>
> * * *
>
> The continuing education of the adult population is carried on by many agencies, by some as a deliberate aim , by others as a by-product not always recognized as education. But the colleges and universities are the best equipped of all the agencies, from the standpoint of resources, to undertake the major part of the job. Education on a near adult level is their business, and they have, in some measure at least, the necessary teachers and facilities.
>
> The present status of university extension services makes it painfully clear that the colleges and universities do not recognize adult education as their potentially greatest service to democratic society. It is pushed aside as something quite extraneous to the real business of the university.
>
> This attitude is fostered by the necessities of adult education. It takes place outside regular college hours and usually off campus. It makes use of faculty members in other units of the university, and for these men extension or correspondence courses are usually extra chores they agree to

add to their regular teaching load in order to supplement their inadequate incomes. In this frame of mind, many of them candidly get by with a little expenditure of energy as possible.

This state of affairs cannot be permitted to continue. The colleges and universities should elevate adult education to a position of equal importance with any other of their functions. The extension department should be charged with the task of channeling the resources of every teaching unit of the institution into the adult programme.

Adult education, along with undergraduate and graduate education, should become the responsibility of every department or college of the university. It should be the duty of the English faculty or the physics faculty, for instance, to teach English or physics not just to those who come to the campus, but to everyone in the community or the State who wants to learn, or can be persuaded to want to learn, English or physics.

To this degree every college and university should become a "community college". Then extension teaching would be accounted a part of the regular teaching load and would receive its due share of faculty energy and interest.

Granted that this would increase the job of the institution many times over, that it would require more teachers, more manpower in administration, and a very considerable increase in the budget. The principal obstacle to acceptance of the programme, nonetheless, is the limited concept that higher education still holds of its role in a free and democratic society.

It must broaden that concept. It must cease to be campus-bound. It must take the university to people wherever they are to be found and by every available and effective means for the communication of ideas and the stimulation of intellectual curiosity. It must not hold itself above using all the arts of persuasion to attract consumers for the service it offers.

Adult education in the past has been much too inflexible, much too bound by traditional notions of proper educational procedures. Extension activities for years have been stultified by the idea that adult education consists merely of the transmission to mature people of campus courses developed to meet the needs of adolescents.

* * *

A college or university has a triple role to play. (1) It should wherever possible provide a center for evening classes or for any other education activity in its local community. This needs no elaboration. (2) It may prepare teachers and other leaders for effective participation in the community programme. They will be drawn from school and college teachers, professional personnel, housewives, skilled tradesmen, etc. The customary college entrance requirements, and degree requirements, should be forgotten in the case of most of them. (3) It may develop background material to aid all the community programmes in which it cooperates. These might include library collections, educational films, language and other phonograph records, graphic materials and art collections.

As a part of the State-wide plan to be discussed below certain colleges may participate in the actual administration of the programmes in local communities. They may supply part or all of the teaching personnel, stimulate the introduction of new activities, and serve in a consultant capacity to the local teachers and other leaders.

Against this background of general recommendations from the President's Commission, let us now look at the specific objectives of two major institutions, one a state university, the University of California, the other a private institution, the University of Chicago.

The University of California. The educational services of University Extension at the University of California are organized around three primary aims: to help men and women advance professionally; to aid them in meeting their responsibilities as citizens of a democracy; to assist them in their pursuit of intellectual interests.

Although the University of California Extension is increasingly designing its services for the adult who has been to college, most of its classes, correspondence courses, short-term institutes, and lectures are open to any man or woman who seeks some form of higher education but has found it impossible to take up residence at the University.

These aims are amplified by Baldwin M. Woods, Vice-President of the University of California in charge of University Extension, as follows:

> Four of today's realities have effects on the continuing education of adults. All of them affect adults as a group, but it seems

evident that they are of greatest concern to the best educated men, to those who assume major responsibilities in our national life.

First, the child starts, not where his father and mother left off, but completely ignorant. Once I remarked to a philosopher friend of mine concerning my then seven-year-old son, "It's amazing how much a boy has to learn." He replied, "How much he has to learn? He has everything to learn."

Second, the average man has an expectancy of twenty or twenty-five years more than the man of a century ago. The life span in America in 1840 is reported as thirty-nine years. The corresponding figure for the present time is substantially above sixty years. It has been assumed by educators that the increased length of life will permit earlier retirement from active employment and lighter duties for people through wider division of tasks. I doubt whether this will occur. It is possible that the burdens of those having responsibility in the professions will increase and that the period of their service will lengthen. The increasing desire to keep older statesmen in service is evidence of this possibility.

The third reality is the higher speed of technological advance. We recognize how slowly our thinking adapts itself to change and how slowly we adjust. For example, the American city is still fifteen to twenty-five years behind adjustment to the automobile.

Every student leaves college or professional school before even the formal part of his education can be finished. This is the fourth fact of today. What is the best time for a student to leave full-time supervised education? Only recently have we become aware of the impossibility of providing all of the training that a man needs while he is in college, not merely because of the volume of material which would need to be covered, but also, because, no matter how much is done, changes in the profession come so rapidly that any course will prove only a partial foundation. The need for a broad and sound basis in college is thus greater than ever.

Can there be a question in anyone's mind today that the problem of learning is lifelong? What can university extension do about it?

First, in the universities it is becoming clear that the shortcuts to understanding and knowledge which civilization has developed must be utilized to the full—those elements of education which are recognizable as basic and which have wide application in life. In the college of liberal arts, for example, emphasis is being placed upon education rather than training, giving the youth a sense of values, an internal compass as it were, by which to steer his course, rather than a detailed map.

Recently, the educational secretary of the American Medical Association noted that about one third of the practicing physicians of the nation are now attending annually short courses, clinics, and similar educational activities—a partial answer to a statement made several years ago by a professor of the Harward Medical School that, "if the doctors now practicing knew one half of the advances in medicine which the recent graduates know, medical practice would advance overnight by about twenty years."

Business-administration education lists three current problems: how to reduce the severity of the business cycle; how to administer the business enterprises of America so that they occupy an unchallenged position in the world as the best plan civilization has to offer; how to develop and administer international economic policy so that American economic power may be used to the advantage of the entire world while adequately meeting its home needs.

Advanced schools of administration, to which students of exceptional ability and high promise of initiative might be admitted, have been proposed. Results, of course, would not be felt for perhaps twenty years. Hence, "What shall we do for those who carry the problems of today and will carry them during the next twenty years?" We can't wait.

In the field of law, the American Bar Association has recently encouraged leaders in the Bar to undertake through the American Law Institute an educational programme of continuing education of the Bar. Public education has recognized the necessity for continued training of teachers and educational administrators in service and has developed promotion plans and programmes coordinated with educational requirements designed to show professional advancement.

If education is considered as a continuous lifetime process, the student on graduation assumes the direction of his own curriculum. He finds it important to include among his teachers the employer, the professional society, the scientific and professional publication, the public library, and the job itself. It is to be expected that it will require several years for the graduate to recognize the nature of the new approach and to plan adequately his continued development. Some of the elements, and perhaps some of the most important, are those which his university is best able to provide for him. Generally speaking, only an educational institution with multiple facilities can provide services over a broad front.

* * *

University extension has an obligation, it would appear, to bring the best of university thinking and knowledge to provide solutions for these problems. University extension in this field, as in others, will depend upon the sources of knowledge and experience which the university provides and not on an ideology which it develops independently.

With the help of the university the professional man may reasonably face the educational realities of today after graduation from college and professional school. Familiar with a body of knowledge which is sound, he may gain sufficient understanding of civic and personal problems to be "on top of" his job and to retain peace of mind in the midst of change. The additional twenty or twenty-five years he is to live will prove a period of continued development and not one of stalled progress or retrogression. If he is successful in making these adjustments, and if we provide him with usable services to aid in meeting his own curriculum, he may still find time for high achievement, although he starts with everything to learn.

The University of Chicago. University College in its effort to define its goals has stated four broad purposes which it proposes primarily to serve:

1. *To provide the liberal arts of reading, writing, speaking, and listening to the end of a more rational solution of men's problems.* These are complex arts of a fairly high order and determine the extent to which men's individual potentialities grow. It is also true that the extent to which man can develop his society through the communication of ideas is contingent upon his mastery of these basic arts.

2. *To provide adults with an opportunity to increase their*

understanding of the world through the humanities, the social sciences, and the natural sciences. The welfare of a democratic community depends in no small measure upon the general possession of a common body of knowledge. Man today is the inheritor of the achievements in art, music, literature and philosophy. He has his place in a complex political, economic and social order. He lives in a world largely built by science. The history of civilization, as portrayed in the humanities; the growth of our greater social order, as viewed through the social sciences; the modern techniques and methods of scientific development, as indicated in the natural sciences, are therefore essential to an understanding of the world in which the adult lives.

3. *To offer adults an opportunity for improvement of professional competence through advanced training.* The downtown Center recognizes that the greater breadth of experience of mature persons opens new areas of knowledge and brings into sharper focus deficiencies in earlier educational experiences. The offerings at the Downtown Center are therefore geared to provide advance training to the adults who already hold an established place in the political, economic and social life of the community.

4. *To enable adults to discharge those responsibilities which the circumstances of mature life have brought them.* The political and social responsibilities of parenthood, election to public office, voluntary public service and other activities which affect the life of the community create needs among adults for information and assistance which the Downtown Center should provide.

Not much evidence is available as to the characteristics of the public which university extension divisions serve. In 1951, however, a detailed study by Lawrence K. McLaughlin, of the student population in University of California Extension at Los Angeles produced the following results.

The purposes of this study were: (1) to determine certain basic characteristics of students to whom the existing class programme of University of California Extension appeals; and (2) to obtain certain reactions from the students enrolled in University Extension classes which relate to the educational service rendered through the class programme.

The questionnaire survey which was conducted in order to achieve the purposes of the study took place in the Southern

Area of University Extension's statewide operation during a three-week period in the spring semester, 1951. The questionnaire was anonymous and was designed for easy administration during class time. For tabulation purposes, the answers to the questionnaire were recorded by the students on Mark-Sense, I.B.M. cards. The questionnaire was administered *once* to all classes in process during the three-week period. Only those students in attendance at the time of the single administration in each class were included in the studied population. The total number of students reached was 6,560 out of approximately 8,500 to 8,900 students enrolled. The data for the obtained population were categorized and tabulated according to twenty-seven fields of interest and fifteen geographical locations of classes. Forty-four per cent of the students in the obtained population were new to the class programme during the spring semester. About 77 per cent of the students in the obtained population were taking but one class.

The obtained data were of two types, i.e., "census" and "student-reaction". The census data were: age, sex, marital status, formal schooling, income, work status, work hours per week and occupational status. The student-reaction data related to service factors in the class programme, such as: publicity, guidance, new courses needed, plans to take additional courses, location of classes, and scheduling.

The summarized data for the total population revealed the following facts:

1. There were almost twice as many males as females enrolled in the class programme.
2. Over 60 per cent of the reporting students were 35 years of age or under.
3. The ratio of married to single students was about two to one.
4. About 45 per cent of the students held bachelor's degrees or higher degrees.
5. The income bracket, \$3,001-5,000, included a larger percentage (44%) of the reporting students than any other two-thousand-dollar bracket.
6. Over 85 per cent of the reporting students were either employed or self-employed.

7. Seventy-eight per cent of the students reported that they worked a 36-40 hour week or more.
8. The programme of classes in operation during the survey period appealed primarily to the professional or semi-professional person.
9. Sixty-six per cent of the reporting students enrolled in Extension classes because of the perceived benefit the instruction would give them in either their present or future main line of work.
10. The largest number of students reported University Extension class schedules, pamphlets, and leaflets as their first source of information about the classes they were taking.
11. Seventy-two per cent of the reporting students indicated their intention to take additional courses through Extension in the near future.
12. About 40 per cent of the students; indicated that there were courses which they would like to take which are not now offered through University Extension.
13. Eighty-two per cent of the reporting students indicated that they would work toward a degree within extension if it were possible to meet all the requirements in Extension.
14. About three-fourths of the students preferred week-day evenings as the one best time for taking classes in Extension.
15. About one-third of the reporting students felt the need for guidance in planning their educational programmes in University Extension.
16. More reporting students came to the classes they were taking from home rather than from work.
17. Eighteen per cent of the reporting students rated the location of the classes there were taking as inconvenient.

From these data, the administrative staff in University Extension at UCLA has been able to modify offerings and administrative practices so as to serve more effectively the needs of the population that attends University Extension classes. Similar studies in other extension divisions and more inclusive investigations of other branches of extension divisions would enable us to generalize more accurately than is now possible about the characteristics of the additional thousands throughout the country who participate in extension activities.

The Organization and Administration of University Extension

A special committee of the National University Extension Association published a preliminary report on adult education in the modern university in which an answer was attempted to the question: "How is adult education administered within the university?" The difficulties facing one who attempts generalization about this question are underscored by the following excerpt from that report.

In the original questionnaire sent out by the committee, the seventh question dealt with the manner in which adult education is administered by the colleges and universities belonging to the National University Extension Association. An examination of the replies indicates wide variation in the manner in which extension work is conducted among the constituent members of the association.

One should mention first those extension divisions which as yet are not well organized and where the extension work is carried on by many different agencies and schools. Often this situation exists in the universities and colleges in which an extension programme has been in operation only a short time. Most of the directors responsible for extension in these institutions are of the opinion that action should be taken to place all extension and adult education under the direction of the extension office.

Some older universities, such as Iowa; report that the responsibility for a given extension project is assigned to the unit best qualified to carry it on. Much of this work is done by the extension unit; some of it is not. According to the report of the director at Iowa, the system works well and should not be changed. At Washington State, the library, the registrar's office the publications office and many of the academic departments have interests and outlets in the community which they serve with the help of the extension division, which acts as a clearing house.

* * *

In the National University Extension Association there are a considerable number of privately endowed institutions, such as Chicago, Harvard, Columbia and to some extent, the

University of Pennsylvania. These institutions vary in their conception of what should be done in the field of adult education, and their extension departments—if such they can be called—exist for the purpose of serving a quite specialized need.

At Harvard, a Commission on Extension Courses offers twenty-nine late afternoon and evening classes. In addition, it assists the Massachusetts Departments of Education in its adult education programme by permitting professors to teach classes and by making rooms available on the Harvard campus. Pennsylvania's extension programme is limited in scope and practically all of it consists of credit courses. Chicago has a varied programme of extension activities. Most are channeled through University College which conducts classes in a downtown center and administers the Great Books Programme and the Correspondence Study Department.

At Columbia, the School of General Studies has taken the place of the Extension Division and offers a credit programme leading to a Bachelor of Arts degree. It seems that the term "extension" ceased to be descriptive since Columbia gave up its extramural centers and its correspondence courses. Columbia offers comparatively little adult education as the term is used in the questionnaire. It offers noncredit service courses to students seeking some special skill or trying to advance in their own fields.

* * *

In state universities and land-grant colleges such as Pennsylvania State, North Carolina, Wisconsin, Minnesota, Michigan, Nebraska, California, Virginia, Rutgers and several others in which the extension division is well established and its functions are well defined and understood by the administration and faculty, most off-campus work is carried on through the extension division. In every case, however, there are a few adult education activities outside of extension.

By far the majority of directors expressed themselves as not at all alarmed about this situation. In fact, one director says that though certain activities in his institution should really be placed under his direction, he "hopes to heaven" they will not be as he and his staff are now too busy to take on additional duties. It is pointed out by several directors that all activities of an adult education nature will eventually replaced in extension. They expressed themselves as completely unworried about the situation and are lending their facilities to other organizations carrying on adult education programmes within their universities.

There are some institutions, such as Indiana University, in which reorganization has recently been made. Indiana was not placed in the category described in the foregoing paragraph because of its recent reorganization. The Division of Education and Public Services of Indiana, which came into existence a few years ago, has by order of the administration taken over practically all the adult education activities of that institution. There are some other newer and smaller universities such as Wyoming in which the extension division was made an administrative agency through which all departments and colleges are authorized to carry on the programme to serve the people of the state. This is an instance in which a young university has endeavoured to start its extension division properly.

One of the authors has had the opportunity of making a special study of organizational and administrative problems in three university extension services: the Pennsylvania State College, the University of Chicago and the University of California. All three of these institutions favour and reflect a vertical form of extension organization—that is, unification of the administration of most of the adult education functions of the institution (except agricultural extension) under the extension division. A few descriptive paragraphs about each of these institutions may be useful.

The Pennsylvania State College. The administrative officer responsible for the university extension of the Pennsylvania State College is designated as Assistant to the President in Charge of Extension. Counselling the President is an Advisory Committee on Extension Services, composed of the Assistant to the President in Charge of Extension and the Deans of the undergraduate schools. Counselling the Assistant to the President in Charge of Extension is an Administrative Committee on Extension Services, made up of the undergraduate-school extension directors. Virtually every undergraduate-school Dean has an assistant in charge of extension for his school. This assistant is generally called a director of extension and has a staff of full-time and part-time supervisors. These school extension divisions are responsible in consultation with the various resident department heads of the school for the programmes offered through extension. They help to maintain high standards of instruction, being responsible for the approval, academic rank, teaching load and supervision of the teachers; the subject matter taught; the textbooks, course outlines, syllabi, and necessary instructional equipment; and in some instances the preparation of examinations.

To aid the Assistant to the President in Charge of Extension to coordinate the work of these school extension divisions, the Central Extension Organization has been set up under an Executive Director responsible to him. There are three main divisions to this central staff organization: the Division of Instruction, the Division of Community Colleges and the Division of Business and Records. The Division of Instruction includes formal class work as well as informal study, correspondence study, instructional aids and management training. The Division of Community College has responsibility for the administration of twelve extension centers, four of which offer full freshman and sophomore programmes carrying college credit and six of which offer full-time technical curriculums. Evening technical work is offered in fifteen centers.

For administrative purposes the state is divided into eleven geographic areas. Each has an administrative head who is responsible for the development, organization and operation of all general extension activities in its area. The programme offered in each area depends upon the need and upon the nature of the requests which have been made by communities in that area. This area organization insures complete coverage of the state and an administrative field staff which can both report needs from the field and promote wider use of campus resources throughout the state.

Staff communication is aided by statewide *Extension News* and by periodic staff meetings attended by area officers. Divisional staff members in the Central Extension Organization also keep in touch with area officers by frequent field trips. The area administrative officers have considerable autonomy and freedom to develop programmes which will meet the needs of their areas most effectively. Annual reports from each of the areas keep the Central Extension Organization and the school extension division acquainted with problems and trends within the areas. Staff communication is further aided by a staff bulletin, issued twice a month to some six hundred members of the extension and college staff.

Policy decisions are explored in periodic meetings of divisional heads, the Executive Director and the Assistant to the President. Questions involving relationship with the undergraduate schools are normally explored by the Administrative Committee on Extension Services. Policies requiring action by the Board of Trustees are normally explored first by the President's Advisory Committee on Extension Services. In addition, practically all the departments and section in the Division of Instruction utilize the services of advisory committees. Moreover, every area officer has an advisory committee composed of outstanding citizens in the communities concerned.

University of Chicago. The administrative unit through which the University of Chicago operates its extension services is known as University College and the Dean of the College reports directly to the president of the University. Administratively, the College functions through a Downtown Center, a Home Study Department and the Radio Office. The heads of the Home Study Department and the Radio Office report to the Dean of University College, but that officer himself administers the programme in the Downtown Center with a staff to which he delegates certain specialized responsibilities.

The activities at the Downtown Center include regular courses, special programmes, lectures, seminars and general educational services. Offices of the Dean of University College and the members of his administrative staff for the Downtown Center are located in the heart of the Loop district. Unlike the administrative pattern in operation at both Pennsylvania State College and California, that of University College permits a comparatively small and compact staff with fewer communication problems and with coordination made possible through the Dean of the College himself. A staff officer in charge of student services, known as the Dean of Students for University College, is administratively responsible both to the

Dean of the College and the Dean of Students on campus. This ensures that personnel policies, although adjusted to the needs of adult students, are nevertheless developed within the framework of campus policy.

University of California. The extension division at the university of California is called University Extension. Its head is vice-President—University Extension. He reports directly to the president of the university and has statewide responsibility for the administration of all extension programmes of the University other than that of the college of Agriculture. Both the President of the University and the Vice-president—University Extension call upon the Extension Advisory Board which represents the faculties at Berkeley, Los Angeles and Santa Barbara, to review policies and give advice on the development of extension services.

The central staff organization within University Extension is designed (1) to assist the Vice-President in the administration of statewide programmes and advise him on statewide policies, and (2) to facilitate administration of extension activities within the three areas into which the state is divided. Collectively this groups becomes a Programme Committee, meeting two days each month for the consideration of statewide and area problems. Statewide policy is formulated by the Vice-President on the basis of these discussions.

The members of this Programme Committee are, in addition to the Vice-President, an associate Director with primary responsibility for the northern-area activities, with headquarters at Berkeley, an Associate Director with primary responsibility for southern-area activities, with headquarters at Los Angeles, Assistant Directors at Berkeley and Los Angeles, and an Assistant Director with primary responsibility for area activities centering on the Santa Barbara campus of the University. The Business Managers for the Northern and Southern Areas are also members of this committee. Staff functions of other administrative officers in University Extension are specialized according to the nature of the activity for which they are responsible.

In all departments except correspondence study, duplicate departments are in operation at Berkeley and Los Angeles. Similar functions are handled by a smaller staff at Santa

Barbara. The correspondence Study Department operates through a single office and staff in Berkeley. Film libraries are in operation at both Berkeley and Los Angeles. Major departments deal with class organization and conferences and special activities.

As at Pensylvania State College, staff communication problems arise not only among the three areas into which the state is divided but also among departments within each area. The California pattern differs from the one at State College in that it is more decentralized and consequently more varied structurally within the areas. Intra-area communication among department heads is accomplished primarily through periodic staff meetings. Communication among areas depends primarily upon intercampus visits, the meetings of the Programme Committee, and the *Director's Letter,* issued periodically to all instructors and staff members of University Extension.

Significance of These Three Patterns. Here are a few generalizations about the organizations of university extension in these three institutions:

1. The importance of extramural services within the modern university, whether private or state-supported, is indicated by the fact that in all three institutions the administrative officer in charge of extension does have direct access to the president's office and is involved in the policy-making group which advises the president on university-wide policies and decisions.
2. Statewide programmes, as represented at Pennsylvania State and California, and as compared with the more concentrated services provided by the University of Chicago, require a rather elaborate administrative framework, the complexity of which seems to increase in direct proportion to the quantity, variety and geographic area over which the services are rendered.
3. Although the extension directors in the three institutions have high status within the university administration, the magnitude and complexity of the operations in which each is engaged require more than physical access not only to the president's office but to administrative faculty committees, which are often concerned only peripherally with operational problems and policy questions affecting administration of university extension. Although

theoretically the advisory-committee pattern at State College and California is intended to improve the administration's understanding of extension problems, the infrequency of meetings and the sheer lack of time prevent adequate exploration of extension problems.

In theory, extension directors obtain instructors of extension courses from campus faculties. In practice, at least two factors cause extension directors to acquire many instructors from other sources. First practitioners from business, industry and the professions are often a good influence in the extension teaching force. Secondly, members of campus faculties are often too busy or simply disinclined to do extension teaching. As a result of both these factors, members of the campus faculties of the University of California, for example, make up only about 20 per cent of the total extension teaching force.

Reference has already been made to the use of an advisory committee composed of faculty representatives as an instrument for maintaining relationships between campus faculties and extension divisions. In addition, all three of the institutions cooperating in the Carnegie study regularly obtain the approval of the appropriate academic department for the offering of both noncredit and credit courses, and approval of extension instructors who are not members of the campus faculties. At Pennsylvania State College, as has already been indicated, each undergraduate school has a director and supervisory staff with responsibility for extension work in that field of knowledge. At Chicago, a programme such as the one for executives is worked out cooperatively between the Dean of University College and the School of Business on campus. At California, the relationship with academic departments is maintained chiefly through appointment of liaison officers in extension, who simultaneously carry academic status and usually some teaching responsibilities in the department which they represent. These officers are largely responsible for organizing and supervising courses and for nominating and obtaining departmental approval of instructors.

Indiana University has come to the conclusion that cooperation between members of the campus faculties and members of the extension division must be founded on mutual respect, which, in turn, must be based not only on active association but also on equality in rank and salary. Accordingly, it is seeking joint appointments, by both extension and the appropriate campus department, for all full-time extension administrative, teaching, and staff (for example, audio-visual department) employees, with rank and salary equal to rank and salary attached to equivalent position in the campus department or administration. This policy is the result of a recommendation which emanated from a university survey. It has now been carried through for about one third of the extension employees at Indiana. The University of Michigan also favour joint appointments.

Our three institutions show wide variation in their policies regarding graduate credit for extension study. At Chicago it is theoretically possible to earn a master's degree in any of the University's divisions through extension study alone. In practice a full list of courses for the master's degree is regularly offered only in business administration, education and social work. Two full curriculums for the Master of Business Administration degree are offered, and most extension students who are working for a master's degree are doing so in business administration. At California limited graduate credit is allowed for extension study when certain conditions set by the Graduate Council are met. Pennsylvania State College once had a rather liberal policy on graduate credit for extension study, experienced some difficulties and virtually dropped the plan, and is now beginning cautiously to redevelop its programme.

In view of Chicago's policy and Clark's study, which shows that 21 of 56 universities queried permit 25 per cent or more of the work for the master's degree to be earned through extension study, a more general shift of policy in support of graduate work in extension may be expected. The probable solution to this problem is already in the making. A number of extension divisions are developing strong programmes of graduate work in fields of study in which conditions are peculiar favourable. Thus Chicago has developed two programmes for the Master of Business Administration degree and Illinois one for the master of Public Administration degree. Pennsylvania State College and the University of Virginia are developing similar work in scientific fields in cooperation with industrial and governmental-enterprises where advanced research under the direction of distinguished scientists is in progress.

With the possible exception of legislative representatives, university extension administrators, more than any other university staff members, occupy positions of high visibility as far as the university's public is concerned. They are frequently called upon to interpret and explain university policies, many of which were designed for campus administration and the protection of campus standards. The attempt to apply these literally to extramural work frequently causes difficulty for the administrator and frustration for the off-campus public. Resistance to change in the direction of liberalizing campus requirements and extending service programmes to the general public can often be traced to a lack of information about what extension is trying to accomplish and the educational results already achieved. Such reasoning brings us back once again to the responsibility of every extension administrator for giving high priority to the job of interpreting and explaining the university's extramural programme to its regular faculty and administrative officers. Until this challenge is met effectively the concept which the late President Van Hise of the University of Wisconsin first expressed in his view of extension as the instrument for making the boundaries of the campus coterminous with the boundaries of the state cannot flourish elsewhere.

Just as the extension administrator must frequently react to or resist pressures from within the university to modify his administrative policies, so must he be a public-reactions expert in his negotiations and relationship with agencies of adult education outside the university, including public schools, libraries, professional societies, community organizations, and civic agencies. The use of advisory citizens' committees in the Pennsylvania State College community centers, the offerings in the field of chemistry as worked out by the University of Chicago and the Chicago Chapter of the American Chemical Society, and the community representative system in operation in California all represent attempts to provide a bridge between the extension administration and the public it seeks to serve.

The development of professional and specialized courses in all three of the extension division described here illustrates how this kind of cooperative relationship grows. Whether a demand is for a continuing educational programme for the bar, a postgraduate programme for business executives, or a short-term institute for members of the Steel Workers' Union, it is obvious that cooperative relationships have to be set up with the agencies representing the professional or lay group seeking help. Indeed, the practice of offering extension courses and institutes in cooperation with the organization which wants the service appears to be replacing the practice of simply offering services for the general public. It may be argued that university extension has done its most effective work as a servant to and cooperator with such groups, usually occupational in nature. Extension has been less universally successful in its relationships with total communities in themselves heterogeneous but on common ground in their search for university help in the development of community-improvement programmes. The area administrators in the Pennsylvania State College extension programme and the community representatives in the California pattern can become the channel through which this kind of consultant help can be given.

The relationship between the extension programme of the state university and the extension programmes of state colleges, teacher' colleges, and other private institutions of higher learning is still to be defined in detail. In the same category would be relationships between the state university and the adult-education programmes junior colleges and public schools.

The pattern of administrative cooperation worked out in any given state or community will depend, of course, upon local conditions, but, in general, it would seem to be reasonable in the light of experience to date to state as a guiding principle that where local resources are fairly well developed, the role of the university through its extension division is to supplement and strengthen the programmes of existing agencies. It can certainly be argued that any university worthy of the name will command resources in teachers, research facilities, and equipment which no other agency of adult education can conveniently or economically reproduce. If these resources can constitute the potential contribution which the university offers to the improvement of existing adult-education programmes in the communities which it serves, then certainly we can expect that on this two-way street of relationships the local agencies of adult education in return will provide not only the continuing support which every university needs but also the laboratories for field observation and experimentation and the facilities for the extension of public knowledge which will at least partially condition the university's growth.

Thus far, all of California's community representatives are administrators of the public-school adult-education programmes in their localities, and some of them also have responsibilities in the local junior-college adult-education programmes. By virtue of their appointment as community representatives of University Extension, they are in a position to strengthen their local adult-education programmes with extension services. University Extension goes into their communities only on their invitation. Thus possible competition and duplication are replaced by cooperation. This California plan will be of interest to many extension division as they face the inevitable growth of public-school and local college adult-education programmes.

Programme Trends

There are important new trends and targets in university extension work which deserve more than the honourable mention which it is possible to give within the limits of this chapter. There is, for example, the growing recognition of the need for postgraduate extension training in the professions. The impossibility of providing in university curriculums all the training that professional people will need is clearly apparent, and the offerings which university extension divisions have developed in cooperation with professional groups constitute in themselves an exciting chapter in the history of the movement. Law, medicine, dentistry, business, engineering and education are among the professional groups now being served. The growing practice of planning short but intensive institutes and conferences, in which, through informal study and discussion, professional and civic groups utilize the expert resources of the university staff, deserves specials mention. The work of the university of North Carolina's Bureau of Research Interpretation has demonstrated how a university can aid in bringing research and education into closer correspondence with the needs of people.

Two of these programme trends have been selected for

more than passing mention. In the report on *Adult Education in the Modern University* already referred to, extension directors were asked to state their aspirations or plans for adult-education development. The largest response to any single item for improving and extending methods of services was the expressed hope of thirteen directors for a resident center for continuation study. This demand is, of course, a tribute to the phenomenal success of the Center of for Continuation Study at the University of Minnesota. In 1951, a Center for Continuing Education opened at Michigan State College in East Lansing. This Center, made possible through a grant from Kellogg Foundation, has the most extensive facilities for residential institutes and conferences now available in any university.

Some indication of what extension division can do when such facilities are available is apparent from the following description. by Julius M. Nolte, of the work of the University Minnesota center.

The center for Continuation Study of the University of Minnesota, recently has finished its twelfth year of operation. Physically, the Center is a three-story fireproof brick building on the main campus. It is a residence college, with lounge library, chapel, seminar and class rooms, dining room and dormitory (bedroom space for 78 persons). There is a heated garage in connection. To this building individuals and groups repair for continuation study in specialized departments of knowledge. When they come as individuals, they make arrangements in advance for study under the direction of appropriate faculty members. When they come as groups, the University conducts for them a course responsive to their needs. In all cases, the registrants pay a tuition fee based on the cost of the instruction. They also pay for lodging and meals.

In its first 12½ years, the new department conducted 812 "schools" or courses for a total of 40,252 persons. The courses varied in length from two days to a month, with the average seven days. The registrants have come from all parts of the United States. Most of them have been residents of Minnesota (31,120), but about a fourth have come from other states (8,708). In all, the census of Center enrollees includes representatives from 48 states, from the District of Columbia, from six Canadian provinces, and from several other foreign countries. Among the enrollees, men have predominated: there have been 24,773 men and 15,479 women. Of the 40,252 registrants, 29,193 have had college training; 9,358 have baccsalaureate degrees, and 12,636 have advanced or professional degrees.

The subject-matter of the courses offered has been varied indeed. Strange to relate, the ministerial profession, from which came the idea for the venture, has not been among the frequent users of the building. There have been, however, many courses for educators, ranging in content from problems of revising elementary and secondary-school curriculums to improvement in the methods of preparing and selecting teachers. There have been many courses for physicians and surgeons and for persons working in hospitals and institutions associated with the medical profession. There have been many courses for public employees in position which, because of direct impact of their duties upon the public welfare, have decidedly professional qualifications. There have been a number of courses for engineers, civil, mechanical and mining. There have been several courses for social-welfare workers, in both public and private agencies. There have been courses for dentists, pharmacists, for lawyers. And there have been some courses which might be classed as civic or cultural, which although they have been conducted upon a professional level, have been attended by many who took them less from a professional interest than from the equally keen interest of the enlightened amateur: courses in government, child health and guidance, photography, Scandinavian culture, creative writing. Of the total of 812 courses, approximately 70 per cent have been given for professional persons actively performing or practicing in the professional occupations studied in the courses. If a housewife can be considered as a professional in her attitude toward the problems of her home, or a citizen professional in his attitude toward the problems of government, this percentage will be larger. The age distribution of the enrollees indicates that the appeal of the Center is strongest for those of middle age, and those approaching or at the peak of their powers. The arithmetical average age is about forty-five years; the median average age is nearly forty-three years.

Satistically, the record of the Center is not impressive. After all, 40,252 persons are not many when set beside the multitudes who throng to adult-education centers of various kinds throughout this country. But when it is remembered that the Center is in a real sense the graduate school of the adult-education movement, and that its registrants are a selected professional class with little interest in entertainment and with no further interest in academic or professional degrees, the fact that in 12½ years some forty thousand successful and competent persons have visited the Center in order to receive expert guidance is impressive. It abundantly justifies the foresight of President Coffman in assuming that a university department devoted to the continuing educational needs of already well-educated persons would be patronized, and it is significant of the direction which our education is likely to take.

A second major programme trend has developed in the general area of community service and community development. The tendency to regard the community as a direct client of university extension is relatively new. The traditional practice has been to provide programmes which will meet the needs and interests of individual adults or of groups of adults but to give little emphasis to activities designed to help communities help themselves in action programmes leading to the solution of community problems. There are many reasons, not all of them historical, which explain this reluctance to enter the community-development field. In a study of university extension supported by a grant from the Carnegie Corporation, one of the staff committees of the three cooperating institutions (Chicago, Pennsylvania State and California) which participated in the study devoted special attention to the field of community service.

Speaking of the tendency of most universities to limit community service to bringing leaders to the campus for training and information rather than working with local leaders in their own communities on the problems peculiar to that community, the committee presented the following hypothesis.

There are a number of reasons why things stand thus at so many institutions. Some of these reasons are concerned with tradition and inertia. Teaching, particularly at the university level, has emphasized the giving of information. The man whose gizzard is chock full of facts and who scratches diligently for more facts is honoured; the practitioner is not. Informational courses have been at a premium, skill courses at a discount. To talk learnedly about juvenile delinquency in a class or institute on the campus is easy compared to helping John doe and Rachel Roe do something about juvenile delinquency in the town of Crossroads. There the familiarity with the mechanisms of small communities, leg work, an immunity to chicken croquettes and mashed potatoes, and maybe a good hand at poker or a guitar. Indeed we may well ask ourselves whether we know enough about human relations and community work to take on this responsibility. Where would you look for a community-development specialist if you needed one tomorrow?

Classes and institutes in the sanctuary of the campus are also safer than an action programme in Crossroads. In fact, one of our three institutions has a regulation that "No formal action may be taken, or resolutions or recommendations presented or adopted at any session" of its extension institutes.

And they are also a good deal cheaper. There isn't a community-development programme in the country, that we know, of that comes anywhere near paying for itself. Industry knows that special-interest training can pay off in results (*e.g.* Chicago's Harvester Project). Communities either haven't found this out, or don't really want an action programme, or can't pay the bill. This fact alone makes a tough problem for an extension director whose division must be largely self-supporting. Penn State has done what it has in community development despite the fact that the entire extension division receives only 14% of its budget from the parent institution.

One other reason is our tendency to see community development as the one shot service that many of our other extension services are. A community asks for some information, or a study, or a training course, may be gets it, and that's all. Whereas successful community development is much more likely to be a long, slow process that partakes of the consultant relationship.

What will effective programmes of community development look life? We are beginning to see some answers to this question in the descriptions of successful programmes which are now commencing to appear. At this point we could stand more reports and good deal more research in this young and growing area of extension service.

Meanwhile, by way of summary, we shall restate here some

of the ideas and procedures we've run across in our examination of our three institutions and the literatures of community development. Extension divisions can help citizens improve the communities they live in by:

1. Setting up a special service within the extension division to handle community development, if this seems wise. It has been found desirable by the universities of Indiana, Michigan, Montana, Nebraska, Oklahoma A. and M., Purdue, Virginia, Wisconsin and Wyoming.
2. Establishing a field organization to serve as a means of community-university communication. California, Indiana, Penn State, Wisconsin and other extension division have experimented with different patterns of field organizations.
3. Selecting well-qualified community representatives.
4. Appointing one or more competent travelling specialists in community development, such as those employed by the universities of Indiana, Michigan, Montana, Nebraska, Penn State, Purdue, Virginia and Wisconsin.
5. Encouraging the formation of community councils. Indiana and Michigan have done much of this.
6. Using a coordinated rather than a piecemeal approach to problems of community development... Penn State believes it is wise to set up an all-university committee, representative of the several colleges, whose function it is to guide community development projects. Establishment of such a committee can lead to better understanding within the institution of the objectives of the community-development programme, place wider resources at the disposal of the programme, and enable the institution to present a unified approach when working in a community.
7. Finding out about and soliciting the cooperation of other agencies which are carrying on programmes of adult education in the community. Penn state emphasizes the importance of this point.
8. Employing suitable means to bring the service to the attention of communities. A community news letter is used for this purpose by the universities of Indiana, Michigan, Nebraska, Purdue, Virginia, Wisconsin and Wyoming.
9. Publishing the results of their experience as guides to

the rest of us as has been done by the universities of New Mexico and Virginia.

We can add to this list, as Points 10-17, some suggestions from the University of Virginia:

10. Awakening the individual to a realization of his importance disturbing his indifference or complacence, and stimulating him to play the active role which democracy demands of its citizens.
11. Helping the community to discover and train potential leadership and to use, to the best advantage, official, professional and "hereditary" leadership which already holds an accepted place in its life.
12. Helping groups of citizens, their officials and professional workers in agencies set up to serve them, to analyze community resources in relation to needs and aspirations, and to determine effective programmes of action growing out of such study.
13. Supplying factual information, materials for study, and suggestions for procedure to individuals, committees, study groups, organizations or agencies concerned in community development programmes.
14. Providing leadership from its own staff or drawn from various departments of the University of other agencies for community study in relation to specific needs.
15. Putting citizens in touch with research agencies and helping them to adapt the materials of research to their own needs or to translate them into language and form meaningful to the average person.
16. Bringing problems or needs of communities to the attention of research or service agencies, thus setting in motion the two-way process that can assure the submitting of problems to scientific study and the application of results of research to living.
17. Reaffirming and demonstrating to educators and professional workers, as well as to a citizens in their communities, that adult education must be a two-way process and that, to the degree it achieves this, it becomes effective as a way of helping communities to help themselves through the efforts of their own citizens.

Any college or university which seriously wants to help the citizens of its constituency to improve the communities they live in should consider a community-development service as a means of doing so. There is little evidence that "university extension as usual" makes any dent in community problems. There is considerable evidence that through *this* kind of extension service, community improvement can begin *now*.

Point 7 in the list above stresses the importance of soliciting the cooperation of other agencies which are carrying on programmes of adult education in the community. This point deserves further consideration since it raises the whole question of what should be the relationship between university-sponsored adult-education activities and those initiated by local public and private agencies. One way of meeting this problem is outlined in the following selection by Paul Sheats:

What should be the relationship between university-sponsored adult-education activities and those initiated by local public and private agencies? A carefully thought-out answer to this question is fundamental in the long-range development of adult-education services in the United States. It would seem to this writer that in spite of temporary setbacks in some sections of the country, the trend toward state support of public adult schools is fairly well established. The patterns of state support now operative in California, New York, Pennsylvania and Wisconsin may differ in detail, but there seems no disposition to question the assumption which underlies the commitment in each of these states to financial support of adult education as an integral part of the public education system of the state. In California, state support this year will make possible a programme serving about one million citizens. Approximately one hundred fifty adult-education administrators will be at work in California communities, inventorying community needs, developing classes, organizing forums, and conducting institutes and training programmes. If, within the next ten years, these procedures become typical in even the more populous states, university-extension divisions which now operate extensive off-campus programmes may find the experience of the University of California helpful.

Operating on what might be called a theory of abundance rather than scarcity as applied to adult education, University of California Extension... under the directorship of Baldwin M. Woods, has encouraged in every possible way the development of the local adult school programmes. The pattern has been one of cooperation in a common effort to meet community needs more fully without fear by either party that the saturation point in adult education will shortly be reached.

This co-operation has been implemented officially at two levels in the following ways: first, at the state level, by join representation of University Extension and public-school adult-education directors on a State Advisory Committee on adult Education, appointed jointly by the president of the University and the state superintendent of public instruction; second, at the community level by appointment of certain directors of public-school adult education as resident representatives of University Extension in that school district. In addition there is the informal and unofficial type of co-operative relationship which develops out of shared responsibilities among University Extension staff members and public adult school officers in the programmes of state adult-education associations, of which there are three major ones in the state at the present time.

A further word about implementation at the community level may be helpful. There are at present six communities in the state in which this type of relationship has been formalized by University appointment of the local director of adult education or a staff member named by him as resident extension representative. In no two communities is the administrative pattern exactly alike, but in general the arrangement is as follows: a request for such an appointment is usually initiated by the superintendent of schools, who recommends that his director of adult as extension representative in the area. In some instances, appointment implies sharing with the school district in the compensation of the local representative; in other instances, financial support is provided by the University through the employment of additional administrative or clerical staff...

The mechanics of these co-operative arrangements are perhaps less important than the operating results. In effect, the arrangements mean that University Extension recognizes the primary responsibility of the local adult school staff for identifying local community needs. Many of these needs can be met adequately and most efficiently by the provision of free services to adults under the state system of public support. Other needs, parti-cularly those of college and university graduates for refresher work and advanced professional training, can best be met by tapping the resources of the University through Extension. The important point is that the pattern outlined here does operate to eliminate competition and overlapping of function as between University Extension and the local adult school. Major responsibility for the development of well-rounded community programme of adult education rests where it belongs—in the hands of the local adult school adminisrator. In practice, in California, the arrangement has operated to extend extension services to the people of the communities in which these resident represen-tatives are appointed, particularly on those levels and in those areas where University resources can be used to best advantage.

The whole problem of how relationships among adult-education agencies of this country can be worked out in the best interests of a well-rounded programme of community adult education will be given further attention in Chapter 13, on programmes planning and coordination of community resources.

Historically and currently, as we have seen, universities and colleges have played a major role in the developing and growing adult-education movement in the United States. Extension divisions, evening colleges, municipal universities, and small liberal arts colleges are in part at least meeting the challenge laid down by the President's Commission on Higher Education. The problems of adjusting to the widely varying needs of the mature adult policies formulated primarily with full-time resident students in mind are not easily solved. Nor is it a simple matter, within the limited resources of these institutions of higher learning, to add to the acknowledged responsibilities of on-campus instruction and research the larger obligation of public service inherent in any meaningful commitment to adult education.

On the other hand, both for their own salvation and the common good, the need of the wider spread of existing knowledge and maximal use of university and college resources in improving citizen competency cannot and will not be ignored. The Adult Education Association of the U.S.A. can perform no more important service to the adult-education movement than to focus public attention, as it is now doing in its efforts to develop area organizations, upon the key role which the universities and colleges must play in the years ahead.

11

Voluntary Agencies

If one looks about him in whatever community one may be, one of the outstanding features will be the number of organizations which help to make up the life of that community. Observers of America have, for more than a century, been moved to comment upon the great number of organizations to which men, women and children belong. We are supposed to be a nation of joiners; if there is anything that needs to be done or undone, we form an organization and recruit members.

To say that our nation is made up of a vast array of organizations is both an understatement and an overstatement. On the one hand, it does not include the web of informal organizations, about which we shall have more to say later. On the other hand, it fails to reveal the large segment of our population which belongs to no one of these name organizations. Community studies seldom show less than 25 per cent in this group of nonmembers, and the percentage may run as high as 60.

Regardless of its exact scope, the organizational network is a vital part of our concept of adult education. With a clearer understanding on the part of the members of the groups and of the leaders of adult education regarding ways of cooperating, these organizations will play an even more significant part. A few communities have experimented sufficiently with the possibilities of programme service to establish the activities of groups beyond doubt as a vital part of the community educational programme for a democracy.

Consider what a resource this organizational network provides. Here is a series of ongoing activities, many of which are directly educational in nature and virtually all of which have some educational aspects, if we use the term in the broad sense of helping people learn how to do better something they want to do. If in some way assistance can be given to the leaders of these group activities through help on planning programmes, getting pamphlets, films and resource persons, improving the methods used, and beginning to evaluate results, the groups will have more satisfaction because it will have done a better job and the community will benefit from the improved quality of learning on the part of a significant number of its members. This kind of educational assistance to organized groups is known as programme service and is one of the significant developments in adult education. This service may be provided by a library, the public schools, a college, or some other resource group which can make professional help available. The Schenectady programme provided through the public schools is described in Chapter 7.

The readiness of groups for help of this kind has been dramatized in *Adult Leadership* through the story of a programme chairman which typifies the situation faced by most such persons. They have no experience upon which to draw and they tend to repeat many of the errors of their predecessors.

Dan and Gretchen Matthews had joined the Moorestown Current Affairs Club five years ago when their friends, Ben and Helen Levin, were on the membership committee. They thought some of the meetings were dull, but they hadn't disliked them enough to drop out of the Club, and last year Dan had been membership chairman himself. This year the Executive Committee said it was his turn to be programme chairman. When he said yes, it seemed the only thing to do. As a matter of fact, there had never been any chance for him to say no. And it was an honour in a way, it really was—not that he wanted to see his name in the paper. But it meant that everyone had confidence in him—well, knew held do a good job, or at least try hard. Besides, they liked him!.

* * *

At lunch the next day, Dan and Mr. Harper, the President of the Current Affairs Club, got together to begin planning the programmes for the season. "What we need is some variety," Jim Harper began, gesturing with his cigar to indicate variety, and Dan agreed, "Absolutely! That's exactly what I was thinking!"

"But you know, Jim," he continued lamely, "I don't know that I should have taken on this job. Pretty busy, you know, and I don't know anything about it. Not the first thing."

"Nonsense!" Jim boomed. "you've been a member for four or five years, haven't you? One of our most reliable members, I might add. You've been to a lot of meetings, you've heard a lot of programmes. You know what's good, what a good programme is. You know what our members like—I dare say a lot better than some of us old war horses who've been running the show. You've been out there in the audience, out there where you could tell if a programme was lousy or if the members didn't like it."

"Well—" Dan wasn't at all sure he knew what a good programme was or what the members liked. As for being in the audience, half the time he was thinking about something else and wasn't even conscious of where he was—and (he remembered one meeting last year his friends thought was wonderful and his thought was terrible) maybe he didn't think the same as the other, anyway. Who was right? How could he know if a programme was good?

One important feature of programme service is that it leaves to the organizations the full responsibility for policy determination. The leaders from any group can, through programme service, broaden their ideas of the kind of programmes possible, they can carry them out more effectively, and they can, if they wish, relate them to other programmes in the community, but it is entirely in their hands as to whether or not they do. The way in which service to organizations broadens the community programme will be dealt with in greater detail in Chapter 13.

Voluntary Organizations

In one sense the term "voluntary" is not a definitive one. In a democracy all organizations have a certain amount of voluntary-ness. What are some groups that we do include as voluntary and some that we do not? Included are women's groups, such as units of the General Federation of Women's Clubs, League of Women Voters, and Junior Leagues; men's luncheon clubs, such as Rotary, Kiwanis and Lions; citizens' groups associated with the schools, such as parent-teacher associations; groups associated with churches; veterans' organizations; consumer groups; garden clubs; age groups, such as Golden Years Clubs or Young Adult groups; special-interest groups, such as health groups. Not included are organizations associated with areas covered by other chapters in this section: schools, colleges, libraries, museums, organized labour groups. The line is not sharp, and we do not want to press the distinctions. The important thing is to find in the community as many groups of these kinds as possible and to increase their values for the adult-education programme.

Something of the potentialities and problems of these organizations is given in the section on "Men's and Women's Clubs" in the *Handbook of Adult Education,* which treats those groups that are for women only or for men only and points out certain broad differences between the two kinds. Although the differences between men's and women's groups are useful to recognize in dealing with such clubs, the important point is the value of these groups for adult education. This value they share with mixed groups, such as foreign-policy and parent-teacher associations.

The article from which this selection is taken began with a general introduction and a brief historical treatment of women's clubs. The article then continued with the problems of women's clubs.

An interesting and very fair postwar appraisal of woman's organizations in this country is presented in a magazine article by Margaret Culkin Banning. In this article, Mrs. Banning discusses the American movement in the light of the attention it has attracted, since the close of World War II, as a possible model for similar women's movements in other countries.

Mrs. Banning's diagnosis of the weaknesses of women's organizations is both competent and thorough. At the same time, she points out that the efficiency of women's work on ration boards, for the Red Cross, and in many other types of wartime service, was undoubtedly due in large part to their having had valuable practice in working together in their peacetime organizations. And although she reports regretfully that "at the end of the war, women went back to words instead of deeds," she sees certain emerging trends which she interprets as a challenge to, if not a promise of, future worth-while achievements.

Recent Trends

There have been many signs, both before and since the Second World War, that organized women's groups have come to be regarded from several points of view as at least potentially powerful forces in our society. A variety of institutions and agencies, including university extension departments, public schools, business organizations, and newspaper and magazine publishing companies, have set up women's club bureaus or services, motivated at least in part by a desire to help women's groups to improve both their study and action programmes. Whether these services have been selfish or altruistic in purpose, the results have unquestionably been beneficial so far as they have aided women's groups to discover and develop their talents and resources for the common good. When, on the contrary, the club services have encouraged the acceptance and use of cut-and-dried, prepared programmes that make a pretense of spontaneity, their contribution to sincerity, independent thinking, and effective group action is dubious, to say the least.

Most helpful of recent developments in the women's club movement are the purely self-help organizations such as the Nassau County (Long Island) Woman's Forum, which aims to substitute cooperation for competition among women's groups.

Men's Clubs

Unlike American women's clubs, which Dorothy Confield Fisher says "are as native to our soil as the sugar maple and the Ford car", the men's clubs in this country can be traced back directly to the eighteenth century men's groups that met in London inns and coffee houses to share food and drink and talk.

The oldest known American club is the Junto of Philadelphia, founded by Benjamin Franklin in 1927. It was

Franklin's idea that the Junto hold weekly discussions on morals, politics and natural philosophy, and that these discussions should led to action which would be beneficial to the community. In this latter respect, Junto has fully justified its founder's hopes. The American Philosophical Society, The Franklin Institute, the University of Pennsylvania, the first American public library, and the first Philadelphia mutual fire insurance company are all outcomes of Junto discussions.

Junto and the other American men's clubs of the eighteenth century represented only the beginning of a movement that broadened and deepened rapidly, as cities multiplied and new ideas spread across the country. However, the men's club movement has never even approximated the record made by the women's movement, either in the number and variety of groups organized or in the total membership enrolled.

Frank Earnest Hill, who made a study of the educational activities of men's clubs in 1938, lists the following objectives most frequently given by men as their reasons for joining clubs: (1) to develop friendships, (2) to get occupational knowledge, (3) to render "service" to the community, (4) to find relaxation, (5) to gain prestige, (6) to improve intellectually, (7) to get business.

Contrast Between Men's And Women's Clubs

This list of self-acknowledged purposes confirms the general impression that sociability and a natural desire to get together are much more impelling and conscious motives with clubmen than with clubwomen and that, in a majority of men's clubs, the educational programmes, if any, are incidental. Mr. Hill's estimate, which other students of the subject consider very generous, places the total of men's club members affected by educational activities somewhere between two and three million.

In regard to the attitude of most men's clubs toward educational programmes, as compared with the typical attitude of women's groups, Mr. Hill writes:

> Insistence upon the direct approach to education seems to me to be typically masculine. Women, in contrast, feel an obligation toward culture. They work out programmes consciously designed

> to promote study. They even attack dutifully subjects in which they have little interest and about which they know almost nothing. The obligation to perform and the satisfaction of performance are often sufficient incentives for them. Men will work as hard—at their best they will perhaps perform with greater brilliance—but they reject a direct approach and usually take no pride in serving culture with a capital C. Their impatience with anything labelled as study is both unquestionable and of the highest importance in any effort that may be make to improve the character of the masculine contribution to education in America.

And here is Mr. Hill's final judgment on the effectiveness of this "indirect approach to education", preferred by men:

> On the whole, the weakness of men's groups as educational agencies may be thought of as lying in the relatively passive character of a large part of the work (too much listening and not enough participation), in the uneven nature of many of the more promising activities, in the narrowness of range which the clubs generally show, in the emptiness of a considerable amount of the speaking heard, and in the relatively small amount of studying done even by those who are participating. As discussion clubs, art clubs, music and crafts clubs grow in number, if they do, and as individual members of service clubs and business organizations take on an increasing share of activity (and this on the whole seems to be their tendency), the clubs should become more important cultural influences.

Advice to Adult Educators

Of the potential usefulness of clubs, both men's and women's, as agencies of adult education, there would seem to be no question. It is clearly evident, too, that there are club leaders who see and are trying to correct the weaknesses that prevent these potentialities from being fully realized. But, obviously, the responsibility for bringing adults education and men's and women's clubs into a more effectively cooperative relationship rests as much upon adult educators as upon club leaders.

Informal Groups

In addition to the formal, name organizations that are so prominent in our society, there are, as we pointed out at the opening of this chapter, a large number of informal groups, often without a name and generally without an organizational structure. The great importance of these groups for adult education has been shown in a few experimental programmes which have been able to work with them. Because of their informal nature, they are not easy to discover and are generally overlooked. Hurley Doody's study tells an interesting story of how one investigator was able to get his first clues and of the ramifications caused by linkages among these auntonomous groups.

Mr. Maria Rogers, the secretary of the Committee on Autonomous Groups, has summarized some of the main points in the *Handbook of Adult Education:*

> Discussion of "autonomous" groups brings to the foreground the importance of classifying human beings. There are two different ways. The first is by categories. In this type of classification, human beings are grouped according to one single criterion or a combination of criteria. Veterans, adolescents, factory-workers, parents, capitalists; these are similar categories of people, having in common some mutual experience or attribute—participation in war, age, type of employment, and so on. These categories refer to single aspects of individuals, who may, and do, vary greatly in personality, and who may feel no impulse to associate with others just because they are members of the same category. Individuals within these categories may even dislike one another and would find it difficult to work together for a common aim.

The other way of classifying human beings is by natural groups. In this type of classification, which is the older and more persistent, individuals are grouped according to their affinities and definites. All successful organizations, all enterprises that are effective, are based on these natural groupings.

* * *

They exist in rural communities, and there they can be found without much effort. In cities, however, they have to be sought for. Categorical groupings based on "interests" appear to outweigh the natural groups in importance. This is an illusion and a dangerous one. Therefore, a concerted effort must be made to bring the natural group to the attention of social workers, educators, businessmen, and all other specialists whose work requires organization or instruction of human beings. Lack of knowledge of natural groups causes specialists to attempt to group human beings in artificial ways which negate well-meant efforts to improve and maintain social institutions. For it must be emphasized that natural groupings are a *sine qua non* for constructive enterprises and successful organizations.

* * *

The discovery and scientific study of intimate groups have started a revolution in education. It is in the intimate group, we have now begun to see, that the individual's personality develops, his habits of cooperation are formed, his social skills are practised, his creativity is released. With the recognition of these all important truths, emphasis is shifting from the techniques of teaching to the processes of learning. Or, to describe this emergent trend in simpler terms: the function of the teacher can now be seen as that of working with natural groups, within which real learning takes place, *assisting* them to perform their functions more ably, from the point of view both of the individual and of society.

* * *

Natural Groups in Adult Education

The revolution in education brought about by the new understanding of groups will have marked repercussions upon adult education. Coming late on the scene as a conscious movement, adult education borrowed almost its whole equipment of philosophy, techniques and assumptions from formal education. It aimed to reproduce among adults the situations that had been developed for children and adolescents. However, adults were not subject to a compulsory education law; they did not have to go to school unless they chose. And most of them did not choose to subject themselves to the strait-jacket of conventional educational methods and operations. Because adult educational enterprises had to *luure* students into their activities, they modified to some degree the severity of their approach. But it was a *modification,* not a completely new direction.

The most enthusiastic and sincere of adult educators have always been concerned about the fact that the bulk of educational courses sought by adults are *vocational* in nature; the arts, and cultural activities in general, play no very impressive part in rolling up attendance figures. The explanation of this phenomenon becomes clear when the orientation of adult education is shifted from the benefits of education for the individual to a view which includes the delights of companionship in natural groups. Then we begin to see and understand that an individual, in order to advance his economic position, will surrender the pleasures of association with congenial companions. But when it comes to pursuit of the higher amenities of life, the same individual finds the going too chilly if he has to register alone for a course of instruction and join a class of students who are strangers to him. He prefers to pursue a more rambling exploration of these pleasures with companions of his own choosing, and to go without benefit of instruction if his natural relationships must be surrendered to obtain it.

Before adult education became a full-fledged "movement" in the early 1920's, it had a healthy, vigorous development in the United States. And this development was an achievement of natural groupings. Throughout the pioneer period in our country, natural groups of individuals banded together to explore any subject matter which interested them. "Study groups" existed before the name for them was invented. Some of our most charming stories of adult educational activities are to be found in local records of New England towns. Neighbours met in one another's homes or in the village hall to hold discussions about philosophy and concerns of mutual interest. Many a time, Ralph Waldo Emerson talked to his neighbours at such meetings. And he came to listen to other neighbours who had something to say about ichthyology, botany, mechanics, history. The extraordinary ferment of intellectual activity which produced new ideas and inventions and a great rate in the United States in the early part of the Nineteenth Century was a product of the functioning of natural groupings.

* * *

In these natural groups, individuals feel secure; they can communicate with one another without fear of misunderstanding; they have common attitudes and a common pool of convictions upon which to draw for interpretation of new points of view. Everyone in such groups can be easy and relaxed. Adult education is carried on as an expression of sociability and of the human propensity for association.

* * *

As Franklin, Socrates and Pierce behaved, so do we all. If we are interested in ideas, we prefer to discuss them with friends whose company we enjoy. Whatever we like to do, from playing bridge to climbing mountains, we wants to do with friends. Individuals without intimate friends constitute only a small and pathetic fraction of the human race. This fraction the sociometrists distinguish as *isolates,* individuals who reject others and are rejected by them. There is strong ground for suspicion that it is to this fraction of isolates in every population that the conventionally organized adult education activities make their strongest appeal. It is therefore obvious that if adult education is to attain the volume and to achieve the ideals which its leaders envision, adult educators must find the way to link up their skills with the ongoing structures of human society and adjust their methods to the needs of natural groups.

* * *

The Committee (on Autonomous Groups) has found that recognition of the transcendent importance of intimate groups does more than point the way to helping groups that conform to our mores. It also leads to new methods of solving "social problems". A case in point is a very successful project for the reduction of juvenile delinquency in Chicago. There it was demonstrated that aid to groups to which juvenile delinquents belong goes far in leading them to change their codes of behaviour, to adjust to and accept socially approved standards of morality. This experience helps to validate the theory, advanced by Dr. Frank Tannenbaum and other students of crime, that the attack on delinquency should be on the group which the delinquent counts as friends; that the aim should be to change the *group's* attitudes, ideals, interests and habits. The juvenile delinquent, like the criminal, is adjusted to his own social group and violently objects to and evades any social therapy that would make him maladjusted to it.

Adult educators have moved out into the community in the effort to aid citizen organizations to solve social problems. It is essential that they carry into their community work awareness of the central importance of natural groups and knowledge of techniques for aiding the development of such groups. Equipped with this knowledge and understanding, adult educators can be very effective in an area which has so far resisted the efforts of battalions of "community organizers" and social workers.

Few groups are so self-satisfied that they do not wish for help. Most of them want to become more efficient in carrying out their expressed or latent purposes, in making a better integration with the larger community. But they want the help to be given in a way which enables them to preserve their dignity and their sense of group-identity. They want the cultural and educational agencies that give the help to respect the group's own leadership. They want any educational programme that may be set up for the group to be geared into the felt needs of its members. Groups can not be dictated to; they can not be imposed upon. When agencies attempt such domination, however tactfully, the group disappears, to re-form in a more congenial atmosphere. It is because these natural groups thus cherish and protect their autonomy that the Committee feels this characteristic of theirs must be emphasized continually. It has thus chosen to call them "autonomous" groups.

The Contribution of Voluntary Organizations to Community Development

Throughout this volume we have stressed the community base for adult education. We have viewed the educational services for adults as those which are needed to help the members of the community live a richer life. In this larger pattern of living the voluntary organizations play an important part—a part that is increasing in significance as we see what is involved in making democracy work.

Our next selection sets forth a philosophy of volunteer service as worked out by the Junior League, an organization devoted to helping make the community a better place in which to live. In this selection the reader will note the references to the interrelation between the volunteer and the professional, a problem of major concern to persons interested in community development.

The rent that we pay for living in a free society is not the financial contribution that we make but the giving of ourselves. Voluntary effort is the very substance of a democracy and working together has always been a part of the American way of life. This pattern offers the opportunity for each of us to share in community service, which is not only a democratic obligation but also a democratic privilege.

The place of the volunteer in social welfare has followed a fluctuating pattern. Many years ago, social welfare services were performed entirely by volunteers. This was an outgrowth of the neighbourliness of our pioneer days and seemed sufficient for the need of that time. Later, as life grew more complex and urban populations increased, more people needed help and it became necessary to develop specialized services and establish agencies to meet the social problems. There was a need to employ trained personnel to carry part of the load. "Charity" gave way to social work; the practitioners in the new field acquired special techniques and training and a new profession evolved.

As this new profession earned recognition and importance, the place of the volunteer in community service diminished year by year until social welfare became the responsibility of the professionals. In many instances, the layman's part in the welfare programme consisted of raising money for causes not too well understood.

However, it wasn't long before the professionals themselves began to realize the need for more citizen participation. They saw that valid community planning must originate with the people who live in the community and must evolve from the joint efforts of the professional and the volunteer. As a result, new opportunities for volunteer service developed, and once again volunteers began to play an increasingly vital part in community service in both voluntary and governmental agencies. This required a knowledge and understanding of community problems on the part of citizen participants, as well as a willingness and determination to meet these problems adequately and successfully.

Today the most dynamic, well-rounded community service programmes include professional leadership and citizen participation. The professionals have come to appreciate the importance of the volunteer and both her actual and her potential contribution. The volunteer is well aware of the need for community services and of her place in them. She realizes the importance of the professionally trained workers in the community agencies. The trained workers give her the stimulation of working with people who can interpret not only the individual services but their relation to the whole community picture. Furthermore, the volunteer is aware that her life is closely bound to the lives of the people in her own community, as well as to the lives of people in remote parts of the world. Because she realizes that constructive volunteer service is one way of strengthening the resources of her community and because community boundaries are constantly being extended and effaced, the results of such service are felt far beyond their immediate locale.

Inherent in the philosophy of voluntary service is the belief that the development of the individual is meaningless unless it results in a tangible contribution to the world in which she lives. The sustaining satisfaction in this individual participation derives from the ability to take a constructive part in community affairs and assume the responsibilities as well as the privileges of citizenship.

This same fundamental concept of the importance of the volunteer in democratic life is expressed in a handbook of the Federation of Protestant Welfare Agencies.

In a democracy it is not essential, nor even desirable, that citizens should agree but it is imperative that they should participate. Opportunities for participation fall into two major categories, namely (a) political action and (b) action on behalf of voluntary institutions and agencies. A true citizen of a democratic society such as we enjoy in the United States is one who shares in both types of participation. He feels a sense of responsibility for his government and also for that vast constellation of private or voluntary institutions which supplements public agencies.

We often use these terms—"public" and "private"—as though they stood in opposition. Indeed, we frequently find ourselves saying "public *versus* private". This latter phrase appears to carry the meaning that an inevitable conflict exists between those services performed under governmental auspices and those sponsored by independent, voluntary bodies. This seems to me to constitute a serious error which, when carried to extremes of action, threatens the future of democracy. Democracies may be said to be moving towards a healthy state when official or governmental agencies and voluntary or private agencies function as though they were involved in a genuine partnership.

But a partnership is strong only when both partners are strong. If one is powerful and the other weak, there can be no true partnership. Many thoughtful Americans have come to recognize this truth and have thus assumed greater responsibilities in bringing strength to private or voluntary agencies and institutions. They have dedicated themselves to a new kind of participation, participation which is no longer desultory and haphazard but which on the contrary takes on the semblance of a task which demands their finest talents.

The selection above referred chiefly to the field of welfare services. The same problem of lay participation is central in the public schools, and a similar cycle of participation, lack of participation, and now a strong movement toward participation has been evident. Herbert Hamlin has pointed out this varying pattern of responsibility and some of the factors relating to it.

There is a growing realization that public schools are *public*. They belong to the public. The public pays their costs. They should be conducted in the public interest. They should serve the total public.

The American public school system developed in an atmosphere of public interest and concern. Laymen have had a large part in its development. Our earliest public school buildings were often built by the local people. Patrons boarded the teachers. Members of boards of education and parents supervised the teachers and examined the pupils. The limited funds for schools were voted at town or school meetings which all might attend and which were well attended.

Later, lay participation in public education declined. The development of large cities and large school districts made it more difficult for individuals to influence school policies. Colleges acquired and long maintained controls over the secondary schools. Powerful state departments of education, buttressed with large state schools funds, were developed and state officials assumed some of the responsibilities formerly held by local laymen. A teaching profession arose with conceptions of "academic freedom" and a sense of professional expertness which separated the professionals from the amateurs in education. Professional school administrators were employed and boards delegated many of their functions to their administrators. Administrators were commonly expected to organize the schools from the top down and to assume the principal responsibility for public relations.

Thus we developed many school system which were largely managed by professional administrators and teachers. Boards of education in these systems became necessary evils, useful primarily in helping to get from the public the funds required to carry out the ideas of state and local professional workers. Laymen became almost unnecessary to the schools, except to furnish the students, elect a board of education, and pass on occasional bond issues. In at least one extreme case, parents were barred from visiting the schools their children were attending. The school's programme of public relations was to "interpret the schools to the public", that is to tell the public how good the school were and how much more money would be required to keep them excellent.

A code was developed, and enforced in some states by withdrawing state approval of schools if violated, which provided that teachers should work only with school administrators and that only administrators should have access to boards of education. Thus board members, the representatives of the public, were effectively isolated from teachers. In many situations strong local organizations of teachers developed and boards were obliged to deal with their representatives in matters of salary and teacher welfare, but teachers had other contacts with boards of education only as administrators allowed them.

Under such a system the administrator's lot became an unhappy one. He was caught between the board and the teachers. Board members might consider him a special pleader for the teachers. Teachers might think him the board's stooge. Often the administrator was the loneliest man in town because he was victim of a system which gave him a status and, with it, prerogatives and responsibilities he should never have had.

Arrangements which gave administrators too much authority and responsibility developed in some school systems because boards of education were interfering with administration and teaching. Neglecting their tasks of general policy making, many boards, especially those in the smaller schools, were spending their time bargaining financially with individual teachers, passing on school disciplinary problems, buying supplies and equipment, and dealing with other matters better delegated to the professional staff.

Having lived through a series of undesirable arrangements, we are now possibly able to set up a new one in which students, teachers, the administration, the board and the public share in policy-making, in appropriate ways, and in which all of these groups, or their representatives, have the systematic, face-to-face contacts essential in the harmonious development of policies that are fair to all.

The trend away from lay participation in public education has been arrested, and in some cases it has been turned back. In many instances it has been painfully discovered that the public pays the bill for public schools and that it wants something to say about the kind of schools it gets for its money. Voters long left out of school planning have finally refused to vote adequate funds for school support.

One of the voluntary organizations that has taken an active part in the development of better education is the Parent-Teacher Association (PTA). It has frequently been criticized for involving itself in matter which appropriately belonged to the governmental body, the board of education. It has therefore endeavoured to define the respective responsibilities of the school board and the parent-teacher groups.

The school board's obligations—

(*a*) To welcome and act upon constructive suggestions or recommendations from the parent-teacher organization concerning the educational needs of the community.

(*b*) To regard the parent-teacher association as an able ally, ready to enlist community support of school board action.

(*c*) To remember that it is elected or appointed to serve the *whole* community, which probably is more completely represented in the parent-teacher organization than in any other community group.

Responsibilities of the parent-teacher unit or council—

(a) To deal directly with the school board in controversial matters regarding school policy and abstain from meddling in internal school administration.

(b) To appraise the work of the school board constructively.

(c) To arouse community interest in school affairs and school election issues.

(d) To refuse, as *an organization*, to endorse school board candidates or seek their removal.

With intelligent leadership within the parent-teacher group and in the school administration, there can be a very effective working relationship which is of great assistance to the educational programme in the community. The 1946 Yearbook of the American Association of School Administrators, *School Boards in Action,* had the following to say regarding the work of parent-teacher organizations:

> Few organizations have the emotional stimulus passed by the parent-teacher associations. Organized as they are on a local, state and national basis, they represent potency and power exceeding that of almost any other interest group so far as public education is concerned. While they have no direct authority to interfere with the legal structure of public education or to dictate what the board of education or its employees shall do, the members can, as individuals, claim the right to appraise the work of the schools. They do have the power to create and develop public opinion for the purpose of influencing community thinking with respect to its educational needs.

When proper relationship are maintained between the PTA and boards of education, the combination will bring about greater understanding and better cooperation than could be attained by either group working independently. Frequently the parent-teacher association is the board's strongest ally. A most effective demonstration of this fact was observed during the late depression when schools were able to maintain much of their educational programme, in the face of strong opposition, because of the unusual efforts of the members of parent-teacher groups dedicated to the solution of educational problems in terms of the welfare of children.

The parent-teacher association is primarily a clearing-house for the presentation and discussion of educational problems out of which may grow an interpretation to the community of the purpose, the worth, and the needs of the public schools. Although it is outside of the legal organization of the school district it has a definite place in the functional organization and should be considered as an advisory and cooperating group of first importance. It can act as an agency through which essential parental education is carried on with the result that definite attitudes and ideals may be developed which will affect the people of the district as a whole.

If either the board of education or the PTA attempts to direct, threaten, or cajole the other, the educational programme of the community will suffer. Both groups must recognize the basic principles upon which the National Congress of Parents and Teachers is founded. So long as it acts solely as a voluntary cooperating agency there should be little justification for conflict. The functional concept of the parent-teacher organization can be made effective, however, only under an intelligent and careful leadership capable of commanding the respect of board members and the public. An attitude on the part of the board to use the organization as a vital and valid agency in its public relations programme will, under normal circumstances, result in better community understanding and appreciation of the purpose, the achievements, and the needs of the schools.

When conflicts arise they should be traced to their sources as quickly as possible and attempts made to remove the causes. Many conflicts are the result of either personal differences or a mistaken concept of the function of the PTA. The most general cause is poor leadership and a lack of cooperative effort, which allows special interest groups to "take the wheel" and to employ "pressure tactics" as a means of attaining their goals. Trouble is likely to ensue whenever the relationship between the board and the parent-teacher group becomes anything other than a cooperative partnership.

It should be emphasized again that the amount of participation in broad community affairs by the voluntary organizations will vary. Each group is free to determine whether its programme is directed entirely to its own members, whether it is almost entirely a service to the community, or whether it is some combination of these. Our concern in adult education is to be certain that education is available where needed.

In many communities it has been found profitable to combine forces on the selection, training, and placement of volunteers. Volunteer service, if it is to be satisfying to the giver and useful to the agency and the community, must be worked out carefully. A number of communities have had experience with central volunteer offices, and the process of locating, training, placing and rewarding participants is beginning to take shape. Some steps in the process are:

(*a*) Informing citizens widely about the kind of opportunities for volunteer service. This involves agencies to get the jobs adequately planned so that volunteers can derive satisfaction from doing them.

(*b*) Interviewing citizens who respond in order to determine their qualifications and to help them understand the opportunities.

(*c*) Providing basic training for the job after a person has made a positive choice regarding a volunteer service.

(*d*) Introducing the volunteer to the job and working with the agency and the volunteer to anticipate some of the possible problems that are likely to arise, such as illness in the volunteer's family, transportation failure, changes within the agency.

(*e*) Providing additional on-the-job training where this is needed.

(*f*) Moving volunteers to position of added responsibility when they show special abilities and moving them sometimes merely to avoid excess monotony in less interesting jobs.

(*g*) Giving appropriate recognition to volunteers who have good service records.

(*h*) Working with the volunteers to seek constant improvement in the process.

From the wealth of material that is available from various agencies, we have taken two selections. The first one illustrates the way in which one agency has worked with community groups to describe the kinds of work which volunteers can do. We have selected material on one agency; the original source has similar material for a number of the agencies in that community.

Oahu Council of Girl Scouts

The local office is maintained by funds from the Community Chest. The primary purpose of this organization is the development of traits that enrich the personalities of the participants and assist them to become active, informed members of a democratic society. There is a place in Scouting for anyone who wishes to help girls, from seven years of age through high school, and learn to use, in a practical way what they already know and encourage them to develop new abilities and appreciations, and most of all, to help them develop a healthy attitude towards life and a set of true values. The organization, being composed of over 90% volunteers accomplishes its aims by finding the proper place for all those who choose to work with it.

Qualifications for volunteer work are as follows:

(a) Must be over 21 years of age.
(b) Must be the type of person who believes in the ideals of democracy.
(c) Experience and skills in group work, out of doors, nature, arts and crafts, etc. are assets to the job, but not half as important as a genuine liking of the girls and a willingness to learn with and from the girls.

Duties are as follows:

(a) To set aside two hours a week for troop meetings.
(b) To set aside an occasional Saturday for hikes, excursions and special events.
(c) To be prepared to give the time necessary to prepare for meetings.
(d) To take the basic training course that is offered by the organization.
(e) To act as a guide for the girls in planning and executing activities.
(f) To be an adult friend to the girls.
(g) To work with the troop committee and arrange and carry out a satisfactory programme.
(h) To cooperate with the national and local organization in maintaining high standards within the troop on all phases of activity, health and safety practices, badge requirements, registration procedures and reports that are requested.

Job Classifications:

(*a*) *Troop leader*. A key position as all other people work to make the leader's experience more satisfactory both to herself and the organization as a whole.

* * *

b. *Troop Committee members*. This is a very necessary part of any troop. There are three to five adults who assist leaders of the troop by relieving the leaders of the mechanics of troop organization so that they can devote more time to the development of girls thru the troop programme activities.

c. *Transportation and Telephone*. A job for someone who must stay at home a great deal. She does all the telephoning for the leader and arranges transportation for special events.

* * *

d. *Programme*. The things girls do as Scouts are called "programmes". This position helps the leader find interesting things for the girls to do or finds people who know about the things the girls are interested in. She see that the troop is represented at Island-wide events.

* * *

e. *Special Jobs*. There is a place for everyone in Scouting. If you cannot become interested in the above job descriptions, come to the office and talk to the staff. There are many little individual ways in which the staff would appreciate help. Posters and the monthly bulletin cover drawings are important volunteer jobs.

The field of volunteer service offers great opportunities for adult education. In San Francisco the public schools have undertaken to provide services for the Volunteer Bureau in the ways indicated in the next selection.

The Volunteer Bureau of San Francisco is the city's official recruitment and training center for volunteers for accredited agencies where payless help is properly used. The Community Chest helps support the Bureau because most of San Francisco's civic, cultural and welfare agencies get their volunteer workers through the Bureau's system of recruitment and screening. The Adult Education Division of the Public Schools helps support the Bureau because each volunteer is trained to do his or her job, and because volunteer service itself is education in good citizenship. Since its inception six years ago, the Volunteer Bureau has served 172 agencies and 7165 volunteers have passed through its doors.

Volunteer work is a process of adult education. Three aspects of educational activities conducted by the Bureau are: training the volunteer, during his initial interview, in the responsibilities of community service, conducting classes for volunteers and for supervisors of volunteers; and equipping college students for community service.

Some courses are given regularly each year by the Bureau such as a three-week course on community service for Junior League provisional members and for other interested volunteers, a course of five sessions for new members of the Infant Shelter Auxiliary, an orientation session for new members of the Volunteer Bureau Advisory Committee and a series of training sessions throughout the year for volunteers who take part in the programme of the Volunteer Bureau.

The Bureau also conducts courses related to special phases of volunteer activities. A Board Member Institute was designed to educate persons on the responsibilities involved in serving on boards and committees. It was attended by 194 individuals representing 67 agencies. A Workshop for Supervisors of Volunteers was the first workshop held in San Francisco for professional staff who have responsibility for training and supervising volunteers. A Workshop on Programmes for Senior Citizens was designed to stimulate agency use of volunteers in work with senior citizens. The Bureau also presented a session on volunteer programmes to the Group Work and Recreation Council of the Community Chest. This gave the Bureau an opportunity to reach lay and professional representatives of over 50 agencies using volunteers.

Other special training courses were arranged for volunteers who were trained to interview USO hostesses, for volunteers who were trained to serve as receptionists at the literature table for a Mental Health Society conference. In order to reach those interested in volunteer service who work during the day, the Bureau presented a series of evening sessions on the general subject, "Know Your Community".

The programme for college students is an increasingly important aspect of the Bureau's educational activities. Sessions for students majoring in Education are held three times each year at San Francisco State College. These sessions are planned by the Volunteer Bureau in consultation with the college and with agencies using volunteers. Since September 1949, when the course began, through February 1952, the Volunteer Bureau has trained 1727 students.

These courses are designed to give students an opportunity to know children outside the classroom and to acquaint students with community service. As most students are on the threshold of citizenship, an introduction to community service is considered vital in shaping patterns of future civic participation. (This programme should not be confused with the placement of graduate students in field work for professional social workers accredited by the Graduate School of Social Welfare, University of California.)

Through the use of the Volunteer Bureau, duplication of effort has been eliminated, saving a great amount of work for the college and providing a wide scope of opportunity for the students. The college course, as well as all the other courses described, was planned and coordinated by the certificated staff of the Volunteer Bureau.

The Power of Voluntary Groups

If adult-education workers become somewhat discouraged in facing the tremendous tasks posed by our communities, the antidote is to visit a community with a good volunteer programme and then to think of the potential resources available if the number of volunteers could be still further increased. Among the citizens not now participating can be found a variety of talents. Democracy is the form of government which can give these talents full opportunity to contribute, and the American genius for organizing should make it possible to combine them into effective working units. The thought of what might be accomplished when we are able to expand our volunteer programmes should give increased incentive to adult-education leaders. The statement in a handbook of the Montgomery (Pa.) County Federation of Women's Clubs is apt at this point.

The community work done by clubs is a complex job. The need for training is becoming more apparent to thoughtful members. In the early days ... club members had to learn through trail and error what to do and how to do it. Today they have access to so many sources of knowledge which were not available to club pioneers that they no longer depend on trail and error. A wealth of publications, such as books, pamphlets, brochures, and periodicals are available for study of club methods and for information on various department and division programmes of work. The next step forward is to organize this wealth of new ideas and material into leadership training programmes.

Another long stride forward will be an increased willingness to change club practices so that they keep pace with the new knowledge being gained... People are unnecessarily slow in the application of scientific knowledge. Club members have it in their power to take the lead in putting this scientific knowledge into practice for the benefit of their community. For example, it would be possible to eliminate entirely smallpox and diphtheria and greatly reduce the incidence of tuberculosis if members would put the full force of their influence behind the campaign to end these plagues. Or, if they did their part in interpreting the principles of mental health until they become part of people's everyday thought and living, they would be doing much toward preventing mental illness, which today is steadily increasing. Future club members will perceive in all this one of their great opportunities to be of service.

There are indications that the future will see greater cooperation between organizations, more frequent joining of hands for mutual advancement and carrying-out community projects. Clubs will remain, separate, as now, in the specific functions that pertain to them alone, but will unite with other local organizations in large action programmes which no one group working by itself could hope to accomplish.

It seems probable, also, that as the newer and more effective methods of work become common in clubs, a larger number of persons will take a real part in the activities of the programme. They will cease to be merely listeners and spectators. If this happens, it should mean a great upsurge of interest in the clubs. True interest is kept alive when members are occupied with meeting real problems and overcoming real difficulties. Sitting on the sidelines is not nearly so interesting as wholeheartedly putting gifts and talents to work.

* * *

As these changes occur, more and more persons will want to participate in this wider movement of thought, planning and implementation. Out of the new knowledge and vision gained through club membership will appear new opportunities for progress and usefulness to the community. Members will be inspired by the common purpose of raising the standards of living, promoting physical and mental health, enlarging the concepts of social justice and extending public education for all of the children of all of the people. They will have provided a foundation on which to build an ennobling future.

As the technical skill of our society grows, each of us has more time outside of the hours he spends in paid work. This time will be distributed among a variety of activities, but certainly a major one should be that of improving our communities. As was pointed out above, this service is the lifeblood of democracy. It gives the giver the satisfaction of sharing in the building; joined with the services of his fellows, it provides an ever richer way of life.

Paul Essert has suggested that community service is as simple as one plus one. If each citizen would volunteer a minimum of one hour off service and one hour training for that service each week, we would soon have a tremendous budget of community power. In a small community of 2000 adults this would amount to 100,000 hours a year of volunteer action and the same amount of educational time. At a rate of $1.50 an hour, this action time is worth $150,000. For a city of 30,000 this volunteer service would amount to $2,250,000. In ten years, think what this could mean.

12

Workers' Education

Workers' Education is an important part of the current adult education picture, and it will be an increasingly important part in the years to come. At the local and national levels there is growing awareness in the unions of the need for education and for more adequate provision for leadership in securing it. Universities are expanding their services to the unions. National organisations make available a variety of help for the educational efforts of the unions—materials, training, consultants.

The Range of Activities in Workers' Education

What kind of activities go on in workers' education? Visits to union groups across the country would reveal the same range as in other parts of the adult-education picture. Many unions would have nothing that could be designated as educational. Many would have some small beginnings, such as helping one or two members attend a class or a workshop in union leadership methods or a small group of the members getting together for a few meetings on bargaining procedures. At the top of the scale would be the extensive variety of activities utilized by a considerable percentage of the membership as illustrated by the programme of the International Ladies Garment Workers Union. Hilda Smith has described something of the flavour of these varied endeavours:

> To look in on a workers' education classroom is to observe a cross section of American industry. In the larger industrial centers there are often skilled workers from the building trades, or from transportation, together with men and women from the

clothing industry. Here is a Scotch carpenter who has had long years of experience, struggling valiantly to hold his own in a discussion of unemployment problems. A vivid, dark-haired Italian girl, a milliner, is seated next him, in a low voice adding a few impressions of her own experience in looking for a job. In the next room a little group of garment workers is clustered around a big relief map of the United States, which they themselves have made. "I never had an idea of what America looked like before", one of them remarks.

Change the picture to a Southern industrial village, where textile and tobacco workers have gathered for an evening class. They have come early, these tall, lean men and women, in order to gather wood and build the fire in the stove, to take the chill of the little rural schoolroom. Here is a cotton mill worker, a thin young woman with bent shoulders. Before the coming of the codes she worked eleven hours on a night shift in her mill. During the operation of the N.R.A., getting off after an eight hour day, she reveals in the chance to go to school at night, a privilege she never enjoyed before. What does she want to learn: She asks her teacher for some book on labour history, for she has recently joined a union and is eager to learn more of the organisation. In one corner, where there is a blackboard, the teacher is surrounded by a group of tall young men in overalls, almost illiterate, who are combining the study of English with the discussion of their own economic problems. "Wages" is written in large letters on the black board, and the English lesson turns into economics as these young American-born workers old American stock, try to trace the factors in the wage situation as they know it, getting practice in grammar and spelling as they do so.

Now it is a Thursday afternoon, in a mid-western city, and a dozen domestic workers are meeting in a Y.M.C.A clubroom. It is their afternoon off, and turning away from the movies or soda fountains, these women are coming to school. Here the discussion turns on the most urgent problems of the domestic workers, together with those of her employer. Questioned as to their own work, the sense of inferiority often found among these women is apparent. "I am only a cook," says one. "I'm only a laundress," says another. To become aware of the importance of all workers in the social structure, and to know that many other women, and the government itself, is concerned with their conditions of work is for these women an illuminating experience.

Up in the mountains of Pennsylvania, a group of young miners decided they would like to know something of the world around them, and of the physical universe. A science teacher offered his time, but no place for a science class could be found. Finally one young worker discovered an old garage, out of repair, at the end of a long alley. Possession was granted by the owner, and the gang went studying charts which show the natural resources of America, and the ups-and-downs of the coal industry. Simple laboratory equipment has been made, and the miners, still rather grimy from their day's work, are experimenting with oxygen and examining a model of a hydraulic engine.

Look in at the shoe workers' union headquarters where a workers' class is meeting, and you will see labour drama in the making. Episodes from the mill, from the street, or the union meeting are acted with spontaneous enthusiasm and criticized by the shoe workers in the audience. Gradually the scenes assume the proportions of drama and are given with at least some knowledge of dramatic values.

Sometimes the public school is not available to workers' education, and no settlement, club or union headquarters is available. In such a case, as in one Southern State, teachers and workers must practice ingenuity. One group, unsuccessful in finding a meeting place for classes, took to the road in an old automobile. When they found a secluded spot with a bit of woods, they stopped and set up their classroom around the car. The blackboard strapped to the rear was proposed against a tree. Teacher and students sat on the running board or on the ground. Discussion started, taking up workers' education itself as the topic of the evening. Pioneers in education, these young men and women from the cotton field and the mill know what it means to struggle for learning; know what it means to get down to the facts, in education and in life.

Characteristic of all these groups is their eagerness to learn. Workers walk miles to attend classes, or go without supper to supply the necessary carfare. As they sit around the table in the class, or gather in a social science workshop, their faces are alight with interest. American-born workers and foreign-born, trade unionists, unorganized workers, or members of an Unemployed Union, they are alike in their desire to discover more of the world around them; to understand what is happening in their own lives; to catch some glimpse of what might happen in the future in their struggle to gain economic security for themselves and their children. To the teacher of the workers' class, it is the spirit of the workers-student which gives the instructor new courage and hope. The workers themselves are instilled with the feeling that instruction will one end with the classroom; that what they learn will be of use in meeting the urgent problems of their own existence, and in bringing about a better economic world for all.

We can get a more comprehensive overview of the programme from Mark Starr's summary of the findings of a survey of union education, conducted for the Fund for Adult Education. Requests for information regarding "current and immediate future programmes" were sent to labour unions; to labour-education bodies such as American Labour Education Service (ALES), the AFL Workers' Education Bureau (WEB), and the CIO Education and Research Department; and to universities. From the results obtained Starr presents the following picture.

While the major share of the activities is borne by the unions themselves, aided by the WEB and CIO Education and Research Department, a number of the programme are carried on by, or in cooperation with the American Labour Education Service and through industrial relations courses in certain university departments and schools, and their extension divisions. There are also increased cooperative relations with those public libraries interested in services to labour groups and with organisations which work with labour in the anti-discrimination field, such as the Jewish Labour Committee, the National Labour Service, the National Conference of Christians and Jews, and the National Urban League.

The educational programmes surveyed include a rich variety of activities:

Week-end institutes and conferences;

Workers' evening classes, whether weekly for several weeks or months or year-round or in short concentrated blocks of consecutive evenings;

One-and tow-week resident full-time training institutes and labour schools, as well as a new and significant one-year programmes of whole time study leading to employment by the union upon successful completion of the theoretical and practical work;

Use of films and filmstrips and other audio and visual aids;

Field trips;

Participation in community projects; and the educational aspect of such regular union activities as membership meetings, shop steward sessions, the union paper, and the work of union committees both inside and outside the plant.

While a great deal of this educational work is concerned with training of members, new and old, and of local leadership for immediate union service, such training often involved education in background material such as labour history, economics and labour-management relations. In addition, the survey found promising educational efforts carried on in a variety of fields with wide social implications—such as national and international affairs, combatting discrimination and promoting participation in community affairs.

Starr then analyzed the content of the programmes reported in terms of three areas of communication: (1) the area of the union itself, (2) the area of the community at local, state and national level, and (3) the area of international affairs. The illustrations he provides in these three areas will make specific the general categories given above. In these illustrations the reader should note the nature of the educational activity the resource agencies, and the kinds of problems that arise in relating union activities to the total adult-education picture.

(1) Internal Union Communication and Self Education

The first of these, education for more effective participation within the union, is clearly the major emphasis of most of the union education programmes carried on at this time. Obviously, in a well run union its very operation, its grievance settlement procedure, the making of its contracts, the running of its meetings, its journal and conventions, are basic and valuable learning-by-doing education for the participating members. Workers' education makes this a more conscious and enriching effort. The summaries show the current extensive need for this type of effort which has come about with the great increase in union membership from about 3 to 15 million since 1933. The union journal especially show this change, and the information given is by no means confined to the union's own activities.

New members' classes, training of shop stewards and union officers are prominent in all the courses, institutes, and schools run by the unions and by the universities active in the field. Cornell and Rutgers Universities, for example, in their extension classes deal with specific and immediate problems of National Labour Relations Board elections and the making of contracts. The same applied to full-time study carried on through longer periods, such as the Trade Union Fellowship training programme for three months' resident study at Harvard, and the part-time nine-month training project for local union presidents and top level union officers run by the University of Chicago. In the union with the longest record, the International Ladies' Garment Workers' Union, the educational work ranges from teaching English to new members recently from Puerto Rico, and providing varied and extensive cultural and social opportunities, all the way to officers' qualification courses for members wishing to run for full-time office. Most recently, the ILGWU has established a full-time study programme in a twelve-month training institute, with final eligibility for elective office where necessary, and immediate appointment upon completion of training....

The changing role of the unions is well indicated by the time-and-motion and job evaluation courses noted by our survey in institutes and classes. Thereby communication between the labour union and management is improved. To the extent that cooperation between labour and management increases, the joint study of industrial relations will increase. Individual courses of this kind, and classes in industrial relations, not mentioned in our survey because they are not specifically directed to trade unions, are to be increasingly found in the curricula and special institutes at many of our colleges....

(2) Integration with the Community

The second type of communication—strengthening the relationships between the union and the community—has been given special encouragement through the work of the CIO Community Service Committee, and in both the AFL and the CIO by the newly awakened interest in political action and citizenship on the local as well as the national level....

The growing interest of the union in serving the union

member in his out-plant problems (as an individual person, as a member of a family group, and as a citizen) as well as his on-the-job problems, is significant and makes for the best kind of public relations for the labour unions.

The counselling activity carried on by the trade unions is well expressed in a mimeo guide issued by the Ohio CIO Council, "Talking with Workers About Their Problems". Obviously the advice given in this guide has grown out of the definite need of the workers to know more about the facilities of the local social work and other similar agencies. A study of the institutes run in the Labour Programme at Rutgers shows a similar trend....

Items noted in our survey include: cooperation with other agencies in campaigns against polio, heart disease, cancer, arthritis, and industrial accidents; courses in mental health and psychology; and health education carried on in conjunction with many health centers and clinics of the auto workers, men's and women's clothing workers, electrical wrokers, etc....

Workers' education has thus far not integrated the activity of the unions into the life of the community as well as it might have done. It needs to train more counsellors for *out-plant* problems, who will serve when necessary as referral agents for social work and community agencies. In addition to such immediate welfare service, workers's education should do more to interest union members generally in the basic principles of good government. This would in effect be applied civics for adults and would aim in time to raise the present low standard of political life, to remove the civic corruption which has aroused justified alarm in recent times and to secure more and better participation in political and community affairs. A body such as the National Civil Service League could give valuable *technical* guidance in setting up programmes and there are a large number of groups, such as the non-partisan league of Women Voters, which would gladly cooperate. The Labour League for Political Education, AFL, and the Political Action Committee, CIO, could deepen and enrich the education content of their activity on a year-round basis.

(3) International Understanding: World Integration

While the main emphasis of union education, particularly in the unions with new or less developed programmes, is understandably on union matters or local problems, there is a growing desire for a better understanding of international affairs.

The terrible pressures of hot and cold wars, the extensive role that labour personnel plays in the ECA and other agencies abroad, the activity of the U.S. Department of Labour, and the appointment of 30 labour attaches by the Department AFL and CIO are playing in the International Confederation of Free Trade Unions—these are some of the obvious factors that have brought international affairs closer to union members. The educational problem is a great one: how to develop, out of this awareness of confused and tragic events, an understanding of complex issues, a sense of human brotherhood and world community transcending national boundaries.

Many beginnings are being made. A great many of the labour institutes include one or more seminars dealing with European problems, the crisis in the Far East, labour's role in the world scene, etc. At least three union bodies—ILGWU (AGL), Packinghouse Workers of America (CIO) and the Michigan State CIO Council—and one university (Harvard's Trade Union Programme) report classes in international problems and labour. The current institutes of the CIO unions have used a manual dealing with international problems specially prepared by the CIO Education and Research Department. We received many reports of single sessions, lectures (for example, "Races and Religions of the World" and "World Citizenship"), film showings, etc. emphasizing world affairs; a number of unions celebrated United Nations Week; the ILGWU arranged trips to UN sessions; many unions, both AFL and CIO, have distributed relevant pamphlets, leaflets, and posters put out by governmental and other organisations, and have given more space to international articles as well as news items in their union papers. Correspondence among workers here and abroad, and the sending of food packages and needed equipment to labour groups abroad have education implications and can be developed further.

Another phase of this programme is the short-term participation of union members in international labour gatherings, including summer schools, institutes, educational conferences and meetings run by the International Confederation of Free Trade Unions, the International Federation of

Workers' Educational Associations, the International Labour Organisation, UNESCO, and other United Nations agencies.

Trade unions are increasingly called upon to provide personnel to serve abroad both as representative of their own labour bodies, and in relation to such government agencies as ECA, the ECA Technical Assistance programme, and the State Department. The direct activity of organized labour, particularly that of the AFL, in the light for free trade unions in undeveloped areas creates increased need for personnel. Therefore workers' education must increasingly take on the responsibility of preparing union members for these new responsibilities.

While reports received show that the unions are increasingly devoting space in their educational programmes and union newspapers to international problems, they are far from utilizing as well as they might the publications and facilities of both government and private agencies. The ALEA Midwest Conference on International Affairs (1951), for example, showed that the wealth of material and personnel available for educating union members about the Marshall plan, the economic consequences of the Atlantic Pact, and similar issues could have been more effectively used if more widely known in union circles.

Workers' education is a comparatively new part of the organized adult-education programme. Earnest E. Schwarztrauber mentions the fact that the Wisconsin Federation of Labour introduced a resolution in 1905 urging activities in workers' education but it was not until the founding of the Milwaukee Workers' College in 1922 that anything came of it. The Workers' Education Bureau had been established in 1921, and in 1924 the AFL recommended a levy on members to help support its activities. The Woman's Trade Union League likewise had, since early in the century, included education as one of its purposes but it was not until 1921 that Bryan Mawr, with the advice of the Leauge, set up its Summer School for Women Workers in Industry. Hilda Smith stresses this point in the article from which we quoted earlier.

Workers' Education a Pioneer Movement

Workers' education in the United States is comparatively

new. We have no such intensive and extensive projects as have been developed in England, through the tutorial classes; in the Scandinavian countries, through the fifty-year old movement for resident folk high schools, where people from farms and factories can attend with the help of government funds; on in Russia, where it is taken for granted that workers will educate themselves through systematic attendance in classes. Starting as an outgrowth of the labour movement in America, through the interest of local unions and State Federations of Labour, workers' education has its roots in the labour movement in this and other countries, and must always be thought of in relation to the educational needs of a labour movement. As developed through various organisations in this country, it now includes local evening classes under the auspices of trade unions, independent committees, and various political parties; a group of resident schools, some with their won buildings, others borrowing empty college or university buildings, and conducting classes on a college campus. Short institutes, week-end schools, conferences and teachers training projects, coordinating agencies such as the Workers Education Bureau of America and the Affiliated Schools for Workers have all played their part in the development of workers' education as it is interpreted in this country. Whatever workers' education may be, it is safe to say that this new movement in education is dynamic, full of vitality, developing rapidly to meet urgent needs.

The development of workers' education is, of course, an integral part of the development of the organised labour movement. Therefore Brameld, in his preface to *Workers' Education in the United States,* stresses the way in which the forces in our democratic society have created the conditions for the growth of education for the workers.

The purpose of this volume may better be understood by a statement from each of two brilliant Egnlishmen. One of the necessary conditions to the development of democracy, according to Harold Laski, was this:

> Popular ignorance had to be dispelled, partly by the growth of literacy and partly by the evolution of a consciousness of power in the masses which would enable them to know both what they wanted and how to organize for its attainment. Largely this was the outcome of nineteenth-century development. Popular

> education slowly achieved the first, and economic organisation, especially in the form of trade unionism, did most to secure the second.

The other statement is from Lancelot Hogben:

> At all great turning-points in the history of our social culture the recognition of a new social need has been the signal for the birth of a new science and the birth of a new science has had the backing of a popular movement outside the established universities. Turning-points in cultural history are not times when men seek culture for the passive satisfaction of secondhand living. They are times when men recognize that knowledge brings the power to shape human destiny. In the present struggle between Dictatorship and Democracy the future of Democracy may once more depend on forging new instruments of culture. As I see it there is a worthier task for an organisation like the W.E.A. (Workers' Education Associa-tion) than bringing the culture of the universities to the humblest worker. It can help to salvage Democracy by becoming the instrument of a *new* social culture. By fearless criticism of the shortcomings of our universities it can strengthen the hands of those who...realize what a university could be if it undertook the tasks worthy of its opportunities.

T.R.Adam stresses this same point in *The Workers' Road to Learning:*

> In the early nineteen twenties...there was apparent a new interest and vitality in opportunities for continued education outside the formal institutions of higher learning. It was, according to Charles A. Beard, a period "of intellectual ferment" in which "The nation was turning fiercely upon itself, inquiring whether under the clatter of the machine age there was prophetic meaning not yet divined." Within many local trade unions, educational centers had been established as a part of this quest for wisdom which was sweeping the country. It was in recognition of that interest that the A.F. of L. "set the seal of its official approval upon this popular movement among the rank and file, by recommending in 1924 a levy on members to promote such experiments under the general guidance of the Workers Education Bureau."

Workers' Education and the Universities

The forces which helped to develop the organised labour

movement in Great Britain and the United States were sympathetically interpreted by a number of students of society in the colleges and universities. These persons, in cooperation with some of the leaders within labour, were influential in providing educational opportunities for workers, using in various ways the resources of the institutions of higher education. The majority of these institutions did not respond, but it is significant that workers' education, like agricultural education, has been more closely related to the universities than to any other source of educational assistance. Libraries and public schools have helped to some extent, but the bulk of the load has been carried by the unions themselves and by certain universities.

One of the first and most successful of the university efforts to work with labour was the University of Wisconsin School for Workers. In writing the story of its first twenty-five years, Earnest E. Schwarztrauber describes the objectives of its programme as follows:

> As an introduction to the discussion of the School's objectives, it may be a clarifying device to indicate the objectives of education in some other selected University departments. The School of Agriculture concerns itself with the farmers' needs in combating plant diseases, in fostering improved methods in soil conservation, in developing better livestock and disease resistant wheat, corn, tobacco and the like. The School of Commerce provides for institutes of varying lengths, winter and summer, to industrial groups, intended to aid businessmen in the solution of their individual and collective problems. But whether the problems are those of farmers or businessmen, they are all related ultimately to one vital problem—how a going concern can dispose of its goods and services at a fair price—for unless it can do that it ultimately fails.

Now the chief problem of workers parallels exactly that of a going farm or business concern. The worker, like the farmer or the employer, seeks to sell his product at a fair price. But the only product he has to sell is his labour—that and that alone. Moreover, it is highly perishable. If it not sold today it is gone forever. He cannot store it up and wait for a better market. And if he cannot sell it he must use his savings, if any, or become dependent on others more fortunate than himself. Unlike the employer, however, the worker cannot effectively sell his in competition with other individuals like himself, for as an individual representative of a thousand workers, he will probably meet with a considerable degree of success. At least he speaks as man to a man, and with power matching—to some extent, at least—the power before him.

It is at this point of contact that the worker, acting in his group relationship with his employer, needs in the first instance the educational services that the School for Workers can render. Collectively, workers can hope to sell their product, labour, at a fair price. Even here they may fail in their objective. The School for Workers functions in such situations by helping workers to achieve an intelligent and informed approach to their problems as a basis for collective bargaining. It offers them a way of efficient and judicious use of their collective power. In other words, the School for Workers does for the workers what the School of Commerce does for the businessman and the School of Agriculture for the farmer in their extension activities—it meets his educational requirements at the point of most vital need.

The function, then, of the School for Workers, is first the implementation of organised labour in its aspirations toward the substitution of industrial government for industrial warfare. But in that primary function are implicit others of equal if not ultimately greater importance. One of these is to help organised labour come to recognise that its place in our industrial society must become an ever growing one. Labour must take its place in every aspect of modern economic and social life. In the community, workers must learn to function as members of city councils, school boards and every other activity in which citizens are engaged. In the state and nation, workers have the right and must assume the responsibilities of a working citizenship. Workers must become, therefore, completely integrated into the working bodies, national and international, that effect direction of world affairs. These citizenship relations have to date been largely the monopoly function of middle and upper class members of society. This situation cannot continue if democracy is to grow in meaning and if it is to endure as the working force in a dynamic social order. Hence, the School for Workers raises its sights to a programme as vital as life itself for there is no real life for the individual of any society unless each individual in it is given a place of dignity and respect equal to any other.

The cooperation of labour and the universities has always been somewhat uneasy, punctuated occasionally by major crises. Irvine Kerrison, in discussing this problem, describes the difficulties on both sides.

> Institutions of higher learning which accept the functional approach to workers' education view their work with labour groups as the fruit of a cooperative union-university partnership in education, and have agreed to certain conditions of partnership.

Labour often asks: Can workers' education, when financed from non-labour sources, be guarded from dilution into something innocuous and sterile? And higher education turns this question around and asks: Can workers' education, when entirely labour's operation, escape the atrophy and narrowness which so often is the result of inbreeding? The unions and universities which accept the functional approach have answered these questions to each other's satisfaction.

They have come to the conclusion that the twin dangers of dilution and bias can be avoided if the possibility of their presence in both university-conducted and labour-conducted workers' education is recognized. They agree that, once this possibility is recognised, administrative safeguards can be devised against both dangers.

Earnest Schwarztrauber states that democratic representation in workers's education policy-making, an informed citizenry, and capable direction can provide positive administrative safeguards against biased or poor administration of workers' education programmes. Survey and experience support his statement.

State-financed programmes must give workers a definite voice in policy-making. Labour people should have seats both on boards of trustees of colleges and universities and on advisory councils to workers' education programmes conducted by universities. Labour and the university concerned should agree on such trustee and advisory council representatives. Faculty and students in the workers' education division should be consulted and invited to participate in policy-making, contributing out of their experience and desires to what finally might be decided. Labour-financed programmes must give democratically selected representatives of the rank and file a voice in the administration of programme.

Colleges and universities in workers' education will have to face the fact that the blood pressures of conservative business and industrial leaders, timid trustees and sheltered pedagogues will go up in direct ratio to the broadness of the programme offered. To a broad workers' education programme, controversies and violent arguments are indispensable appurtenances. Economic heresies are heatedly discussed, industry's motives and incentives are openly questioned, and serious proposals for social change made. Out of all this comes not merely the teaching of skills but broader and better understanding of social, political and economic problems facing democracy. Discussion of these things is a part of the role of a university in its community. As our colleges and universities expand and extend broad workers' education programmes, democracy will take on greater reality and new vitality.

It is important for democracy that a common ground be discovered and that more services not only of universities but also of public schools, libraries, state and federal departments, and other agencies be made available to make workers' education the vital force it must be in the total programme. The point we are making here is the same one made in other chapters: all persons interested in adult education have a stake in all parts of the programme. Although those in the colleges and in the unions who are primarily engaged in workers' education have especial responsibilities, all of use must support their efforts and help to ensure a proper perspective relative to the other parts of the community programme.

A number of universities are endeavouring to achieve a balance by working out programmes in which attention is given to the needs of labour, management and the public. Imaginatively conceived, this approach has promise, but there is the possibility that it might spread limited resources thin and fail to achieve anything of significance. There is no hiding the fact that the role of organised labour is a controversial issue to many persons; all of us in adult education, therefore, have the responsibility of creating a better understanding on both sides.

Where the tension factors are as great as they are here, the importance of the teacher is readily apparent. The discussions of this point which we present here are related to the experience in workers' education, but the ideas are relevant in all areas of adult education.

Schwarztrauber begins with the generally accepted premise that a good teacher knows the needs and interests of his students. He then shows the need for skills in knowing what to do in relation to these needs and interests. The good teacher will have both—a point which raises problems for training teachers. This is one of the areas of especial concern in the universities giving attention to workers' education.

A teacher who is to serve workers in their group and individual needs must of necessity know those needs intimately. The idea is that he get his knowledge first hand, that is, by practical experience as a worker. Trade union leadership is inclined to believe that the best teachers are those who have grown up in the ranks of labour, and that such persons alone can fully understand and met the needs of workers. Some go so far as to declare that a teacher educated in the public schools and universities becomes so intellectualized and thereby so insulated that he cannot, even if he would, maintain vital contacts and make any contributions to workers.

It is true that actual work with one's hands in a factory or mine or in the field is a most desirable asset. Not only does such experience supply the practical technical knowledge needed, but it supplies also a psychological approach to the job which cannot possibly be acquired otherwise. The fear of unemployment, for example, the sense of insecurity, the feeling of helplessness, in the individual whose only possessions are his hands and his skills—these inner experience cannot be delivered and transmitted to comfortable individual in the classroom. They come only to workers as workers. But to argue that one cannot be a teacher of workers unless he has been a worker is to argue that one cannot, for instance, teach banking unless he has been a banker, nor business management unless he has been the manager of a corporation or business of some sort. The fact is that were trade unions to apply that criterion and reject all teachers except those trained in "the school of hard knocks", their educational activities would suffer as a result. In actual experience, when unions set up their own formal education programme they find themselves forced to turn to the public schools and to the universities for instructional services. This was true in Wisconsin during the yeas when labour conducted its own local education programme. It is still largely true today where organised labour maintains its own classes.

The point at which the teacher drawn from labour's ranks so often fall down as a teacher is in his lack of a broad and deep educational background. There are self-made men in labour's ranks as there are in the employers' ranks, but big gaps in the final product are quite as likely to be found in the one as in the other. Experience in Wisconsin has been that persons intimately acquainted with immediate trade union problems and needs often lack either the teaching techniques required or else the broad knowledge in allied fields which gives poise and balance in teaching. To this last statement objection has been raised in some quarters. Many labour leaders and others engaged in the field of workers' education are suspicious of the so-called broadly educated person of "poise and balance." They have reasons growing out of experience for such suspicions, particularly if the poise and balance are the products of study in some ivory tower. But when the well-prepared person at the same time keeps in touch with workers and their problems, he has the possibilities for becoming a good teacher of workers.

Irvine Kerrison, drawing on the experience of conference on the problem, breaks down the characteristics of a good teacher into seven points and emphasized the fact that the teacher always has a responsibility both to his student and to society.

At a conference on workers' education held at Cornell University in February, 1946, the following qualifications, listed in the order of their importance, were accepted as essential for university people responsible for a programme of workers' education:

1. Union experience of such nature as to demonstrate sympathy for the social ideals of the labour movement and a knowledge of the structure and functioning of the labour movement.

2. Participation in some form of workers's education activities, especially in programme development, and, if possible, administration.
3. A record of success in group activity, including ability to cooperate with others.
4. Knowledge of the field of workers' education.
5. Knowledge of and ability in group work and educational processes as applied to workers' education.
6. Knowledge of and experience with community organisations and governmental agencies as related to their helpfulness as resources in a workers' education programme.
7. Acceptability to people of known reputation in the field of workers' education.

Current college and university workers' education programme most acceptable to the labour movement are those which use labour people on their teaching staffs. Programmes which use fully qualified teachers who happen to be employed fulltime in the labour movement give tangible evidence of their belief that a class leader ought to be genuinely and fudamentally sympathetic with the problems and interests of the people in his class.

The good workers' education teacher faces a dual responsibility! He is responsible to the workers and to society as a whole. The first responsibility demands qualifications which persons employed in the labour movement, for obvious reasons, most adequately can present. The second is a general responsibility which all qualified teachers can satisfy and which links the workers' education teacher to all true teachers in every field.

Other Resources—ALES, WEB and CIO Department of Education and Research

Although institutions of higher education are very important in the development of workers' education and should, as we stressed, be urged and aided to do still more, they are only a part of the total picture.

Labour itself has provided leadership, both in individual unions, such as ILGWU, Textile Workers of America, and Packinghouse Workers of America, and through organisations whose services are available to groups of unions or to individual unions. The Workers Education Bureau, attached to the AFL, is responsible for helping AFL unions which desire assistance. Similarly, the CIO Department of Education and Research provides services for CIO unions. The American Labour Education Service works with all groups of organised Labour.

The following description of the WEB is based on materials supplied by John D. Connors, Director.

Workers Education Bureau—American Federation of Labour

The Workers Education Bureau serves the Federation as a clearing house of information and a coordinating agency in the field of labour education and related activities. Its activities include planning nation-wide and state-wide programmes, local classes and study groups, lecture courses, forums, advice on setting up scholarship award programmes, developing public relations programmes, assistance in securing the inclusion of courses on labour in the public school curriculum, gaining the cooperation of public libraries, furnishing speakers, aiding on radio and television programmes, and advising on and distributing labour films. In addition it responds increasingly to requests for information, advice, and materials which come from colleges and universities, public school administrators and teachers, government agencies, libraries and other community organisations.

The Bureau has during the year held two conferences of education directors of national and international unions and state federations of labour...

During the past year our affiliated unions have made considerable progress in the use of movies and filmstrips, and it is encouraging to note that they are entering into the field of film production at an accelerated rate...

To service this growing interest in the use of audio-visual materials, the Bureau maintains a film library which includes not only films produced by A.F.L. unions but also those produced by governmental and other agencies on such topics as discrimination, world affairs, foreign trade, the United Nations and its affiliated organisations, labour-management relations, social security, health and welfare and political action. In addition to furnishing films and filmstrips for showing by A.F.L.

organisations, the Bureau also aids them in purchasing projectors, screens, recorders, etc., at substantial discounts.

The Workers Education Bureau News Letters, published monthly, surveys current workers' education projects among A.F.L. affiliates and universities. It also reviews and annotates new films, books and pamphlets. A completely revised and enlarged edition of the Bureau's bibliography *Labour's Library* is out this fall. During the past year the annual supplement *Labour and Education in 1951* was published, as well as the 15th printing of its parliamentary procedure manual *How to Run a Union Meeting* and the sixth of its *Shop Steward's Manual.*

In line with the Federation's expanding programme of encouraging the growth of the free trade union movement throughout the world, the Bureau continues its cooperation with the educational activities of the I.C.F.T.U and the International Federation of Workers' Education Associations. Considerable time has been spent in assisting MSA, the State Department, the Department of Labour and other government agencies in their programmes of international exchange of workers and information. The Bureau is cooperating with the State Department abroad particularly in Asia, to show workers the advantages of free democratic trade unions and how they can help workers to solve their economic problems...

During the past years the Federation has cooperated with the Inter-University Labour Education Committee, which was established to introduce such subjects as world affairs, community participation, and economic understanding into educational programmes for union officers and members which are already in operation, and to assist labour leaders in starting and carrying on additional educational programmes within their own organisations...

The notes on the CIO Department of Education and Research come from material supplied by George T. Guernsey, Associate Director in charge of education. The report indicated that the Education Division during the year 1951-1952 stressed the following activities among others.

(1) International understanding was emphasized through the use of films, pamphlets, posters and classes in its one-week institutes. The department sponsored a special two-week international affairs seminar at Storrs, Connecticut, and a

three-week overseas programme in Denmark, Norway and Sweden for 25 CIO local union officers;

(2) New ground in CIO's one-week institute programme was broken in the New England, Southern and far Northwest areas;

(3) The Department of Education and Research cooperated with the American Labour Education Service and the Inter-University Labour Education Committee in helping them to develop programmes in the field of workers' education financed by grants from the Fund for Adult Education of the Ford Foundation. The department also worked closely during the past year with the Labour-International Affairs Programme of the American Friends Service Committee.

CIO-Danish Workshop

Perhaps the most noteworthy project sponsored by the Education Division in cooperation with the International Affairs Committee was the labour education workshop in Denmark. Twenty-five local union leaders were sent to Denmark, Norway and Sweden for a three-week trip at a total cost to each of $300, including transportation by air from New York City overseas and return.

Guide For Work with Universities

The CIO is firmly committed to the following policies in this field: (1) the union movement must plan and direct its own programme, (2) it must critically examine resources made available to it in developing its education programme, (3) in the use of study materials or teaching personnel, the trade union movement must carefully select the material and the teachers which will help to build an understanding of the programme and policies of the trade union movement and help it make its contribution to building a democratic nation and a democratic world, (4) because many universities have had no experience in the field of labour education and many times have developed labour-management institutes as a substitute for labour extension work, the CIO feels that all universities in this field should establish labour advisory committees which will bring to the programme the background and understanding of experienced labour educators, and (5) in using university programmes, the CIO feels that only those that are open to all CIO members, regardless of race, creed or colour, should be used.

The basic purpose of an educational programme is to build a strong, democratic labour movement in the United States. Any programme must be measured by its success in doing this.

Film Work Expands

The CIO Education Division sponsored a two-day experimental film conference in March 1952 at Harrisburg, Pennsylvania, where local unions using films were able to come together for training in leading discussions with the use of films...

The CIO Film Division now has 110 titles with 225 prints in its film rental library...

Pamphlets and Books Published

The department has continued to publish pamphlets including its new primer pamphlet "CIO Says The Odds Are Up To You", a popular pamphlet on problems of international affairs...

New Education Manual

A new 1952-53 Education Manual was prepared by the Education Division, and has been widely praised by leaders in the field of workers education. It consists of materials which are helpful to union officials interested in developing an educational programme. Divided into seven sections, the manual contains outlines for discussion of many of the legislative problems, voting records of Congressmen, background on court decisions in the field of civil rights and civil liberties, methods of improving our schools, as well as suggestions for carrying CIO's programme to the grass roots. In each section are a list of films and pamphlets bearing on the subject as well as organisations from which additional material may be secured. The following statement on the ALES is taken from the *Union Education Survey.*

The Work of American Labour Education Service

American Labour Education Service is what might be considered a direction-finding agency. For a period of 25 years it has discovered and fostered significant development in workers' education—in developing study materials for adult workers, in establishing resident schools, in research and experimentation in educational method, and in conducting pilot projects for combatting discrimination through union education.

Today ALES is putting more stress on inter-group relationships in the international field...

...Conferences in this country sponsored by ALES have dealt with various aspects of the international scene and early in 1951 a Midwest Conference brought together leaders from 23 international unions to study the problem of how to make international problems "come alive" for union members.

As part of its general programme in inter-group relations, ALES has worked to further cooperation between farmers and workers through education. A series of Farmers' and Workers' Education Conferences has brought together labour and liberal farmers' and cooperative groups, and out of their discussions in developing a manual of educational activities to promote improved farmer-labour understanding of manual problems in local communities.

Another phase of its work is the relation of white collar workers with other wage earners. It sponsors a resident labour school, White Collar Workshop, set up especially for office workers, postal clerk, teachers, librarians, social workers and government workers...

Certain long-term functions...include advisory service to trade unions and other organisations through field trips to initiate activities and advise local groups as well as through suggestion by correspondence; national conferences for co-ordination of work and to provide a forum for those professionally engaged in workers' education; sectional and local conferences to stimulate new activity or focus attention on special problems; preparation of labour education materials including special reports and bibliographical materials; informational and clearing house activities such as a teachers' registry and educational counselling and consultants' services for individuals interested in the workers' education field...

... Through an annual conference of teachers and leaders in workers' education, which brings together some 200 educational representatives of unions, universities and community agencies, ALES provides a meeting ground for those professionally engaged in workers' education.

... As a direction-finding organisation, ALES is working continuously on the study and evaluation of workers' education programmes, helping to integrate new trends and projects in the field with established values based on experience, and acting as liaison and interpreter among labour, university, government and community organisations.

What Lies Ahead in Workers' Education?

The future of workers' education is the future of organised labour, and the future of organised labour is the future of democracy. In our increasingly interdependent society we move ahead only through cooperation. There will, of course, be tests of strength in order to clarify issues and determine directions—these are an integral part of the democratic process. But the fundamental approach must be positive. It cannot be one of eternal opposition. This means that all adult educators, no matter what their direct connection with organised programmes may be, must understand the place of the worker in modern world society.

The excerpts cited below from three statements regarding the basic role and status of organised labour cannot adequately cover the tremendous area that labour presents, but they can encourage further study by the reader.

Earnest E. Schwarztrauber presents the basic logic for accepting the organised labour movement as a part of modern society. For many this may seems unnecessary, but there are still numerous persons in key positions who have reservations regarding it.

The School for Workers assumes, as a first premise, the trade union movement as an accepted institutions in modern industrial society, despite threatening situations facing it at times. In America there is general approval in theory of workers' right to organise and to bargain collectively, but there exists in fact actual resistance to the practice of that right. Nevertheless, in theory and partially in practice, trade unionism has become woven into the fabric of American institutional life. And, barring a catastrophe such as befell workers in totalitarian societies, and continues in some today, trade unionism will become as generally accepted in our country as in England and the Scandinavian countries. In fact, trade unionists will no doubt grow in influence in every facet of American life, social, economic and political. This is as it should be since a social system can not be a healthy one if there exists a second-class citizenship for any group in its midst.

If then we are reasonably right in our first premise, the second should logically follow. That is, trade unionism implies among other things that collective bargaining is a normal relationship between employees and employer. Otherwise the privilege of organisation is largely an empty one...

A further premise of great importance is the essential dignity of all labour, however menial, if it serves human welfare. Few will seriously challenge the soundness of this premise. How many, however, are cognizant of the fact that increasing mechanization in industry tends to reduce many workers to the level of the semiskilled and subjects them to the depersonalizing influenced of monotonous automatic labour?...

A final premise assumes that workers can no longer be looked upon as mere "hewers of stone and carriers of water". That is, events not only at home but abroad indicate that workers are asserting not only their rights but also their desire to assume responsibility in the whole field of community and national life. In other words they are arriving at the stage in their social development where they want and expect to share in the whole of community, national and even international life and action...

Walter Reuther outlines the broad aims of the United Automobile Workers Union, one of the most powerful of the organised labour groups. In the article from which this selection is taken, he proceeds to describe the efforts for old-age security, good health, peace and the strengthening of democracy through such things as a guaranteed annual wage and insurance, which will give a broad security to the worker and his family. All of this involves education for intelligent political action.

We in the United Automobile Workers Union (Congress of Industrial Organisations) have worked hard in the vineyard of collective bargaining, and hundreds of thousands of workers and their families have won for themselves greater security and a richer, fuller life.

While our gains and achievements have been outstanding, we realize that collective bargaining is a never ending struggle to make human progress. Each victory, each gain, must be used to further strengthen and build our union—to educate our members to an understanding of their rights, their opportunities, and their responsibilities and to prepare ourselves to move forward to further achievements. There are still many problems unsolved and still many battles to be won before workers receive their full share of the fruits of American industry.

Perhaps the best way for me to discuss the practical aims and purposes of American labour is to recount some of the major achievement of the UAW-CIO, and some of its major goals and hopes for the future.

The UAW-CIO has worked and fought hard to raise collective bargaining above the level of a struggle between competing economic pressure groups, and to gear it to the good of the whole community. We have clearly understood that we live in an inter-dependent world in which labour cannot raise itself by its own economic bootstraps. The UAW-CIO has had the strength and has generated the loyalty and enthusiasm that have made possible our great gains, because we abandoned the old slot-machine kind of unionism and instead developed the kind of progressive and dynamic programme that reflects the needs of all the American people.

Out of this concept grew the dynamic wage policy which we have developed in the last five years—a wage policy which is directed toward increased purchasing power and real wages, rather than just toward increases in money wages.

The UAW-CIO basic agreements, which now cover more than one million workers, translate into reality the economic and social principles which have been the foundation of the union's programme during the last five years. They recognise that increased purchasing power—not just increased money wages—is the only basis for a higher standard of living. They recognise that workers have a right to a constantly improving standard of living and that they have a right to share in the benefits of greater production, made possible through technological progress, without additional human effort.

Our union was born out of the determination of the workers

in our industry to build for themselves and their families a better life and a more secure future. The workers recognize that they could build a better world for themselves and their children only through the establishment of a powerful, militant, democratic and progressive industrial union with the strength and vision to champion their cause.

Peter F. Druker, an economic analyst of modern society, extends Reuther's idea to show the stake that everyone has in the actions of labour groups.

Never before, it seems, has organised labour been as strong, as powerful, and as accepted, in this country, as today. Yet the American labour movement faces its most serious crisis. It is a crisis of success, not of failure—but that may make it all the more severe. Our union leaders still live in the days when they had to fight for recognition if not for existence. But the problems they really face are those of labour's power and responsibility as a ruling group in industrial society.

True to the traditions of this country, and they are good traditions, in this case at least—the problems will not be solved on the theoretical or abstract level, but pragmatically and case by case. But it is quite clear what the areas are in which the decisions will have to be found. They are: (1) wage policy (2) the "right to strike", (3) union control over the citizen's access to a livelihood, and (4) internal union organisation.

In the final analysis, the problem of labour's role in our industrial society is one of conflict between the position of the labour union in the individual enterprise and the position of the labour movement in modern society. In the individual enterprise, the union is first and foremost a permanent opposition, an "antibody". There are many areas within this relationship where the interests of enterprise and union go together; and the more cooperation there can be in these areas the more effective, and the stronger, will both enterprise and union be. But the union can never subordinate itself to the enterprise's rationale of profitable and efficient production as the final yardstick of decisions, behaviour and policy. Its major function will always be to set against the purely economic goals of the enterprise the economic, social and political goals of the employee.

Society, however, must demand of the union movement

that it take positive responsibility for the strength and success of society and economy. It is not possible for that union movement to claim exemption from this responsibility on the ground that the labour union is just another pressure group—the attitude John L. Lewis has taken so consistently. For the labour movement differs fundamentally from all other pressure groups in that it possesses both coercive and exclusive powers. No farm organisation, however strong, has ever been able to prevent its own members from planting, harvesting, or marketing a crop. No other pressure group, in other words, has ever been able to control either the citizen or society. The labour union, inevitably, can do both. And this means that the labour union, rather than being a pressure group, that is, an economic organisation, inevitably has political and social powers.

Of any such group, society must demand positive responsibility. Society must demand that the labour movement subordinate its own aims and beliefs to the aims and beliefs of society, to the productivity of the economy and the profitability of the enterprise system. But at the same time, society demands that the union act as a permanent opposition within the individual enterprise.

This conflict has not been resolved in any country. It is widely believed that the American labour movement is less mature than some of the older European labour movements. This is a fallacy. In fact, the American labour movement is a great deal more mature than any European labour movement, if only because it has been wise enough not to let itself become the tail of the ideological kite of a political party. But the best that can be said for the American labour movement, and even for its more advanced leaders, is that it is slowly becoming aware of the existence of a problem of labour's role and position in industrial society. On our success in solving this problem within the next generation may depend not only the survival of an independent and strong unionism, but the survival of our productive economy and our free society.

These selections from the field of workers' education indicate that there are two major needs at present: (1) to strengthen and extends services to labour groups along the lines promised by current programmes, and (2) to make workers' education a more integral part of the total adult-education efforts in the community.

Labour education is inextricably a part of community adult education. The fact that there have been and still are suspicions on both sides must be recognised. The central fact which can help to cut through these differences is the role of *work* in our society. Work is a central factor in any society—so much so that it often escapes attention. In society of specialized techniques which permit more opportunities for other things, the role of work—and therefore of the worker, requires re-examination. In this connection the statement of J.B.S. Hardman in *Workers' Education in the United States,* is relevant.

What is Workers' Education?

Defining the Area. Briefly and perhaps somewhat crudely defined, *workers' education is education for workers.* The logic of this definition lies in the fact that when we say workers' education we refer neither, specifically, to the enterprises which seek to Americanize the foreign-born; nor, generally, to the magnanimous efforts which aim to inject a living content into the intellectual vacuums left in some adult heads by education they received in the little red brick school. Only incidental to the concept and scope of workers' education are the activities which help to overcome handicaps of language or adult illiteracy, or which try to train adult workers in skills and trades they did not learn at an earlier age. Basic to workers' education is the effort to help the worker find his location upon the scale of our socio-economic setup, to gain a clear knowledge of all the facts relevant to his condition as a *wage-earner.* By this definition, workers' education aims at equipping the worker with the kind of tools that will enable him to become a better wage-earner, and this means *to make him a union member* and ever a *better* union member. Thus workers' education lands foursquare in the vortex of ideas and interests which center in organised labour. There it properly belongs: workers' education is in this sense different from what is bèing done in the institutions devoted to general adult education or to vocational training.

Conceivably, our accent upon the wage-earner aspect of worker's education may bring up the terrifying spector of *class* education. But this is so only if we insist on an habitual loyalty to accepted, but not at all real, meanings of certain words. The democratic society which has been emerging in recent years, however slow the pace of progress, does not at all preclude a functional relevancy between the terms *union member* and *democratic citizen.* In this respect, the tasks of workers' education are not altogether distinct from those which progressive public education will soon have to deal with. For all too long a time, the interrelation of the workers as citizen, and citizen as worker, has remained neglected under our public education system. Surely there is no basic contrast between democracy and free associations of wage-earners; indeed the relationship is one of integration. Public educators will be obliged to pay much attention to this crucial fact.

At the same time that we build better services for workers' education, we must also move, as a number of universities are doing, to help management and the public. Agriculture, too, will be increasingly involved as technological developments brings into this area the same kinds of problems. Each such area—agriculture, organised labour, management, professional services—has its specialized educational needs; together they constitute the public, which has the task of creating over-all policies which will enable each group to do its work still more effectively.

13

National Agencies

The concern of this book is to help develop a strong programme of education for adults. Since the focus is on meeting the needs of adults whenever and wherever the needs occur, the center of such a programme will be in the local community. Only as we can build comprehensive and competent services as the local level can we accomplish this task successfully. In a totalitarian country it would be possible to do the planning at the top and order the programmes put into effect in every locality. In a democracy we maintain the major responsibilities at a level where the citizens, operating in face-to-face groups, can set the basic patterns.

Anyone who has participated in such a democratic programme knows that the local groups need help with ideas, with materials, with the variety of special skills which are required for programmes which are adaptable to local differences. There is a place in the cooperative approach to local community problems for resources at the state and national levels. The point to keep in mind is that the major purpose of these resources is to build strong local activities.

The theory is straightforward and generally accepted. The difficulties arise in practice. The emphasis upon the central role of local needs does not ensure that localities will automatically act on these needs. Time is short, and the result is often that persons operating at the state and national levels grow impatient. "Tell me what we should do and we will be glad to go to work at it" is a plaint too well known to persons who try to aid local groups. If the outside resource persons succumb to this cry, local leadership is still further emasculated.

One of the major points to emphasize, therefore, is that assistance to the local groups must continue over a period of time long enough to build the necessary leadership. Too often plans are made to finance services for a three-year period. At the end of that time there may be little to show in the way of tangible results, and the aid is terminated when possibly it should be increased. Unless persons at the state and national level recognize that the growth which generally characterizes efforts to foster local responsibility is slow, and unless they ensure continued support for ten-year periods, we shall continue to see a succession of abortive experiments.

Everyone in adult education has a stake in this matter of providing adequate help to local groups. The goal we are trying to reach is the availability of services to all adults in this country, young and old, of all levels of experience and ability, whether they live in city, village or country, north, east, west and south. It is heartening to find occasional places where good programmes have been achieved, but our task is to make these the rule and not the exception.

One of the encouraging signs has been the sensitivity of the Adult Education Association of the U. S. A. to the approach outlined above. In fact, the strong feeling which we as authors have on this matter arises, to a considerable degree, from our participation in the development of policy in the Association. We devote considerable space to selections from the materials of the Association not only because it is the national organisation in adult education but also because it illustrates in a very positive way some of the steps that can be taken to strengthen the partnership with local groups.

The development of the new Association is an interesting effort to apply the concept of democratic participation. The urge to create a single national organisation came from a situation in which there had been two organisations carrying on almost identical activities, neither one having the resources to do an adequate job. When a committee was established to consider the possibilities of a single organisation, it wisely began with a careful examination of the current situation in adult education and the appropriate functions of a national organisation. We shall quote from some of these analysis which the organising committee prepared.

The first selection is taken from a progress report of the joint committee. At this stage the committee was composed of representatives of the two national organisations, and there was a good deal of suspicion growing out of the relations between the two groups. Because it would have been easy to become bogged down, as had some earlier attempts, the approach of the committee was of great importance.

The present endeavour to create a single or a new organisation is an endeavour to find a means of unifying and enriching the professional functions which the American Association for Adult Education and the Department of Adult Education have undertaken to serve in the past.

As the report will clearly indicate, this endeavour does not carry the connotation of "merger", of "absorption", of "amalgamation", or of "federation". The Joint Committee has been actively engaged in making plans for a new kind of adult education organisation that can meet the needs of the adult education field, unify existing leadership, and provide an executive channelling of service between local, state, regional and national adult education programmes.

This first decision of the Joint Committee (to explore the tasks of the adult education profession) was of crucial importance. *First*, it was a procedural decision and thus did not invoke strong feelings of loyalty or the consideration of individual agenda plans in advance of a thorough consideration of all the factors involved. *Second,* this first decision of the Committee established the precedent of moving toward the solution of other problems through a stepladder progression of decisions on the basic and underlying questions. Had the Committee failed to reach agreement on its first decision it would have had nothing to go back. The history of the Joint Committee has been a steady movement forward on the basis of agreements reached. Because of this the Joint Committee is now able, if necessary, to resolve a point of disagreements by going back to a previous agreement and then moving forward again.

The Tasks of the Adult Education Field

The exciting vision of involving all adult educators in the creation of a new, responsive and multi-purpose organisation capable of serving and providing leadership on many fronts captured the imagination of all members of the Joint Committee from the beginning of its operations. In recognizing that the needs for a national adult education organisation had to be ascertained before consideration could be given to the planning of organisational measures adequate to meet them the Joint Committee was at once conscious of its own inadequacy to assess these needs. However, it felt that in order to give a reality basis to its considerations it should at least draw up a tentative list of the tasks performed by adult education in the field.

The Joint Committee therefore decided to approach organisational needs in terms of those tasks of adult education from which organisational needs may grow. The tasks which the Joint Committee has examined and sees as areas of responsibility touching all programmes of adult education are as follows: (It is reemphasized the following is a preliminary listing of the responsibilities of the professional field of adult education—not the functions of a new organisation).

1. Identification of all formal and informal adult education activities and establishing good working relationships.
2. Diagnosis of the real needs and interests of the adult community as a whole and of the subgroups within it.
3. Evaluation of existing programmes and services.
4. Planning more adequate programmes and developing better coordination of community programmes.
5. Discovery, development and utilization of programmes resources such as techniques, methods and materials.
6. Stimulation, involvement and counselling of the individuals and groups served by adult education.
7. Involvement, selection and education and training of non-professional adult education workers.
8. Interpretation of adult education to the public.
9. Development of pre-service and in-service education and training for professional adult education workers.
10. Development of programmes of research in adult education.
11. Continuing development of a functional philosophy of adult education.

12. Development and safeguarding of the professional status, economic security, and academic freedom of adult educators.

Possible functions and services of the proposed Organisation

The twelve tasks listed above indicate in a general way the scope and nature of the responsibilities of adult education programmes. The Joint Committee recognises that the list is incomplete and serves only as a guide to the forthcoming discussions in adult education circles. In examining these tasks in reference to the implications they hold for the formation of a new national, professional organisation, the Joint Committee suggested the following possible general functions and services of the new organisation:

1. Providing means of communication among adult educators (for example, conferences, committee work, periodicals, handbooks, staff correspondence and interviews).
2. Providing consultation and referral services.
3. Stimulating, conducting, and reporting research and invention relevant to the practice of adult education.
4. Continuing definition of the adult education movement and profession.
5. Encouraging and assisting in continuing evaluation and improvement of the content and methods of leadership training and all aspects of the practice of adult education (such as, for example, materials, method, techniques, programme planning, organisation and administration).
6. Continuing interpretation of the social scene in the light of its effect on the educational needs of adults.
7. Interpretation and representation of adult education to the lay public, to workers on other educational levels, and to public and private agencies in the United States and internationally.
8. Attempting to secure more adequate legal and financial provision for adult education services.
9. Operating a placement service for adult education workers.
10. Defending adult education workers and agencies against infringements of rights essential to the performance of their functions.

Implicit in this list of functions and services are the agreements of the Joint Committee that the new organisation should operate essential programmes as well as serve and coordinate the work of others; that it should provide active leadership of its own as well as support the leadership of others; and that it should provide a balanced and broad programme capable of earning and holding the involvement and respect of workers in adult education from all of the many specialized fields.

What kind of organisation could do all these things? The planning group knew the limitations of the efforts of the existing organisations. It was aware of the special difficulties in the inchoate nature of adult education at this time. It therefore tried to identity some of the issues that would need to be considered and to formulate wherever possible guiding principles to be considered by the founding assembly. It is interesting to note that there are several points on which the planning group was not able to agree. The concept of continuous consideration by the new organisation of all principles of operation was central in the planning.

The statement continues:

Principles of Organisations and Membership

The above list of possible function and services is sufficiently ambitious to require dependence upon the establishment of a sensitive and communicative relationship between the workers actually engaged in adult education and the policy-making officials responsible for directing the activities of the proposed organisation.

The following principles have, therefore, been considered by the Joint Committee as consistent with its thinking about an organisation which is quickly responsive to the changing demands and requirements of adult education carried on in the field. The Joint Committee has also been aware that implicit in the operation of a professional organisation intent on serving the interests of a wide-spread and diversified clientele lurks the constant danger of power pressures exerted by the size, influence, prestige, wealth, or some other characteristic of a part of its constituency. In taking this factor into account, the Joint Committee has emphasised protecting "minority interests" in adult education from domination by the larger and more solidly organised groups:

Specifically, the Joint Committee suggests that the structure of a national organisation should be such as to—

(1) Fulfill the functions assigned to it in terms of the needs of individuals and organisations working in adult education.
(2) Provide for the effective participation of the majority of adult education workers.
(3) Provide for the full participation and representation of, and services to, all minority interests in adult education.
(4) Grow and adapt to the changing needs of its constituency.
(5) Establish working relationships with organisations and fields of endeavour (that are not integral parts of the organisation) as the interests of adult education may require.
(6) Integrate its activities closely with those of other local, state, regional, national and international adult education organisations, associations and agencies.

Organisational principles considered but left unresolved include the following:

(1) To what extent should the policies and officers of the organisation be determined directly by the memberships? To what extent by representatives of the membership?
(2) To what extent should membership be open to all individuals and organisations concerned with adult education?
(3) Relationships that should exist between a national organisation and other private educational agencies, such as the National Education Association, the American Council on Education, the Institute of Adult Education at Teachers College, Columbia University, etc.

As soon as it was clear that there was real promise of positive action, the group made up of the appointed representatives of the two organisations began to bring other persons into the planning. The committee held a one-week workshop at Sarah Lawrance College in the summer of 1950 with persons from a number of areas of adult education present. Subgroups were set up to develop the thinking in the various area, such as in-service training, field services and leadership training. These subgroups expanded their memberships and thus brought an additional number of persons into the planning for the new organisation.

The material which follows represents, as did the selections above, preliminary thinking to guide the persons who constituted the founding assembly and, if approved there, the members of the association as they moved forward along related lines. The reader will find from time to time in the issues of *Adult Education* and in other materials published by the Adult Education Association further statements on the progress of these and other committees.

I. Social Interpretation and Direction Finding

In order that the adult education movement may work toward the realization of these and other desirable aims, the national organisation should (a) Re-examine with workers on other educational levels and the members of the various educational and socio-civic groups the educational process as a whole with the implications the expanding opportunities for adult education have for elementary, secondary and higher education; (b) Interpret and anticipate developments in the social scene that create social problems at home and abroad and problems of personal orientation and morale for individuals; (c) Assist local communities in making such interpretations and assessing their adult educational needs; (d) Assist national organisations to make such interpretations and to evaluate and reconstruct their programmes in the light of the characteristics and needs of the social scene; (e) Collaborate with other organisation in stimulating and conducting research in social problems areas.

II. Consultation and Field Services

One of the purposes of the new organisation is assumed to be the stimulation of the developments of adult education both in the expansion of programme opportunities and in the improvement of the educational personnel producing the programmes. The central office would stimulate this quantitative and qualitative improvement by certain services which it would provide for consultation and for work in the field.

A number of these services are outlined below. In envisaging the operation of these services the proposal is that the principle be followed that the national organisation would never perform a task that could be done as well by another organisation. It should also be noted at this point that no clear distinction is made between the function of consulation and the function of field service. It is assumed that there is considerable overlapping in these two functions and that the same staff members would be called upon to perform both types of services.

The following services are suggestive but in no way definitive:

1. Specific types of consultant and field services would include:
   (a) Leadership training.
   (b) Assistance to national, state and local groups in strengthening their organisations from the standpoint of service to their own constituents.
   (c) Legislative consultant service.
   (d) Consultant service on financing adult education projects and programmes.
   (e) Research assistance.
2. The maintaining of a continuous annotated inventory of personnel and services for consultant purposes already available on various levels—national, state and local; and the operation of a referral service where any of these exisiting services can meet the need.
3. The continual assessment of the need for consultant services and field services not now being provided for, and the furnishing of staff assistance directly to groups where satisfactory referrals cannot be made.

III. Communications among Adult Educators

The principal means of communication among professional and nonprofessional adult educators is the journal of the national organisation. Many persons and some organisations will join the new association in order to receive the journal. It should be issued monthly to permit frequent contact with the membership. It should be attractive in format, well-planned in content...

A somewhat less effective but nevertheless helpful means of communication would be the distribution of other types of publication than the journal. Such publications would include pamphlets, and reprints of articles of adult education implications that appear in other publications; for example, in labour journals, industrial journals, teachers' bulletins, research publications, etc.

In addition to serving as a house organ for the national organisation, the journal would contain (1) articles, (2) news items, and (3) reviews of literature and research. The entire contents should be significant and lively, *i.e.*, worthy of attention and discussion by workers in adult education and related fields.

IV. Methods and Materials

A. *Materials.* It is suggested that the national organisation be the focus for assembling of materials and information about the materials (unless some appropriate agency, *e.g.* Office of Education, can be found to take over this function).

B. *Methods.* One of the services of the national organisation can be that of training in the methods of adult education to all groups and organisations that are identified with the adult education task.

V. Leadership Training

In the field of leadership training the proposed new organisation should function primarily as a catalytic agent to stimulate, to promote and to organise on a sharing basis the work of its constituents and cooperating agencies and individuals. It should seek to strengthen already existing leadership services and also open up new directions in leadership training.

Such a function will require (1) an intimate awareness on the part of the organisational staff of leadership training work being done in various areas and institutions throughout the country; (2) knowledge of research being undertaken and needed in the leadership education field and the significant findings and outcomes of the same; (3) a very strong personal collaborative and cooperative relationship with exisiting agencies and institutions in the field of leadership training; (4) proper clearing house facilities which cannot be provided by other organisations.

VI. Personal Services

1. Make an inventory of the various types of opportunities in adult education leadership such as the board of education or community directors of adult education, teaching positions, social service opportunities, personnel work, research assistants...

2. Organise a placement service in co-operation with various component organisations...

3. Work to raise the professional status of those engaged in various types of adult education leadership...

VII. Public Relations and Financial Support

A specialist who understands legislative procedures, financial problems and promotion should be employed in the central office to devote full time to building support for adult education. Included in his work shall be such tasks as the following: (1) Acting as representative of the organisation before congress, foundations and similar sources of funds...(2) Training and consulation services on request to local, state and national organisations and agencies on methods of gaining more adequate financial support. (3) Preparing and assisting in the preparation of promotional materials on adult education for dissemination through the mass media—cinema, magazines, newspapers, radio, television, etc. (4) Helping to determine how to finance pilot projects; gathering information relating to finance as a background for the promotion and establishment of adult education activities.

VIII. Research

A. The Committee makes the following affirmations:

1. The function of research is to assist communities and organisations to get problems solved more effectively...Research is viewed as an integral part of the total local programme, growing out of the work of the local organisation and feeding back into its activities...

2. In viewing research in this integral way it would be important that it be done in long-term units. Adequate weight should be given to basic research as needed.

3. The National Organisation would operate primarily as a cooperating agency and would conduct research only where

either *(a)* no other agency would do it, or only where *(b)* it is such an integral part of the programme that the National Organisation should clearly do it.

The Committee proposes the following kinds of activities:

A. The use of present resources—applying present research to adult education problems, reporting current studies, studying channels to improve use of research, clearing house on resources.

B. The development of attitudes relating to research—bringing about better communication between research workers and practitioners, helping identify practicable problems and getting research resources for them.

C. The development of a strategy of research—defining the various steps needed to accomplish the above and getting appropriate groups to accept responsibilities.

D. The provisions for evaluation—insuring early attention, assisting in developing necessary techniques.

The committee working on the materials quoted above were volunteer and had only limited resources. The statements were intended as working documents and had the inevitable roughness of such papers. It is therefore interesting to see how well they did keep the emphasis on the local groups and the way in which they saw the national organisation in a helping role.

One of the problems that arose in defining the membership plan was to ensure that the power was in the hands of individual members. There was fear that organisational rather than individual memberships might open the way to control by blocs. At the same time it was very important that organisations be actively associated. It was therefore agreed that the many national organisations that were closely identified with adult education and should have definite relationships with the national organisation should become members or a Council of National Organisations. This council would be an integral part of the Adult Education Association. We quote from the materials developed at the meeting to organise the council in February 1952.

Purpose and Objectives

The purpose of the Council of National Organisation of the AEA is to afford an opportunity for national organisations voluntarily to confer, plan or work together more effectively on problems of common concern in adult education.

Structure

As authorized by Article III of the Constitution of the AEA of the USA, a Council of National Organisation is created. Although a constitutional organ of the AEA, this Council shall develop its own policies, programmes and organisation, and shall determine its operating relationships with the AEA.

1. The name of this organisation shall be "The Council of National Organisations of the AEA of the USA.."
2. The governing body of the Council shall be the representatives of Participating Organisations of the Council convened in assembly.
3. Each Participating Organisation shall be entitled to one voting representative in the Council.

Membership

1. For the purposes of membership planning the Council of National Organisations of the AEA of the U.S.A is considered a consultative assembly.
2. The constituents of the CNO are designated as Participating Organisations.
3. The following organisations are considered eligible for election as Participating Organisations:
   (a) those interested in the general philosophy and basic purposes of the AEA of the USA,
   (b) those representing interests that are national or international in scope,
   (c) those actively concerned with and contributing to the educational improvement of the adult population.
   (d) Federal government agencies and sub-divisions thereof,
   (e) those dedicated to broadly acceptable social goals.
   (f) those who maitain standards of integrity and factual accuracy in their educational materials,
   (g) professional and trade associations of recognised standing but not individuals or individual business firms,
   (h) those which are not essentially partisan political organisations.

Programme, Services and Projects

The Council of National Organisation of the AEA should serve as a depository of information on agency programmes, projects, finding, materials, techniques and services.

A survey of organisation programmes and problems is recommended to serve as an initial pool of resources for a proposed clearing house.

It is believed that Participating Organisations in the Council expect to derive two benefits from the Council:

1. An exchange of information on the basis of content.

2. An exchange of information on the basis of educational techniques and materials.

Be it resolved that: Implicit in the programme of the CNO is education for democracy and that one of the first items on the CNO agenda should be an exploration of how to translate this objective into programme.

It is recommended that:

1. AEA and CNO do not set up parallel service and functioning committees without good reason, but that

2. Organisations have adequate representation on committees.

The Adult Education Association of the U.S.A has lived up to the democratic principles outlined above. It is endeavouring to build a strong body of services to adult educators. It publishes two magazines, *Adult Education* and *Adult Leadership;* it has twenty committees working on problems of programme and service; it is developing a regional service programme; and in other ways it is undertaking to strengthen the hands of local practitioners. It is well aware that the national organisation can be strong over a period of time only when there is activity in the local communities.

We have devoted considerable space to the new national organisation for adult education because it is obviously of prime importance to persons interested in adult education and because of the effort it has made to met some of the problems of our complex civilization. The wide acceptance of the importance of local control is not alone enough to ensure the maintenance of such control. There must be administrative plans which can successfully meet the decisions arising. The AEA is seeking to combine the best values of centralization and decentralization through (1) its series of working groups, each concentrating on some special aspect, such as problems of the aging or social philosophy, and (2) a number of offices throughout the country which will enable the association to keep closer contact with local activities and make wider use of persons in the various regions.

This approach calls for strong regional, state and local organisations. It is one of the major functions of the AEA to assist in the development of these organisations, primarily by helping to train the leaders to man the services required. Here we shall merely emphasize again the importance of such organisations in providing comprehensive services to all adults.

The problem at the intermediate level is complicated by the fact that we are undoubtedly in a period of transition from states to regions as far as many kinds of services are concerned. Governmentally, states are the intermediate unit, and services, such as education, libraries and agricultural extension, are organised on this basis. Functionally, however, many services can better be provided on a basis of an area larger than a single state, but we are only beginning to organise governmentally at this level. The TVA and the Southern Regional Council on Graduate Education are important development in this direction. For non-governmental services, we do not have agreement on boundaries, different organisation using different regional plans to divide the country.

The Agricultural Extension Service has worked very effectively on a federal-state-local plan of cooperation, and the experience of this service can provide guidance.

Only a few states—California, Michigan and New Jersey are examples—have strong associations of adult education. Even in these, however, the services to the local communities are limited. Opportunities to share experiences and to join in training workshops are the chief services, plus occasional communications through newsletters. In general, state associations depend upon state education department personnel to carry out the services.

This dependence raises the problem of dividing financial resources between the federal and state agencies and the further problem of getting recognition for regions which could then qualify for governmental personnel services. States vary so tremendously in their wealth that services depending upon state and local financing tend to be very inequitably distributed among the total population, as has been demonstrated many times for the public schools. Adult-education leaders should work for ways of allocating to smaller units taxes collected at the national level so as to permit strong programmes close to the level of the local communities.

Another problem that arises in connection with national organisations is the relation of an increasing number of such organisations to the local community. Very properly the national organisations recognise the importance of action at the local level and frequently they then proceed to organise the local community for the specific activity that they are promoting. If ten, twenty, thirty, or more national organisations all wish to organise local councils, the net effect may be inefficient or, worse, dangerous to the integrity of the locality.

Of the many national organisations with a conscious concern for adult education (in December 1952, the Council of National Organisation had about 100 participating organisations), we shall present brief sketches of two to illustrate the organisational pattern and the services.

The National University Extension Association

One of the major organised services of adult education is university extension. The national organisation which serves this area is the National University Extension Association, generally known by its initials NUEA. The purpose of the NUEA, as stated in its constitution, is "the establishment of an official and authorised organisation through which colleges and universities engaged in university extension, adult education and other public services may confer for the development and the promotion of the best ideals, methods and standards." This is elaborated somewhat in the following paragraphs from a mimeographed statement on the Association:

> The chief benefit of the NUEA is that it serves as the one organisation that has consistently for 32 [38 in 1953] years promoted the interests of the major universities and colleges in the field of public service and adult education. University Extension has set a unique pattern which has developed the

> American University into a genuine public service institution, a significant contribution to modern times, to a civilization that needs as never before a disinterested, relatively free approach to knowledge and understanding.

The Association provides a common meeting ground for educators and administrators concerned with university extension who in other associations are not adequately represented; and its officers and committees have been able to influence national policies in many fields, especially on the federal level in emergency situations calling for initiative and invention. Two examples are the U.S.A.F.I. [United States Armed Forces Institute] and E.S.M.W.T. [Engineering, Science and Management War Training]. Others, less well known, are the remarkable impetus to the proper use of audio-visual techniques, the centralization of motion picture depositories, and the creation of the National Film Council and the Educational Film Library Association. Recent accomplishments have been the inauguration of Training Courses for Extension Workers with the support of the Carnegie Corporation and the expansion of resident extension centers and correspondence courses for veterans.

Promotion of the idea of federal aid for university extension presents a problem calling for consistent study, conferences, and consultation with other associations' policy-making bodies.

The Association conducts an annual conference; publishes a monthly *Bulletin,* the proceeding of the conferences, *Studies in University Extension,* and other materials; and has a number of committees which carry on special or continuing studies and report to the members. The 1951 *Proceedings* carried reports from the following committee: Implications of Atomic Energy for Adult Education, Extension and Adult Education Research, Radio and Television, Studies in Extension Education, Industrial Relation and Workers Education, Institutes and Conferences, Technical Institutes, Institutional Cooperation and Community Organisation.

The NUEA is an organisation of institutions. The sections of the constitution on membership and representation illustrate the way in which this kind of organisation has dealt with the problems of participation. Voting is by institution, with each institution holding active membership entitled to one vote.

Individuals participate in the activities of the Association, but only the accredited representative of each institution votes.

Article III. Membership

1. Consistent with the purpose of this organisation, the membership of the National University Extension Association shall consist of active members, associate members and individual members. Active members shall include those institutions which, at the time of making application for membership, are State Universities, Land-Grant Colleges and other institutions of acceptable standing not included in the above classification.

2. Institutions conducted for financial gain or profit shall not be eligible for membership in this Association.

3. Associate membership in this Association shall be composed of institutional members conforming in all respects to the provisions of Sec. 1 and 2 of Article III of this Constitution but which may not fully meet the criteria set forth in the by-laws. Such members shall enjoy all the rights and privileges of membership, except the right to vote in business sessions or on matters binding the Association.

6. Individual membership in this Association shall be composed of persons in the employ of either active or associate institutional members. Such individual members, at the meetings of the Association, shall be given the privilege of the floor but not the right to vote.

7. Emeritus faculty or administrative extension personnel who are no longer in the employ of the institutional members by virtue of retirement shall hold honorary membership without payment of dues.

Article IV. Representation

1. The principle of representation in this Association shall be institutional rather than official or individual. The number of accredited representatives from each institution shall be determined by the member institution itself.

2. The allotted number of accredited representatives for each institution shall be chosen by that institution in such manner as meets the approval of the president of that institution.

3. Any officer, whether a member of the faculty, the division of extension or of the board of governors of any institution belonging to this Association shall be entitled to all the privileges of a representative excepting the right to vote.

4. Each institution received as a member of this Association shall be entitled to one vote on any question before the Association, the vote to be cast by its accredited representative or representative spokesman.

The American Library Association

The American Library Association, commonly known as the ALA, is one of the major national professional organisation in adult education. It is a comprehensive association with a large staff and it undertakes to serve all the interests of the library movement. There is not agreement on just what aspects of library work are properly considered adult education. The over-all picture of the ALA is given in the statement in the *Encyclopaedia Americana.*

The American Library Association is an international organisation of 15,000 librarians, library trustees and friends of libraries. Most of the membership is drawn from the United States and Canda. Founded in 1876, to promote better library service and librarianship, it is the oldest and largest library association in the world and is affiliated, formally and informally, with more than sixty other library organisations. The association initiated the expansion of the public library movement in America and blazed the trail toward the recognition of librarianship as a profession. The man largely responsible for the organisation of ALA, Melvil Dewey, was also the organiser of the first library school. The growth of library schools, in number and significance, received important stimulation from the ALA Board of Education for Librarianship. Through a grant from the Carnegie Corporation, the board was enabled to establish standards and accreditation, to carry on studies, and to encourage the publication of professional texts.

The association acts as a clearing house for public libraries, school, college, hospital, prison, business and special libraries, as well as for library schools. It sets standards for library personnel, carries on cooperative programme such as cataloguing, the compilation of bibliographies, etc., makes authoritative information available on subjects related to library matters. Through its International Relations Office opened in 1942, the association is concerned with the operation of American libraries in foreign countries, the interchange of librarians and publications on an international basis, and the importation of foreign books and journals. The association opened a national relations office in Washington in October 1945, to "advance and protect the interests of libraries and of people who use libraries, insofar as those interests may be helped or hurt by legislation, regulation or other government action".

The association publishes five regular periodicals—the *ALA Bulletin,* issued monthly, which includes news, articles, reports on association activities, conference proceedings and the yearly directory of members. *Booklist* is a semimonthly guide to the selection and purchase of current books. The quarterly *Subscription Books Bulletin* reviews subscription sets. The *Quarterly Hospital Book Guide* presents reviews of carefully selected fiction and nonfiction suitable for use in hospitals and similar institutions. In addition, the ALA publishers numerous books and pamphlets of special interest to librarians.

The association's policies are directed by an executive board and council of practising librarians. It has several divisions, concerned with specialized fields of library service, each of which enjoys considerable autonomy within the framework of the parent organisation. Some of these division issue specialized publications, for example, *College and Research Libraries,* published by the Association of College and Reference Librarians. Membership dues in the American Library Association are on a graduated scale, based on salary and library income. Besides membership dues, endowments, grants and sales of publications contribute to the association's income. The association holds midwinter and spring conferences yearly. David H. Clift is executive secretary of the association, which maintains headquarters at 50 East Huron Street, Chicago, Illinois.

The ALA has a variety of groups within its overall structure in order to take care of the variety of activities involved in building a strong library service throughout the nation. Adult education is specifically dealt with by the Adult Education Board and by the Adult Education Section of the Public Libraries Division. Special projects, such as the American Heritage Project, are handled by committees. The ALA's responsibilities in this project have been staged by Mrs. Grace Stevenson, who will direct it.

The most challenging achievement of ALA's 75th anniversary year to date is the grant of 150,000 made by the Fund for Adult Education of the Ford Foundation for the purpose of establishing, under local public library leadership, community discussion programme on "The Heritage of the U.S.A. in Times of Crisis". In conducting the project the ALA has agreed to:

1. Plan and coordinate the programme through a central staff, field workers and consultants.

2. Select a group of six demonstration regional and local areas with due attention to variations in location, population density, library governmental structure, economic and educational factors; and allocate funds to public libraries in these areas for staff, materials, transportation and related expenses.

3. Provide consultation and advisory service to these and other public libraries spontaneously participating in the programme.

4. Conduct a training programme through the national staff, field workers and consultants, including national and regional workshops and institutes for library specialists and community volunteers.

5. Identify and develop suitable programme, training and promotional materials based primarily on the New York Public Library experience and will facilitate their distribution to the demonstration areas and to other cooperating libraries.

6. Seek the guidance of other interested national groups through such channels as the Council of National Organisations of the Adult Education Association of the U.S.A.

* * *

One of the end results the programme should strive to achieve is establishment for the future of a pattern of adult community discussion under library leadership all over the country.

The director does not visualize the heritage programme as a flag-waving programme. Its object is not to prove American superiority to the world, nor do we expect to indulge in ancestor worship.

The programme must be big in conception, with the long view—giving the average citizen a chance to examine his heritage and decide what it stands for; to realize where we have achieved the dream of our forefathers, where we have failed, and what we might do about the failures.

Three of the greatest dangers in our national life today are fear, distrust, and the apathy of the great masses of people about public questions. The programme must provide an opportunity for renewal of democratic faith—a confidence that the foundations of our national life have both the strength and flexibility to be translated into meaning for the present so that our democratic principles may fit our greatly changed conditions.

The only way to keep our American heritage alive is by a constant translation of it into the institutions and needs of our times. By an examination and understanding of this heritage, we hope to help today's Americans to accomplish this.

The ALA, like all large organisations, faces the problem of how to get active participation among its members. The matter has been well stated by Clareance B. Graham, president of the ALA in 1950-51, in a report to the Council.

Your problem as members of the Association is that you must not expect your president, your Executive Board, and even your Council, which is elected to represent you—to do your thinking and to solve your problems for you. Periodically, you have an activities committee appointed to do some soul searching for you. I plead for each member of the Association to appoint *himself* a permanent activities committee and do away with these periodic binges of self-righteous reforming.

I have never failed to learn something of importance in even the smallest library I have visited. I have been struck by the fact that librarians are increasingly becoming the leaders in their community. And yet in their own professional association, many are not contributing toward its own militant democracy.

National Foundations

One national group of growing importance to adult

education consists of the foundations. These do not themselves deal directly with the local community except in cases of pilot projects, but they do indirectly influenced activities through their support of universities and other groups that provide services to localities. Because of the extensive role played by the Carnegie Corporation in the support of adult education during the second quarter of this century and the promising role being assumed by the Ford Foundation at the beginning of the second half of the century, we believe it is very important that the student of adult education have some knowledge of this part of the total educational picture.

We choose the present selections relating to the Ford Foundation for reasons which parallel those given for the choice of the AEA earlier in the chapter. The Ford Foundation (on an expanded basis) is new and has recently made a very careful study of its role. It is also closely related to current adult education.

In 1948, when it was anticipated that considerable funds would soon be available, the trustees had a study made as the basis for the policy of the Foundation. The general approach of the study committee is set forth in the following paragraphs fro its report.

Pursuant thereto, a Study Committee was appointed to act as independent consultants to the Foundation. This Committee was made up of men widely known and respected in such fields as education, medicine and public health, the natural sciences, political science and government, the social sciences, the humanities, and modern business and industry.

The Study Committee also agreed at the outset that the purpose of the Study was not to accumulate a comprehensive catalogue of projects which the Foundation might undertake, but to block out in general terms those critical areas where problems were most serious and where the Foundation might make the most significant contributions to human welfare.

The Study Committee also agreed at the outset that it should view the needs of mankind in the broadest possible perspective, free from the limitations of special professional interests, it was to discover the most important problems and opportunities of human welfare. The Study Committee invited each member to ignore the confines of his speciality or profession and bring to the Committee the best thinking in his field concerning the most pressing problems of human welfare generally, whether they lay in his field or elsewhere. By agreement therefore each Committee member respected the boundaries of his own experience and training only for the purposes of administrative coordination.

The Study Committee held hundreds of interviews and conferences and analyzed thousands of pages of materials. It sought to find a "clearer understanding of the term 'human welfare,'" which was central in the Foundation's charter. In this connection it may be noted that Lindeman, in an earlier study of 100 foundations, had found that 90 per cent of their expenditures were for education (43 per cent), health (33 per cent), and social welfare (14 per cent).

The Committee proposed an interpretation of the role of a foundation which is useful to us in interpreting the current situation. It should be remembered that this is a report of a study committee and not an official statement by the Foundation.

The Role of a Foundation

This view of democracy is one of challenge to a modern foundation. By the character of its response The Ford Foundation will determine the degree to which it will help carry toward maturity the modern concept of philanthropy.

The history of philanthropy is the record of a continuously evolving philosophy of giving. At one time the gifts of individuals and benevolent organisations were intended largely to relieve the suffering of "the weak, the poor and the unfortunate". Philanthropy was thought of merely as temporary relief for evil conditions which would always exist and about which fundamental could be done. With the establishment of the modern foundation a much greater concept came into being. The aim is no longer merely to treat symptoms and temporarily to alleviate distress, but rather to eradicate the causes of suffering. Nor is the modern foundation content to concern itself only with man's obvious physical needs; it seeks rather to help man achieve his entire well-being—to satisfy his mental, emotional, and spiritual needs as well as physical wants. It addresses itself to the whole man and to the well-being of all mankind.

A foundation is, by its nature, especially well equipped for this task. It has no stockholders and no constitutions. It represents no private, political, or religious interests. Most foundations may, if they deem it wise, expend their total resources within any period they wish. This freedom from entanglements, pressures, restrictive legislation, and private interests endows a foundation with an inherent freedom of action possessed by few other organisations.

Further, a great foundation possesses an extraordinary stature in the public mind. By law, as well as by its charter, it is dedicated to human welfare. Its responsibility is to the public as a whole. In political and social issues it cannot be partisan. This very nonpartisanship and objectivity gives to the foundation a great positive force, and enables it to play a unique and effective role in the difficult and sometimes controversial task of helping to realize democracy's goals.

The breadth of The Ford Foundation's objectives imposes a duty on it to put its resources at the disposal of those who can contribute most significantly to the advancement of democracy. The Foundation must be constantly alert to the problems and needs of our society; it must continuously stand ready to help in those strategic areas where the greatest progress can be made toward democratic goals, and wherein human needs and aspirations can be most effectively fulfilled.

The needs and problems of human welfare far exceed the total of all available foundation funds. Of the two billions of private monies expended annually in the United States for philanthropic purposes, only three per cent are provided by foundations. Yet foundations have succeeded in making contributions of the greatest benefit to mankind. The real significance of a foundation's spending lies not in the amount expended but in the care and wisdom with which its programme are selected.

These facts clearly indicate the need for the Foundation to concentrate its support upon those problems which are at once the most important and which obstruct progress in the most directions. Successful work upon them is likely to have the effect of a catalytic agent. Such concentration means, of course, that support will not be available for work in other areas; this is an inevitable result of selectivity. The Trustees and officers of the Foundation must at all times remain alert, however, to the dynamic nature of the needs and problems of human welfare and must stand ready to reorient their programmes as conditions and opportunities change.

The Foundation is free to interpret its own function in society and to act boldly in implementing that interpretation. The opportunity is great; the responsibility is equally great. If the opportunity is met with foresight, good sense and courage, it is our opinion that the Foundation can play a vital role in the furtherance of democracy, and consequently in the advancement of human welfare.

The Foundation proceeded to set up a number of autonomous funds to handle specific areas. One of these was the Fund for Adult Education, which takes the responsibility for projects most directly relating to adult education. The basic approach of the Fund of Adult Education is set forth in the Annual Report for 1951:

The goals for Programme Area Four ("Education in a Democratic Society") were given the following description:

> The Ford Foundation should support activities to strengthen, expand, and improve educational facilities and methods to enable individuals more fully to realize their intellectual, civic and spiritual potentialities; to promote greater equality of educational opportunity; and to conserve and increase knowledge and enrich our culture.
>
> Education must meet the needs of the human spirit. It must assist person to develop a satisfactory personal philosophy and sense of values; to cultivate tastes for literature, music, and the arts; and to grow in ability to analyze problems and arrive at thoughtful conclusions.

To carry out the above commitment in the general area of education, the Ford Foundation established two independent organisations separately administered by their own Boards of Directors: The Fund for the Advancement of Education and The Fund for Adult Education. To the first Fund was assigned the responsibility for activities addressed to formal education in schools; to the second was assigned the responsibility for activities dealing with "that part of the total educational process which begins when schooling is finished." This latter phase of the educational process was considered to have as its aim "the expansion of opportunities for all adult men and women to continue their education throughout life in the interests of mature and responsible citizenship"—bearing in mind that "in today's world civic responsibilities are political, economic and social in scope."

The Programme of the Fund for Adult Education

It is against this background that the Fund for Adult Education conceives its special task as that of lending support to programmes of liberal adult education for free citizens in our free society.

In the Fund's definition *education* stands in contrast to training on the one hand and indoctrination on the other. It is concerned with the development of the whole person, not merely specialized functions. It is concerned with developing the ability to think independently and well, not with the passive acceptance of ready-made, prescribed opinions. Teaching how to think, not what to think, is the aim. It is a life-long precess with institutional education only the initial phase.

The *liberal* characteristic of education the Fund considers to adhere in processes and product rather than in content or material. The process is free thought and communication; the product is the mature and responsible citizen in a free society. The Fund recognizes that achieving education of a liberal character depends mainly upon the skill and imagination of the educator.

Education of a liberal character is no longer class education. Formerly its objective was to prepare the few for both the rights and the duties of freedom—freedom from the necessities of labour and for leisure; freedom for the privileges and obligations of rule. In the United States today almost no one is free from labour, but almost everyone has increasing opportunities for leisure. Almost all adult citizens share the responsibilities of rule. Liberal education, therefore, should now apply to the many and not merely to the few.

The Fund regards the continuing process of the education of *adults* as demanding materials and methods attractive to adults. The relationship between group leader and group members is not between the presumably immature as in the education of children and youths, but between equals of different life experiences. Accordingly, both materials and subject matter should be designed to capture and retain the interests of persons already having many competing uses for leisure time. There can be no compulsion on adults to participate in educational programmes. They must give their time and energy freely or not at all.

The Fund conceives of liberal adult education as addressed to *free citizens*—individuals who are simultaneously ends in themselves and participating members of their society. It therefore follows that those to whom programmes of liberal adult education are addressed have the privilege and responsibility of sharing in the shaping and carrying out of those programmes.

From the fact that the Fund operates within, and in the service of, a *free society* stem additional determining factors. The free society of the United States in the mid-twentieth century is based on the assumption that the fullest development of the individual is the end in view and that the same individual is the means for its preservation. It is necessarily a self-examining and self-improving society. With universal suffrage the political base of the society, an enlightened adult citizenry is a fundamental requirement. From the consequent need to reach as many citizens as possible a programme of adult education, to be fully effective, must employ all the media of communication the society makes possible—in our technological age the mass media as well as all the traditional channels.

Given the contemporary fact of world-wide interdependence, any educational programme looking to mature and responsible citizenship must recognise that the citizens of the United States face the danger of war and loss of freedom. If these perils are to be averted, the American people must act with knowledge, courage, and wisdom in a host of complex situations. Therefore, it is to education in world affairs, political affairs and economic affairs that the Fund directs its primary effort. At the same time there is recognition that these affairs must be understood broadly, in relation one to another and in the perspective of time. Accordingly, it is assumed that genuinely liberal thought and action in these spheres require a continuing attention to the heritage of humane insight and wisdom embraced within the humanities. In short, what is incontestably urgent must never biot out what is permanently important.

Certain Operating Principles

Just as the broad purpose of the Fund requires that it address itself to certain general categories of activity rather than others, so the inherent nature of the Fund requires that it be highly selective within the framework of the general categories. Clearly the Fund at best can hope to address itself to only a limited segment of the total sphere of adult education in a free society. Rigorous selectivity is accordingly inescapable, and selection, in turn, must be on the basis of the relative contribution of a proposed programme to the controlling aims of the Fund coupled with its relative appropriateness as a Fund-supported activity.

Given the nature of the organisation and its commitment, and given the society within which it operates, the fundamental approach must be to seek out, encourage, strengthen, develop and expand appropriate agencies and resources already existing rather than to bring into being new operations and agencies. The latter, nevertheless, will be regarded as appropriate when diligent investigation points to their necessity in the interests of the total programme of the Fund.

Given the Fund's role as a philanthropic organisation within the society and its commitment to the society in its totality, political non-partisanship is necessarily incumbent within the fundamental dedication to democratic values, institutions and methods.

The activities which the Fund for Adult Education has undertaken have been described by its president, C. Scott Fletcher, in an article in *Adult Education:*

> During its first six months the FAE has concentrated on two tasks essential to a proper grounding of long-range policy planning and procedure: (1) a comprehensive stock-taking of existing adult education activities and agencies with regard to their aims, scope, policies, methods, resources, accomplishments, and potentialities; and (2) the support of initiation of specific projects promising to offer guidance for the development of its long-range programme. The Fund's work undertaken to date can be catalogued under four headings—Fact Finding, Television and Radio, Community Discussion and Test Cities.

I. Fact Finding: Research Studies and Evaluation

An appropriate starting point appeared to be an evaluation of the liberal education programmes for adults offered by the evening colleges.

Programmes developed by business management, labour and agricultural groups offered another important area requiring study. Other fruitful lines for investigation will be provided by college and university extension programmes, the public schools, fraternal organisation, clubs and civic groups.

Certain cities such as Denver and Cleveland have developed successful adult education programmes. Therefore, the Fund had planned to get the facts and to disseminate them by means of the printed word and the motion picture.

* * *

Because of the value of having the results of all these surveys and studies under one cover, the Fund will retain an outstanding writer to collate the findings into a related whole. This will provide a source book for all people interested in improving adult education in this country.

II. Television and Radio

The Fund will utilize the channels of television and radio as fully as is consistent with its aims and with the most effective development of its programme. In television and radio two approaches will be made: (1) through commercial channels and (2) through educational channels.

* * *

Educational radio stations have always had great need of professional assistance in developing stimulating educational programmes. The grant made by the Fund to the National Association of Educational Broadcasters is making it possible for this groups of 107 educational radio stations to obtain competent professional help. Financial aid in developing programmes, as well as the loan of equipment, has similarly been granted to the only educational television station in the country, WOI-TV at Ames, Iowa. Support of the work of the Joint Committee on Educational Television is resulting in legal and technical advice and assistance to educational institutions which want to apply for television channels from the F.C.C.

Because the field of radio and television presents such a variety of difficult problems, the Fund plans to arrange for a survey to help in appraising the future of these most modern forms of communication.

III. Community Discussion

The Fund is convinced that in the last analysis "face-to-face" participation in viding various aids to discussion leaders and groups and (2) supporting several discussion programmes conducted by existing organisations. Preliminary findings of the surveys currently in progress under Fund auspices reveal that programmes of adult education in the United States, numerous though they are, suffer from the lack of trained manpower and adequate funds.

Assistance in planning programmes for adult discussion groups and in leading such groups is much needed by laymien in the field. The grant by the Fund to the new Adult Education Association will be used for the publication of a magazine designed to help the non-professional people who are engaged in adult education work.

For professional adult educators, the Fund will provide a number of scholarship and fellowships. As Cyril O. Houle wrote in the *Adult Education Bulletin* of April, 1949, "In the rapidly expanding field of adult education, the greatest bottleneck now is–as it has always been–the production of qualified and capable teachers."

The Fund seeks to use the medium of the 16mm. film in a number of ways. The Film Council of America, which promotes the wider and more effective use by community organisations of film materials for the general welfare, has been given financial assistance. The Fund is exploring the possibilities of producing a film on the importance of continuing education throughout life. It will produce a film on the Cleveland programme already mentioned.

The lack of adequately trained discussion leaders has made it abundantly clear that the programmes of existing organisations cannot move as rapidly to reach a maximum number of people as the Fund believes imperative. Therefore, the acute need for inventing new methods and providing new opportunities has become apparent. Two special projects have been initiated and developed by the staff of the Fund. These will provide materials and assistance for more widespread group discussion.

IV. Test Cities

The community is the point of greatest impact of adult education programmes supported or initiated by the Fund. The community is the unit through which most adults will be reached and in which coordination should occur. In order to augment and coordinate adult education activities in the community, the Fund has devised the Test Cities Project.

The ends of the Test Cities Project are as follows:

(1) To test old, and invent new, methods of stimulating and integrating adult education activities at the community level.

(2) To determine the extent to which Fund-supported programmes are useful educationally to various groups and various segments of the population within the community.

* * *

The Fund hopes to develop, in the Test Cities, patterns which other communities might wish to adapt to their own needs. It will attempt to establish in the minds of the people the importance of continuing adult education throughout life. It will indicate ways whereby they can participate in a variety of programme and benefit from their participation both as individuals and as a community. It hopes to demonstrate that to the extent adults become involved in such a coordinated pattern, they become well-informed, mature and responsible citizens. It is through an informed citizenry that the community improves itself and, at the same time, becomes aware of its world relationships, thus contributing to international understanding and a free world at peace.

The development of smooth-working relations in which strong national organisations provide services to local communities and help to channel action proposals to appropriate decision points and in which vigorous local groups help furnish the stimulus and support which keep national organisations growing is not easy, but there is nothing impossible in it. The major need will be to ensure that there is time and inclination to maintain adequate communication among the leaders. We have found the proposals of the AEA on this matter eminently promising.

There may be some question as to whether we need all the national organisations with which we are currently blessed. If limitations were to be imposed, however, by whom would they be determined? It is better to keep available the opportunity to organise freely than to impose any kind of censorship.

In the long run it is likely the development of strong local communities will take care of the matter. Once we achieve ways of considering the various questions which changing conditions create, there will be fewer uncared-for aspects which seem to call for an organisation to do something. Where clear needs are indicated, support will be available through the local groups.

As in the other chapters, we emphasize the fact that these organisations of the kind described are the concern of everyone involved in adult education. This does not mean that everyone is to join every organisation. It does mean that at the policy level each person must have a clear picture of the kind of cooperative pattern he believes to be desirable and that he work to make this possible.

14

International Programmes

Although an effort was made after the First World War to set up an international organisation through which adult-education leaders from many countries might exchange ideas, little came of the effort. A World Association for Adult Education, which was formed in 1919 and held a world conference in Cambridge, England, in July 1929, served as a clearinghouse for the collection of information and issued a variety of publications. The coming of the Second World War aborted these efforts at international cooperation, and it was not until the United Nations Conference in San Francisco in 1945 that the effort was officially renewed. This conference led to the establishment within the UN system of a specialized agency called the United Nations Educational Scientific and Cultural Organisation.

Both at San Francisco and during the three years immediately preceding that event, many prominent educational leaders from the United States participated in the effort to define the objectives and functions of such an international organisation. The lay representatives of important national voluntary agencies had a great deal to do finally with the adoption at San Francisco of provisions in the UN Charter which authorized the creation of a specialized educational agency. Constitutionally organised in London in 1945, UNESCO has throughout its brief history given a prominent place in its programme to adult education activities. If "it is in the minds of men that the defenses of peace must be constructed", it could scarcely do otherwise to attain its purposes.

In this chapter we shall include reports on the major adult education activities of UNESCO.

At both the second and third general conferences of UNESCO, at Mexico City in 1947 and at Beirut in 1948, respectively, resolutions were passed calling upon the Secretariat to organise an international conference on adult education. Such a conference was held at Elsinore, Denmark, in June 1949. The following report, by one of the members of the American delegation, describes some of the highlights of this meetings.

First of all, a few facts about the conference itself. This was a UNESCO-sponsored meeting on the grounds of the International People's College in Elsinore, Denmark, with the Danish Government acting as official host. It was attended by representatives of almost 30 nations and approximately 25 international organisations. Some 125 delegates were in attendance with official observers and visitors in addition. The conference lasted for 10 days, from June 16 to June 26 inclusive, and the bulk of the conference time was spent by the delegates in four commission meetings: one on materials of adult education; one on agencies and problems of organisation; the third commission on methods and technics; and the fourth on means of establishing permanent cooperation in adult education.

* * *

The organisation, management; and methodology of international conferences represent an area of needed research and experimentation in adult education. On the basis of the experience in Denmark, it would be my hunch that special technics will have to be developed if the advantages of face-to-face communication in the work-type conference with which we are familiar in the United States are to be achieved in international meetings. I do not think this is simply a matter of overcoming the obvious blocks to communication in respect to language differences. To a large extent these can be overcome by simultaneous translation. Facilities to permit this at Denmark were not available.

More serious is the lack of common purpose and the perception of common problems. This heterogeneity of purpose is bound to be in evidence in a conference where the delegates' problems range all the way from literacy education for nomadic tribes in Egypt to evaluation of efforts to communicate the social implications of science through museums and exhibits. It may well be that a regional approach to problems in adult education may advantageously preface efforts to identify common needs and common problems on a worldwide scale.

The principle of public support for adult education is, on the whole, well established throughout the world. In Great Britain grants from the Ministry of Education and local education authorities to adult education are estimated currently to approximate 2 million dollars. Norway will put almost 1 million dollars into direct state support, and state aid in Sweden will exceed $3\frac{1}{2}$ million dollars in dollar equivalence. Differences arise, not over the principle of state support, but rather on the method of channeling this support into the bloodstream of private and public agencies of adult education. There was a definite cleavage within the conference over the role of voluntary agencies. On the whole, the Scandinavian delegates would give priority to demands of voluntary groups on the public funds available for support of adult education. In England, although the principle of support of voluntary agencies is well established, it is now obligatory under the Education Act of 1944 for local education authorities to secure for their areas all the facilities necessary to meet the demand for all forms of "further education."

In this country we are firmly committed to the principle of channeling public funds to public agencies. In the field of adult education this may mean that the vitality of the voluntary movements is reduced unless our public adult schools conceive as part of their community responsibility, the rendering of service and assistance to the numerous autonomous groups which carry on adult education activities.

One cannot visit the folk high schools of Denmark or hear about the success of similar institutions in Norway and Sweden without wondering if we in adult education in the United States have adequately met the needs of the younger age groups of adults, especially those not served by our colleges and institutions of higher learning. The folk high school movement in the Scandinavian countries has been adequately reported in documents now translated into English, and those of us in public education could profit from a careful study of these materials.

In a democratic society adult education, can best be carried on in small face-to-face groups; in fact, democracy depends upon the vitality and virility of these groups...Adult education can become the instrument for the harmonizing of interests within and among groups at home and across national boundaries. Adult education must become a world movement because essentially the problems which thwart man in his struggle for a better life are world problems. These ideas, as proposed by Sir John Maud of Great Britain, deserve to be pondered by each of us. Have we come to rely too dependently upon mass media in the United States? To what extent is adult education as a movement devoting its energies to the improvement of group process and group functioning? Have the resources of adult education in the United States really been channelled into a nationwide attack on political and economic illiteracy, particularly as it affects American public opinion on world problems? If not, why not? And, if not, has the time now come when the special interests and resources of university extension, public adult schools, libraries, museums, agricultural extension, and workers' education, can be merged and integrated, at least so far as international cooperation and UNESCO's programme are concerned?

I should like to repeat here, in closing, what I have said to many of my friends since returning from Denmark. One comes home after an experience of this sort with a new appreciation of the responsibilities which being an American entails in today's world. It is a responsibility not without privilege, and those of us who are engaged in adult education will, I hope, in all humility be the first to ask, how can we help by our efforts at home, and by sharing our experiences, our successes, and failures with our colleagues aboard, to bulwark the foundations of a world society in which man may live without fear?

The conference made a number of recommendations: "to send missions from countries where adult education is more highly developed to those less advanced; to organise visits, international summer schools, study tours; to arrange international seminars on vital and urgent problems; to speed up exchange of information." The conference decided against recommending that an international organisation outside of UNESCO be created and suggested that UNESCO serve, at least for the time being, as the link between national organisations and leaders in the field of adult education.

After the conference, a Consultative Committee on Adult Education was established to advise the UNESCO Secretariat and particularly the staff of the Education Division at Paris. The American member of this committee was Dean Herbert C. Hunsaker, of Cleveland College, who has also attended the Elsinore Conference.

Two major publications in addition to the summary report already referred to have been issued by UNESCO as a result of the conference's recommendations: a volume on *Adult Education, Current Trends and Practices,* was published early in 1950, and a draft edition of an *International Directory of Adult Education* was issued the same year. The latter volume is to be finally published when corrections and additions have been received from member states.

Two special seminars have been held since the Denmark meeting. One, on the role of libraries in adult and fundamental education, was held at Malmo, Sweden, in July and August 1950, and the other, on adult education methods, in June and July of the same year near Salzburg, Austria. The two following selections give the highlights of these two seminars. The first is by Helen Steinbarger, a member of the American delegation to Malmo. The second is by the U.S. Delegation to the Austrian meeting.

Dr. Cyril O. Houle, the dean of University College, University of Chicago, was named the director of the Seminar. He worked in close cooperation with UNESCO staff members and with Miss Ingeborg Heintze, director of the Stadsbibliotek and her staff. All meetings were held in this library, modern in its operational facilities and adequately supplied with room for meetings of any size...

Forty-eight delegates from 21 countries were in attendance...

Democratic procedures were followed throughout the Seminar. After every plenary session held during the first week, questions were raised and general discussion followed. During this period, the entire membership considered the philosophy and principles of adult education, and agreed on this definition: "Adult education is an effort put forth by a mature person to improve himself by acquiring new skills, information, understanding, attitudes or appreciations or the effort of an agency to present the opportunity and the encouragement to mature persons for improving themselves or their community."

* * *

The diversity of interest, the positions held, and the type of library represented by the delegates, necessitated the division of the body into main discussion groups. These groups, in turn, were divided into committees and sub-committees to consider in detail questions which arose during the major discussions. All meetings were thought-provoking. If a statement was made, it had to be substantiated by citing cause, methods used, and results. The results of the deliberations proved to be rewarding.

* * *

Under the leadership of Dr. Houle, assisted by Mr. Munn, Group I considered the basic character of adult education and the necessary essentials to the development, publicizing and evaluation of an adult education programme in libraries where library services are reasonably well established.

A brief result of the findings of this group will give the highlights of the discussion. It was generally agreed that the library is a center for research, aesthetic appreciation, recreation and education, and that all staff members have a part to play in the development of a successful programme in any of these areas, particularly adult education. It was decided that formal education is not the function of a library but libraries should assist agencies conducting classes or help agencies in establishing programmes by loaning material and furnishing professional consultant services.

If a library has no adult education programme and wished to develop one, the need for a community survey was stressed, the plan always taking into account library resources, staff, printed materials and budget. There should be both long-term and short-term planning. The first should define the scope and purpose of the over-all programme, the second should define certain projects.

The necessity of an annual evaluation programme was emphasized in order to determine success or failure; whether additional services should be developed or existing services curtailed; what the programme involved in working with a particular group or individual; what influence the programme had on individual or community thinking or action.

It was agreed that the net result of working with community groups, by reaching more individuals at their interest level, is an increased use of library materials and professional services. In addition, attention is focused on the library and this often encourages other agencies to plan programmes which require library cooperation. It is important that librarians belong to community groups as individuals and act as official represen-tatives at meetings of others.

Although community involvement was stressed, work with the individual was given due consideration. In order to give competent reading guidance, it was recommended that librarians should have received special training, must know techniques and books, if they expect to raise the reading level of the reader to that having definite educational value. Courses in psychology and sociology were recommended as invaluable aids in understanding the reader and his needs.

* * *

Mr. Lachlen F. McRac, chief librarian of Fort William Public Library, Canada, led Group II, which discussed types of audio-visual materials, methods of use and their adaptation to a library adult education programme.

It was the consensus that such a programme falls within the scope of a modern public library, as these mediums are useful in education at all age levels. For this reason the librarian, whether he is able currently to use audio-visual aids or not, should have as part of his training a knowledge of their possibilities as an educational medium and the techniques involved in their use.

It was suggested that, because of the cost involved and because the popular appeal of films, etc., carries with it a certain danger to library standards, a survey should be made, applying the criteria accepted in planning the over-all adult education role. This will furnish information on "how effectively the community will be able to use audio-visual aids, what authorities outside the library are able to help toward effective utilizations and how heavy will be the strain upon the facilities of the library itself."

Members decided that library service in this field might fall within three categories:

1. A minimum programme which a library of any size could and should follow. This would take the form of an effective community film information service.

2. A median programme, sponsored by the library, which would include as part of the all-inclusive adult education programmes the public showings of films, concerts of recorded music, radio broadcasts, etc. It would include number one, above.

* * *

Mlle. Yvonne Oddon, librarian of the Musee de l'homme, Paris (and formerly consultant in UNESCO's Fundamental Project in Haiti), was the leader of Group III which discussed the establishment of library service as an aid to fundamental education in underdeveloped regions. This was a difficult and all-inclusive subject. From their deliberations came a number of significant recommendations directly addressed to UNESCO. As the content of the first three form the first three of the recommendations submitted by the entire membership, these will be reported later. The others are as follows:

(4) that Unesco should promote in consultation with librarians, the making and publication of every type of educational material, particularly simple reading matter for adults, both in local and official languages.

(5) that a practical textbook on the making and use of educational material at the fundamental level, should be edited in cooperation with a library specialist. It should include such topics as simple recording, the making and use of slides and filmstrip, the use of museographic techniques and characteristics and the choice and publication of typical adapted reading matter.

(6) that UNESCO should recommend the inclusion of professional librarians on the national commission of each member state.

* * *

Although little in this Seminar is new to librarians in this country, yet it was illuminating to realize just how new the findings were to those from many of the other countries. It is felt, quite conclusively, that changes will be made in existing programmes, if any, and that new programmes will be planned. The composite of the thinking and discussion during the Seminar is reflected in the following declaration and resolutions transmitted to UNESCO headquarters in Paris:

The Malmo Seminar records its conviction that public libraries can be and in some cases are, among the most effective agencies now existing for the continuing education of great masses of the people. The Seminar also recognizes the great potentialities of public libraries are too seldom realized and that in most parts of the world library services to fundamental and adult education are only now beginning or have not yet begun.

This Seminar therefore recommends to UNESCO that its programme be expanded to allow for the promotion of public-library development on a much wider front, as required by the realities of the situation. To this end it specifically recommends:

(1) that a course on library establishment, operation and development should be included in courses organized in fundamental education centers for the training of experts.

(2) that, as a follow-up to the present Seminar, regional seminars or conferences of a limited number of librarians and other experts should be organised at intervals to discuss specific topics such as organizing library campaigns, rural library service in fundamental education areas, special training for fundamental education library service and problems of wider library cooperation.

(3) that UNESCO's fundamental education preliminary surveys and missions should not be launched without the services of a professional librarian who should remain until sufficient professional staff has been trained to carry on and supervise the newly formed libraries;

(4) the production of a film demonstrating the best public-library practices;

(5) the enlargement of the *Unesco Bulletin for Libraries* to include information on material issued by other sections of UNESCO which might be used in library programmes of adult education and information on sources of national material available for circulation internationally, such as exhibitions, films, filmstrips, photographs, etc.;

(6) that UNESCO promote the development of public-library adult education programmes for immigrants and displaced persons.

The following excerpts deal with the Austrian Seminar.

The seminar was an outgrowth of a recommendation made at last year's international conference on adult education at Elsinore, Denmark. Its purpose was an exchange of experience and ideas among adult educators of many lands on methods of adult education, with special attention to means of promoting international understanding.

There were fifty delegates from 19 countries...

Director of the seminar was Sven Bjorklund, dean of the People's University of the University of Stockholm, Sweden...

* * *

The seminar was organised along the lines of the "work conference" which has recently become prevalent in the USA and other countries. Its core was four working groups which met every morning. In the afternoon there were workshops and at night either educational or social programme. Nearly every week-end there was a field trip or excursion. An excellent library contained many hard-to-get items brought by the delegates or borrowed from UNESCO's own library. The seminar governed itself through a general assembly and numerous committees. English and French were the official languages.

The four working groups were essentially discussion groups whose purpose was to exchange experience and seek points of agreement in four areas of adult education: (1) organisation and administration, (2) intellectual and scientific training, (3) economic and social training, and (4) approach to the arts and the educational use of leisure time. Each delegate belonged to one of these four groups. They had from 8 to 12 members and met daily.

The workshops were also discussion groups, but were concerned with more limited aspects of adult education: libraries, film production, music, popularization. One or two of the workshops met throughout the seminar. Others met only a few times, being organised to take advantage of the presence of some visiting expert. Most of them were small, say half a dozen persons, though the one on international understanding, organised by Shepherd Witman, attracted over twenty. They usually met twice a week.

The evening programmes were both educational and recreational in nature, their content varying from a panel discussion on the Korean situation (which developed while the seminar was meeting) to an evening of folk-dancing. There were usually two evening programmes each week.

There were perhaps a dozen plenary sessions. Like the evening programmes they gave visiting experts a larger audience than could the smaller workshops, but their more important function was to give the members of each of the four working groups a chance to find out what was going on in the others.

* * *

The general assembly was the legislative arm of the seminar. Its purpose was to set goals, to discuss and improve progress toward these goals, to hear and act on reports and recommendations. It met about eight times. All seminar members had the right to vote in the assembly.

The executive committee was the coordinating arm of the seminar. It attended to announcements, regulated the calendar, received suggestions, disposed of matters not important enough to go before the assembly and reported more important matters to the assembly for action. It consisted of one member elected from each of the four working groups, one from the staff and one from the secretariat. It met daily.

The functions of the other committees are obvious from their titles or from the following parenthetical remarks: (1) Reception and Welfare, (2) Leisure Time (excursions), (3) Evening Programmes, (4) Research and Reports, (5) Co-op (to start and run a store to sell necessities to the delegates), and (6) Publicity. The last-named committee had four sub-committees to take care of: a mural journal (daily announcements), a newspaper, a "radio" programme (produced, recorded and then "broadcast" over a public address system during the dinner hour), and press and public relations.

Several other committees were added in the course of the seminar: an evaluation committee to solicit the opinion of the delegates on the organisation and operation of the seminar, a follow-up committee to propose means to help the delegates keep in touch with one another after the seminar, and four coordinating committees to collect the main points and recommendations which were appearing in the four working groups and to rework these for consideration at the final session of the general assembly. These four coordinating committees were concerned with, respectively: leadership training, cultural problems in relation to adult education, methods of adult education and the relationship between adult education and other levels of education, and means of promoting international understanding. The coordinating committees consisted of delegates chosen from each of the four working groups. During the last week of the seminar the working groups were replaced by the coordinating committees.

* * *

The seminar made a number of recommendations designed to advance the world movement of adult education. Among the most important of these were resolutions calling for: (1) establishment of an international center for adult education and of as many regional centers as are found desirable, (2) collection of all significant experiments in training leaders for adult education, (3) preparation by UNESCO of a glossary of adult education terminology for use at future international meetings and a bibliography of books and materials on adult education, and (4) publication by UNESCO of a periodic bulletin on adult education.

The seminar also made several suggestions to international organisations and member states of UNESCO, urging (1) exemption of educational activities and materials from taxation, (2) production and wide distribution of mass media materials and their free flow between countries, (3) termination of propaganda broadcasts, (4) development of language teaching programmes, folklore organisations and tourism, and (5) establishment of closer relations between fundamental education and adult education.

Finally, the seminar approved a number of general principles which should guide adult educators: (1) While it is important for adult education to continue to help the individual increase his understanding, develop his creative powers, deepen his appreciation and enlarge his ability for critical thinking, it is equally important for adult education to help people solve the problems they face as citizens of their communities and of the world. (2) Although the adult educator must begin with the interests and needs which people consider important, he must accept the responsibility of building bridges from such interests to community and world needs. (3) Those who participate in adult education should share in determining the goals toward which they wish to work and the ways in which they will work. In any given community, the larger the proportion of the people who can be drawn into the adult eduction enterprise and the more representative they are of the various strata in the community, the greater are the enterprise's chances for success. (4) The progress of adult education programmes should be continuously appraised. Mere numbers of people are no proof of success. The only valid criterion of success is that the changes at which the programmes aims are in fact being realized in action. (5) Progress toward the goals of adult education can be accelerated if adult education and pre-adult education join forces and work together. (6) Adult education must use the best leaders it can find wherever it finds them; they will often have to be given special training for their duties. (7) Adult education must use methods appropriate to adults and make full use of their interests and experience.

* * *

In our opinion the single most valuable result of the seminar was the personal and professional friendships which were formed there. Through these friendships, through the programme of the seminar, and through mutual visits and correspondence after the seminar many of the delegates acquired a good deal of information about adult education programmes in one another's countries and indeed a deeper insight into adult education in their own countries.

The recommendations, suggestions and principles approved by the seminar and mentioned above should do much to advance national and international adult education movements if they can be carried out. A start was made at the seminar on the glossary of adult education terminology and the bibliography of books and materials. We have heard unofficially that the proposed international center for adult education has been approved by UNESCO and may soon be established in connection with the University of Paris.

Although production of documents was not a major

purpose of the seminar several useful ones came out of it, notably one on suggested methodology for future international conference on adult education. The official report on the seminar is appearing in an early issue of UNESCO's *Occasional Papers On Education*. A film on the seminar was made there and will soon be released by UNESCO.

It is always hard to give proof of changes in attitude. But we could cite several instances of "conversion" on the part of adult educators who came to realize that their concepts of adult education were academic or outmoded and that other ways of doing things might bring better results.

We think it also worth mentioning that there were no instances of delegates voting as geographical blocs.

Finally we were pleased that those who planned the seminar followed the "work conference" pattern rather than the more traditional speech marathon which would have been easier in view of the language difficulties and in which some of the delegates would have felt more secure.

* * *

There never was a conference without shortcomings and there never will be one. But only as we learn to recognise these shortcomings and eliminate them will we have better conferences. It is in this spirit that we make the following comments. First, there was too much talk about education methods, not enough actual demonstration and practice of them.

Second, there was evasion of one of the important concerns of the seminar, namely means of promoting international understanding. Admittedly we don't know much about this. But we know more about it than we gave evidence of knowing at this seminar.

Third, we did not always practice what we preached. For example, Item 3 in the above list of principles states that the participants in an adult education programme should share in determining its goals and ways of working. The seminar gave lip service to this principle but was unable fully to carry it out in practice.

Fourth, we discovered that we have much to learn about how to conduct an international training seminar for leaders in adult education. There were serious failures in planning, communication, involvement of delegates, use of human and material resources and evaluation. Some of these failures can be charged in part to the language problems inherent in an international seminar and in part to poor cooperation on the part of some of the participating governments. Some must be charged to those who planned the seminar. Some must be charged to the simple fact that adult educators do not yet know enough about how to train leaders efficiently, especially in an international setting. Progress along this road was made in the production of the document "Report on Techniques of International Seminars in the Light of the Mondsee Seminar" and in the recommendations calling for a collection of experiments in training leaders for adult education and the establishment of international and regional centers for adult education.

* * *

This seminar had some notable accomplishments. If the above recommendations aimed at eliminating its more serious shortcomings can be followed at future international meetings on adult education, then the seminar will have been a useful first step toward the improvement of international adult education meetings and the urgent task of training leaders of adult education in a world setting.

Other seminars sponsored by UNESCO have had important implications for adult education. Two, for example, have been held on education for international understanding, one in France in 1947 and one in England in 1948. Two seminars in 1949 dealt with illiteracy and fundamental education; one, held in Brazil, took up the problem as it affects the Americans, and the other, at Mysore, India, with the problems of adult education in the rural communities of Asia.

As an international organisation, UNESCO must be concerned with the extension of opportunities for fundamental education to the more than half of the world's population currently illiterate. Accordingly, a large block of its resources and funds have been devoted to the development of training and development centers. One such center, already in operation at Patzcuaro, Mexico, is designed to train workers and produce materials for fundamental education in Latin America. Other centers are proposed for the Near East and Southeast Asia. Some Point Four funds have been made available to supplement UNESCO's budget for this programme.

Another publication on fundamental education is produced

by UNESCO in English, French and Spanish and from time to time special monographs in this field have been made available. In this whole effort at fundamental education, the experience and technical knowledge of American workers, particularly in the field of Americanization and literacy work, can be of tremendous assistance.

In the draft of the UNESCO programme for 1953-1954 is a recommended programme in the field of workers' education. The two aims of the programme will be to improve methods and techniques in workers' education by international means and to increase international understanding through workers' education. A series of seminars and courses dealing with the problems of workers' education has been scheduled, with follow-up meetings in the member states. In these projects UNESCO will cooperate with the International Labour Organisation and International Workers Organisation. This whole effort in the field of workers' education will be coordinated through an International Center of Workers' Education in Paris. Future developments will depend on evaluation and recommendations by the Consultative Committee on Adult Education.

With a total annual budget which approximates 10 million dollars, the amount of direct assistance which UNESCO can give in response to the manifold demands from 65 member states is obviously limited. Fortunately, its achievements need not depend on financial resources alone, although these should certainly be made more adequate than is now the case. It is appropriate to view UNESCO as a symbol of the faith still held in many parts of the globe that education, science and culture can still be made to serve as powerful instruments in the achievement of world peace and security. More particularly, leaders in adult education in the United States can and should work with and through UNESCO to share with their colleagues in other lands whatever knowledge and skills will be of use in the solution of their national and regional problems. Conversely, from such interchange and intercommunication will come new learnings which are relevant to the solution of our own problems. In his view UNESCO thus becomes as bridge over which tow-way traffic is maintained between and among professional groups with common interests, common purposes, and–to some extent at least—common problems.

The domestic arm and cooperating body for UNESCO in the United States is the U.S. National Commission for UNESCO. This organisation was established under provision of the same law (Public Law 565, 79th Congress, 2nd Session, July 30, 1946) which authorized U.S. participation and membership in the international organisation. The membership of the commission was set at not more than one hundred, appointed by the Secretary of State. Sixty of these were to be nominated for membership as representatives of principal national voluntary organisation interested in UNESCO. The remaining forty were to consist of not more than ten persons from the Federal government, fifteen representing UNESCO interests among state and local governments, and fifteen persons chosen at large. The Department of State was authorized to provide a secretariat for the National Commission.

The function of the National Commission in this and other member states is defined by Article VII of the UNESCO Constitution as follows: "National Commissions...shall act in an advisory capacity to their respective delegations to the General Conference and to their Government in matters relating to the Organisation and shall function as agencies of liaison in all matters of interest to it".

In fulfillment of this obligation, the U.S. National Commission has created, on recommendation of its Executive Committee, two major committees—one on programme and one on activities in the United States. The Committee on Programme devotes especial attention to the *ongoing* activities and proposed programme of UNESCO, recommending to the commission the items in the programme which should receive priority support from the United States delegations to the General Conferences of UNESCO. The Committee on Activities in the United States devotes primary attention to those efforts which the commission should promote, sponsor and support in this country. Major items which have been identified as appropriate for commission activity in the United States have included (1) education about the UN system, (2) human rights, particularly increasing citizen understanding of the Declaration of Human Rights and the celebration of Human Rights Day in December of each year, (3) promotion of special activities, such as the UNESCO Gift Coupon Plan, educational reconstruction in war-devastated areas, etc. In addition, it should be noted that the commissions secretariat performs a wide variety of services to the UNESCO staff in Paris, including the collecting of information about American experience in relation to educational, scientific and cultural studies made by UNESCO, arranging for the selection and briefing of United States delegations to international meetings and conferences, locating technical personnel for educational missions operating in various fields and in many sections of the globe under UNESCO auspices.

What does the work of the commission have to do with adult education? It is quite true that many of the national voluntary citizen organisations which have representatives on the National Commission do themselves have extensive activities properly called adult education. Such agencies as the National Congress of Parents and Teachers, the League of Women Voters, the American Association of University Women, and the American Association for the United Nations are clearly a part of the adult education movement. But there are also many organisations in the commission which are not membership bodies and which do not have planned programmes for the education of adults. Such agencies as the Modern Language Association, the American Society for Engineering Education, the National Research Council, the American Council of Learned Societies and many others are of this type. The role of the commission in adult education has been studied by William L. Kimball in a thesis prepared for a Master of Arts degree at the University of California, Los Angeles. He states :

The National Commission has been engaged in adult education as it attempted to recruit people for participation in UNESCO matters or to extend public understanding on these matters. In doing this, the National Commission was neither an old, well established organisation, nor was it working alone in the United States. The National Commission necessarily operated within, upon, and with a vast and varied complex of social communication and influence groups; it also operated as a quite unique body in many respects.

There has been no comparable precedent for the National Commission in the experience of the United States. The National Commission entered the domestic arena as an official representative of a world inter-governmental organisation. The

U. S. Government was not experienced in this type of relationship since it had remained aloof from the League of Nations. Intellectuals and educators were not experienced in official dealings with international educational matters for the same reason. The National Commission was a quasi-governmental body, partly under the control of government but having a large measure of autonomy. The government had consulted with lay groups in the past concerning cultural affairs but only on an informal basis. The lay organisations were almost entirely inexperienced in legal relationships with governmental education, though they were familiar with government-administered programmes. The National Commission must also be counted as an agency of social communication, one of the conscious agencies which has attempted to influence the adult mind in the United States. Its nature is somewhat unique here also. The adult education movement has been largely unorganised at top levels, has been strongly local, voluntary, and autonomous. There has been much voluntary coordination and collaboration at national levels and some even at international levels, but nearly all has been informal and non-governmental. The National Commission is unique in adult education as a cooperative body formed mostly at top levels and formally established by law.

The special place of the National Commission within the area of social communication and adult education can be further described. The Commission must be counted as a special interest group, even though its goals have been generally accepted; it has not been just a broad, general adult education agency such as the public schools or the libraries. The National Commission has been an unusually broad and representative body, even for a cooperative organisation; besides involving many important adult education agencies, it has represented or contacted people in federal, state and local government, in the mass media and in special technical and scientific areas. The Commission thus has brought together those who advance knowledge, those who distribute it and those who apply it. It apparently has been a well-equipped organisation.

The nature of the adult education movement has created both advantages and disadvantages for the National Commission's work in this area. The breadth and variety of the movement have been an advantage in that more channels and approaches to people were available. There probably have been the disadvantages of duplication of rivalry with so many channels and approaches. The heterogeneity and local autonomy may have made it difficult for the National Commission to reach the grassroots and native leaders. Those most likely to be members of the National Commission, the heads of national organisations, government officials and university people, were not always in the closest contact with local conditions. But local strength could be a tremendous advantage if the National Commission developed means for decentralization of contacts.

One of the dilemmas with which the commission has had to come to terms is peculiarly an adult education problem. Being, as Kimball says, primarily a top-level body representing national organisations but realizing that to be effective in relation to its announced purposes it must stimulate grass-roots learning and activity, the commission has vacillated somewhat between placing major reliance on national organisation and promoting state and local UNESCO organisations. On the whole it has favoured working through national organisations and the mass media rather than through field services direct to local organisations in local communities. This policy was dictated in part by the small size of UNESCO's budget and staff and in part by a desire to avoid both the reality and appearance of operations which might be constructed as competing with those of member organisations. On the other hand, if UNESCO's programme and that of the U. S. National Commission are to be successful, it must be a people's programme, carrying with it widespread citizen participation, understanding and support. It cannot be this if it must depend upon biennial national conferences reaching two thousand leaders as its only major avenue of direct, face-to-face contact with the people it is designed to reach.

Kimball identified five major channels through which the Commission has sought to achieve its purpose.

Individuals

The individual members of the Commission were an important channel of contact or education. They were expected to carry out the major part of National Commission activities in attending the regular meetings, in serving on committees and panels of the Commission and in organising and participating in the general UNESCO conferences. In addition to these activities, the members have been valuable resources and agents in the Commission's adult education work. In their geographical region they were of assistance to interested local groups, communities and organisations, including state and local UNESCO councils. Some members aided in establishing these local groups and served in them. Members also acted as individual adult educators in speaking, writing or broadcasting on UNESCO subjects. They also aided in promoting local and national educational campaigns, including such events as United Nations Week and Day. Individual members aided in the education of special audiences through their membership in other organisation or through their profession or occupation.

To this must be added the activities of alumni members and of the Commission's secretariat. Former members have served in much the same way as regular members, except that they could not participate as members in Commission meetings and on committees. The secretariat has always been very active and helpful; the major difficulty has been that the Department of State was not able to employ a larger secretariat. However, the secretariat has prepared most of the National Commission official documents and reports, has served on the Commission's committees, has assisted national organisations interested in UNESCO, and has worked outside of Washington in the field, helping organise the regional and general conferences and advising and assisting the local UNESCO councils and commissions.

Organisations

National organisations, either those only interested and cooperating in UNESCO work or those which are "alumni" of the National Commission, as well as those organisations currently designating members to the Commission have been considered the basic channel in contacting the people of the United States. Those most important in this respect have been the general, nation-wide, non-technical or non-specialized organisations with fairly extensive public membership...

As a whole, these organisations consistently reported from

year-to-year a wide range of activities and varying degrees of activity in adult education. They were able to contact their membership through publications and meetings. They sponsored programmes such as discussion groups, informal seminars, radio addresses and fellowships or study grants. They also cooperated with other organisations, governmental units, state or local UNESCO councils or the National Commission itself in national specific programmes such as United Nations Day or the Food and People programme. Activity ranged from very active organisations whose "complete report [on UNESCO activities] would run into volumes" to others who just requested advice for activities. It would be extremely difficult to measure even the quantity of this activity; a helpful clue is that such organisations could reach, in one way or another, approximately forty to sixty million people or about 50 per cent of the adults in the United States. They undoubtedly have spent millions of dollars and distributed hundreds of thousands of articles and publications concerning UNESCO.

Information Programme

The public information campaign was one of the earliest channels set up by the National Commission. At the first meeting of the National Commission, in September 1946, it was recommended that a Committee on Information be established to ensure that the members of the Commission, interested organisations, and the public would receive continuous and effective information on UNESCO matters. In terms of adult education, the general programme of public information included the activities of national organisations, independent agencies and of individuals, as well as the work of the Commission's secretariat, other State Department Offices and the Committee on Information and its successor in Commission committee structure...

The policy of the National Commission has always strongly favoured this channel. The specific policies for the information campaign were to use all available channels, including the Commission itself, mass media, organisations and the meetings and conferences...

Valuable general publications included posters, pamphlets, leaflets and small booklets, including many produced by the

United Nations, UNESCO, other specialized agencies, or by private organisations whose work related to UNESCO. Important examples of National Commission publications were *The Kansas Story on UNESCO,* which described some very active local work, and *UNESCO and You,* a pamphlet giving a six-point programme for individual action. The Commission also published and distributed reprints of documents, speeches, radio scripts or press and magazine articles.

Mass media material actually prepared by the National Commission included regular releases for radio and press and special materials. The National Commission has not had a regular radio broadcast, published a newspaper or a widely distributed magazine, nor of course, manufactured and distributed films for mass consumption. The regular news materials were a weekly radio news release, the *UNESCO World Review*, and the semi-monthly *UNESCO Features* to news, editorial and feature services and to film producers and writers, with a monthly digest to four hundred weekly newspapers. The Commission also distributed clip sheets and other news materials to all members and to interested organisations.

UNESCO Conferences

This channel was legally required and through the general conferences the Commission has made personal contact with great numbers of interested organisations and indirectly, with whole states and local communities. This personal contact involved in a general conference was an important factor in stimulating participation in the UNESCO programme.

Local Councils

...These groups were in general patterned after the National Commission. They intended to provide coordination of the UNESCO work in their areas and to help stimulate new UNESCO activities. They took advantage of the existing community channels for such work and promoted some work directly themselves. One of the most active, the Kansas Commission, was unique as a broad, active organisation in itself. Here many local, municipal, or county UNESCO Councils were formed as members of the State Commission. In 1950 the Kansas Commission reported as members thirty-eight county

UNESCO Councils, in addition to state organisations and private individuals.

Adult education by the active local groups throughout the country varied. The local UNESCO Councils added local adult education agencies, such as the community organisations, local chapters of national organisations, public institutions—libraries, evening adult schools, municipal activities and near-by universities and the local mass media groups. Many UNESCO Councils, on their own initiative, promoted discussion groups, conferences, forums, study groups and other aids to education about UNESCO for the adults of their areas.

In 1950, six states, California, Kansas, Michigan, Oklahoma, Utah, and Washington, reported continuing state councils. Six New England states functioned under the New England Committee for UNESCO. Four states in which councils had been previously organised were reported to have lost strength. Two new states and the Territory of Hawaii (1949) reported action indicating preliminary steps towards forming UNESCO Councils. In addition to these formal state groups, there were a number of local UNESCO Councils, both within the states having a state council and in other states. Five additional states reported such activity in 1949.

From this brief description of the work of the U. S. National Commission for UNESCO, it is apparent that its adult education activities are numerous. Its concentration on world understanding and interpretation of efforts at international cooperation in the fields of education, science and culture is urgently needed if citizens in this country are to play well the part in the world scene which events have cast. The fact that much of the work of the international UNESCO organisation is directed toward underdeveloped and educationally underprivileged sections of the globe makes even more important the interpretative and educational role which the commission has undertaken. What cannot be learned about through direct experience must be understood by vicarious means and these the Commission has sought to supply. Its effect can and should be improved by the active collaboration of other agencies in the adult education movement and by the best consultant help which can be made available.

❑❑❑